Hidden Costs, Value Lost

Uninsurance in America

Committee on the Consequences of Uninsurance

Board on Health Care Services

INSTITUTE OF MEDICINE
OF THE NATIONAL ACADEMIES

THE NATIONAL ACADEMIES PRESS
Washington, D.C.
www.nap.edu

THE NATIONAL ACADEMIES PRESS • 500 Fifth Street, N.W. • **Washington, DC 20001**

NOTICE: The project that is the subject of this report was approved by the Governing Board of the National Research Council, whose members are drawn from the councils of the National Academy of Sciences, the National Academy of Engineering, and the Institute of Medicine. The members of the committee responsible for the report were chosen for their special competences and with regard for appropriate balance.

Support for this project was provided by The Robert Wood Johnson Foundation. The views presented in this report are those of the Institute of Medicine Committee on the Consequences of Uninsurance and are not necessarily those of the funding agencies.

International Standard Book Number 0-309-08931-X (Book)
International Standard Book Number 0-309-51139-9 (PDF)
Library of Congress Control Number 2003106651

Additional copies of this report are available for sale from the National Academies Press, 2101 Constitution Avenue, N.W., Box 285, Washington, DC 20055. Call (800) 624-6242 or (202) 334-3313 (in the Washington metropolitan area); Internet, http://www.nap.edu.

For more information about the Institute of Medicine, visit the IOM home page at **www.iom.edu.**

"Knowing is not enough; we must apply.
Willing is not enough; we must do."
—Goethe

INSTITUTE OF MEDICINE
OF THE NATIONAL ACADEMIES

Shaping the Future for Health

THE NATIONAL ACADEMIES
Advisers to the Nation on Science, Engineering, and Medicine

The **National Academy of Sciences** is a private, nonprofit, self-perpetuating society of distinguished scholars engaged in scientific and engineering research, dedicated to the furtherance of science and technology and to their use for the general welfare. Upon the authority of the charter granted to it by the Congress in 1863, the Academy has a mandate that requires it to advise the federal government on scientific and technical matters. Dr. Bruce M. Alberts is president of the National Academy of Sciences.

The **National Academy of Engineering** was established in 1964, under the charter of the National Academy of Sciences, as a parallel organization of outstanding engineers. It is autonomous in its administration and in the selection of its members, sharing with the National Academy of Sciences the responsibility for advising the federal government. The National Academy of Engineering also sponsors engineering programs aimed at meeting national needs, encourages education and research, and recognizes the superior achievements of engineers. Dr. Wm. A. Wulf is president of the National Academy of Engineering.

The **Institute of Medicine** was established in 1970 by the National Academy of Sciences to secure the services of eminent members of appropriate professions in the examination of policy matters pertaining to the health of the public. The Institute acts under the responsibility given to the National Academy of Sciences by its congressional charter to be an adviser to the federal government and, upon its own initiative, to identify issues of medical care, research, and education. Dr. Harvey V. Fineberg is president of the Institute of Medicine.

The **National Research Council** was organized by the National Academy of Sciences in 1916 to associate the broad community of science and technology with the Academy's purposes of furthering knowledge and advising the federal government. Functioning in accordance with general policies determined by the Academy, the Council has become the principal operating agency of both the National Academy of Sciences and the National Academy of Engineering in providing services to the government, the public, and the scientific and engineering communities. The Council is administered jointly by both Academies and the Institute of Medicine. Dr. Bruce M. Alberts and Dr. Wm. A. Wulf are chair and vice chair, respectively, of the National Research Council.

www.national-academies.org

IOM Staff

Wilhelmine Miller, Project Co-director
Dianne Miller Wolman, Project Co-director
Lynne Page Snyder, Program Officer
Tracy McKay, Research Associate
Ryan Palugod, Senior Project Assistant

Consultants

Hanns Kuttner, Senior Research Associate, Economic Research Initiative on the Uninsured, University of Michigan
M. Eugene Moyer, Economist, Annandale, Virginia
Elizabeth Richardson Vigdor, Assistant Professor of Public Policy Studies, Terry Sanford Institute of Public Policy, Duke University

Reviewers

This report has been reviewed in draft form by individuals chosen for their diverse perspectives and technical expertise, in accordance with procedures approved by the NRC's Report Review Committee. The purpose of this independent review is to provide candid and critical comments that will assist the institution in making its published report as sound as possible and to ensure that the report meets institutional standards for objectivity, evidence, and responsiveness to the study charge. The review comments and draft manuscript remain confidential to protect the integrity of the deliberative process. We wish to thank the following individuals for their review of this report:

ARTHUR L. CAPLAN, Director, Center for Bioethics, University of Pennsylvania, Philadelphia

HAILE T. DEBAS, Dean, School of Medicine and Vice Chancellor, Medical Affairs, University of California, San Francisco

ALAN M. GARBER, Henry J. Kaiser, Jr., Professor and Professor of Medicine, Director, Center for Health Policy, Director, Center for Primary Care and Outcomes Research, Stanford University, Stanford, California

MARTHE R. GOLD, Logan Professor and Chair, Department of Community Health and Social Medicine, City University of New York Medical School

BRIGITTE MADRIAN, Associate Professor of Economics, Graduate School of Business, The University of Chicago, Illinois

JOHN McCONNELL, Assistant Professor, Emergency Medicine Research, Oregon Health & Science University, Portland

Preface

Hidden Costs, Value Lost: Uninsurance in America consolidates and builds on previous Committee work in order to develop estimates of the costs to our society of tolerating a large and shifting population who lack health insurance—more than 41 million in any single year. Nearly twice as many lack coverage at some point over a 2-year period. Lack of coverage among Americans under age 65 exacts a number of costs that are borne by uninsured people themselves, by their families, by communities and health care institutions, and by the nation at large; ultimately, we all bear these costs in one form or another.

This fifth report by the Committee on the Consequences of Uninsurance immediately precedes our sixth and final analysis, in which we will articulate principles that should guide policy reforms to pursue and ideally achieve universal coverage. In this final report, we will also assess prototypical strategies and gauge their impact in light of these principles. While previous reports have focused on health and social consequences of uninsurance, *Hidden Costs, Value Lost* considers the financial impact of this problem for the nation overall. In part, this is done by "cashing out" what the Committee has learned and reported in its first four studies (in dollar terms when feasible, qualitatively when not). In this report, the Committee considers not only the costs created by uninsurance but frames these costs in terms of the potential benefits that might be realized by providing health insurance to the entire population. These benefits are then evaluated in light of the projected costs of the additional health care services that the uninsured would use if they had coverage and could therefore afford these services.

Hidden Costs, Value Lost takes the broadest societal view of the economic and social costs that our nation incurs as a result of our current health care financing policies—approaches that leaves tens of millions without coverage at any point in time and most adults under age 65 at risk over time of losing their coverage. As with its investigation of community-level effects of uninsurance in *A Shared Destiny*, the Committee again faces the limitations of research addressing many of the costs throughout society that accompany the lack of health insurance. The Committee contended with the problem of limited data by using analytic approaches such as estimating the economic value of healthier life years forgone due to uninsurance. This strategy can be compared with that of governmental agencies that assess the risks and benefits to health and longevity of a variety of safety, environmental and health care interventions. Viewed from the broadest perspective, the lack of health insurance is a health risk at the population level. Likewise, universal coverage, however achieved, can be considered a health intervention at the population level.

We encourage readers of this report to adopt a societal perspective as they consider the costs of uninsurance and to balance these costs against the potential benefits of various reform strategies. Historically, many have argued that we cannot afford to cover the uninsured. Perhaps, after reading this report, many will conclude that we can no longer afford not to cover the uninsured.

Mary Sue Coleman, Ph.D.
Co-chair
Arthur L. Kellermann, M.D., M.P.H.
Co-chair
June 2003

Acknowledgments

Hidden Costs, Value Lost: Uninsurance in America reflects the contributions of many people. The Committee acknowledges and thanks those who participated in its development.

The Subcommittee on the Societal Costs of Uninsured Populations prepared the report for the Committee's consensus review and issuance. James Mongan chaired the Subcommittee. Members included Norman Daniels, Sherry Glied, Jack Hadley, Ruby P. Hearn, Emmett Keeler, Willard G. Manning, Jack Needleman, Gordon R. Trapnell, and Stephen J. Trejo. The members of the drafting subcommittee, through a number of working groups, prepared and analyzed data on costs and health expenditures as well as directed and reviewed the work of consultants and staff. The Committee is indebted to their intensive efforts to bring this work to fruition.

As consultant to the Committee, economist Elizabeth Richardson Vigdor, Duke University, prepared an analysis of health capital losses among the U.S. population due to the lack of health insurance. (The complete study is included as Appendix B.) Elizabeth expertly and graciously conducted additional analysis and derived estimates at the requests of the Subcommittee and Committee. Eugene Moyer, senior economist with the Department of Health and Human Services (retired), and Hanns Kuttner, economist, University of Michigan, also served as Committee consultants, researching and drafting sections of the report and standardizing and updating expenditures and cost projections.

The Committee and Subcommittee benefited from presentations from a number of experts on topics addressed in *Hidden Costs, Value Lost*. Cathi Callahan, Actuarial Research Corporation; Jack Hadley, Urban Institute; Jack Needleman, Harvard University; and John Sheils, Lewin Group, discussed approaches to cost estimation with the Committee at its October 2001 meeting in Woods Hole, Massachusetts. John Grgurina, Jr., Pacific Business Group on Health; Richard Kronick, University of California, San Diego; and Jill Yegian, California HealthCare Foundation, participated in a panel discussion on small business perspectives on health insurance at the February 2002 Committee meeting in San Francisco. Economists Robert Helms, American Enterprise Institute, and Ellen O'Brien, Georgetown University, shared their insight and research on health insurance and uninsurance at the Subcommittee's initial meeting in July 2002. Jessica Banthin, Edward Miller, and John Moeller, economists at the Agency for Healthcare Research and Quality, presented their simulation model of health spending by uninsured and insured populations at the second meeting of the Subcommittee in January 2003. Susan Milner, Maryland State Department of Health, and Hugh Waters, Johns Hopkins University, shared their ongoing research on the costs of the uninsured population of Maryland with the Subcommittee. Timothy Westmoreland provided information to the Subcommittee on the conventions that the U.S. Congress uses to estimate the costs of legislative proposals. The Committee thanks these individuals and their organizations for sharing generously their time, expertise, and work. In particular, the Committee would like to acknowledge the support The Kaiser Commission on Medicaid and the Uninsured has provided to Jack Hadley and John Holahan of The Urban Institute for their research on the costs related to uninsurance, and thanks The Commission for making this work available to the Committee in its study and deliberations.

The Committee recognizes the work of Institute of Medicine (IOM) staff. Project co-director Wilhelmine Miller served as principal staff to the Subcommittee and coordinated the drafting of the report. Project co-director Dianne Wolman advised on and edited multiple drafts. Program officer Lynne Snyder assisted in drafting and editing, and research associate Tracy McKay conducted literature searches and prepared the figures and tables in the report. Senior project assistant Ryan Palugod maintained the project's research database and helped prepare the manuscript for publication. The IOM Board on Health Care Services, directed by Janet Corrigan, sponsors and provides overall guidance to the Committee.

The Committee thanks The Robert Wood Johnson Foundation for its generous and continued support of the work on the consequences of uninsurance and especially acknowledges The Foundation's president, Risa Lavisso-Mourey, and senior program officer Anne Weiss for their interest and assistance with this project.

Contents

Hidden Costs, Value Lost

Uninsurance in America

Executive Summary

The discontinuity of coverage and complete lack of health insurance among tens of millions of Americans every year entail costs for our society in

- lost health and longevity, including health deficits leading to developmental and educational losses for children;
- financial risk, uncertainty and anxiety within families with one or more uninsured members;
- financial stresses for and instability of health care providers and institutions in communities with relatively high uninsured rates that reduce the scope and amount of available health services, including public health services; and
- lost workforce productivity.

As a nation and as public law, we invest in the health of those who have health insurance, through tax subsidies and publicly sponsored coverage. About 85 percent of the U.S. population benefit from this investment. As a society, we also spend substantial public resources for health care services to the remaining 15 percent of Americans—the more than 41 million people who lack coverage every year. Despite this public spending on health services for the uninsured, those who lack coverage have worse health outcomes than do similar individuals with insurance, because dollars alone do not confer the health benefits that continuous coverage does. If all members of society bear certain risks and costs from spillover effects of uninsurance, all should realize some benefit, at least indirectly, from a public policy ensuring that everyone has coverage.

Hidden Costs, Value Lost: Uninsurance in America tallies some of the most clearly identifiable economic and social costs of uninsurance, as described in the

1

Committee's previous four reports. The Committee concludes that maintaining an uninsured population of 41 million results in a substantial loss of economic value that improved health would provide uninsured individuals. The Committee also believes that, as health care interventions become ever more effective in improving health and extending life, unequal access to such care, as documented in *Care Without Coverage* and *Health Insurance Is a Family Matter*, becomes increasingly unjust.

Americans devote more economic resources to health care than people in any other nation in the world, both in total dollars spent ($1.236 trillion for personal health care services in 2001) and as a percent of the gross domestic product (14 percent) (Levit et al., 2003). Access to health care is valued highly and widely throughout American society. In this report, the Committee takes a broad, societal perspective as it examines the performance of economic resources devoted to health care, health insurance, and alternative uses for these resources, which include personal resources, firms' investments, and public monies.

The societal perspective allows the Committee to evaluate our society's failure to invest in health insurance for 15 percent of the population from the standpoint of the public interest, rather than the interest of any particular individual or group within society. Practically, the societal perspective reflects the kind of aggregate, population-based information and national data sets that the Committee was able to use in its analyses. More importantly, as a matter of principle or ethical choice, the societal perspective values the interests of each individual member of society equally and allows the Committee to examine the fairness of the distribution of the costs and benefits of public policies and investments in health (Gold et al., 1996a).

WHAT ARE COSTS OF UNINSURANCE?

What do we mean by cost? This report draws on information developed within several different analytic frameworks because of the breadth of the issues encompassed by the "costs of uninsurance." When uninsured people obtain coverage, their use of health services would be expected to increase as a result of improved financial access. The majority of the costs due to being uninsured that the Committee has identified are not health services costs (that is, uncompensated care or expensive hospitalizations because of delayed treatment) but rather result from the poorer health outcomes of uninsured individuals.

Families with uninsured members bear costs resulting from the financial burdens and risks of out-of-pocket health care spending and, because children's receipt of health care in practice depends on their parents' coverage status, children in families with uninsured parents are less likely to receive adequate services.

The spillover costs of uninsurance experienced within communities result from both the poorer health of uninsured populations and the demands made on local public budgets and on providers to support care for those without coverage. Thus, this report considers both the extent and the source of resources devoted to the care of people without health insurance and the economic cost implications of the poorer health they experience because they lack coverage.

THE VALUE LOST IN POORER HEALTH

Given the key role of health coverage in improving health outcomes, how much health is lost with a population of more than 41 million uninsured? In this report, the Committee adapts an analytic strategy that has been used to assess the value of life-saving and health-improving medical interventions, imputing a monetary value to the years of expected life that an individual is estimated to have in particular states of health (e.g., excellent, fair, poor; with controlled hypertension, or prostate cancer in remission, or no functional limitations).

The present value in money terms of the "stock" of years of life in certain expected states of health has been coined "health capital" (Grossman, 1972; Cutler and Richardson, 1997). This analytic concept of health capital is related to the approach used by government agencies that regulate public health and safety (e.g., Food and Drug Administration, Department of Transportation, Environmental Protection Agency) to evaluate and compare alternative public policies that mitigate risk and improve health. This approach involves estimating the value of averted risk as expressed by the expected number of lives saved (statistical or anonymous lives when the policy is implemented) to determine whether the benefit of reducing a particular risk or harm justifies the costs involved in adopting such a policy. The Committee has applied the analytic concept of health capital to the health risk it has been concerned with—the risk of being uninsured, compared to having coverage. Stated in the converse, the Committee has estimated the aggregate personal economic value that would be added if the entire U.S. population had health insurance coverage, compared with the status quo, which leaves 16.5 percent of the population under age 65 without coverage.

The Committee commissioned an analysis estimating the value of diminished health and longevity within the U.S. population as a result of uninsurance. Economist Elizabeth Richardson Vigdor combined information on the longevity, prevalence of health conditions, and health-related quality of life for insured and uninsured populations. The relative mortality rates for insured and uninsured populations were drawn from the Committee's earlier systematic literature review of health outcomes as a function of health insurance status and reflect a 25 percent higher mortality rate within the uninsured population (IOM, 2002a,b). Vigdor's estimates constitute a range of values for the forgone health of uninsured individuals, based on different assumptions about the relative health status of insured and uninsured populations.

Imputing a value of $160,000 to a year of life in perfect health and calculating the present value of future years with an annual discount rate of 3 percent, Vigdor estimated that the economic value of the healthier and longer life that an uninsured child or adult forgoes because he or she lacks health insurance ranges between $1,645 and $3,280 for each additional year spent without coverage

(Vigdor, 2003). This value differs for people of different ages and for men and women because of differences in underlying health status and life expectancy. These estimated benefits could be either greater or smaller if unmeasured personal characteristics were responsible for part of the measured difference in morbidity and mortality between those with and those without coverage.

The Committee's best estimate of the aggregate, annualized cost of the diminished health and shorter life spans of Americans who lack health insurance is between $65 and $130 billion for each year of health insurance forgone. These are the benefits that could be realized if extension of coverage reduced the morbidity and mortality of uninsured Americans to the levels for individuals who are comparable on measured characteristics and who have private health insurance. This estimate does not include spillover losses to society as a whole of the poorer health of the uninsured population. It accounts for the value only to those experiencing poorer health and subsumes the losses to productivity that accrue to uninsured individuals themselves.

These estimates constitute an initial effort to develop an integrated and coherent framework for evaluating a number of economic costs attributable to the lack of health insurance; they are not definitive but suggest the direction that further research and analysis might take. Figure ES.1 illustrates the costs of uninsurance that the Committee has documented in its work to date. The bracket to the left of the pyramid shows the costs that are captured in the estimate of the economic value of forgone health by those who lack coverage, and the costs that are additional to that estimate.

HEALTH CARE COSTS OF THE UNINSURED

In its analysis of the costs of health care now used by those who lack health coverage, the Committee finds that

• **Uninsured children and adults are less likely to incur any health care expenses in a year and, on average, incur health care costs well below half of average spending for services by all those under age 65.**
• **People who lack health insurance for an entire year have out-of-pocket expenditures comparable, in absolute dollar amounts, to those of people with private coverage. Uninsured individuals pay for a higher proportion of the total costs of care rendered to them out of pocket, however, compared to insured individuals under age 65 (35 percent, compared with 20 percent), and they also have much lower family incomes. Out-of-pocket spending for health care by the uninsured is more likely to consume a substantial portion of family income than out-of-pocket spending by those with any kind of insurance coverage.**
• **The total cost of health care services used by individuals who are**

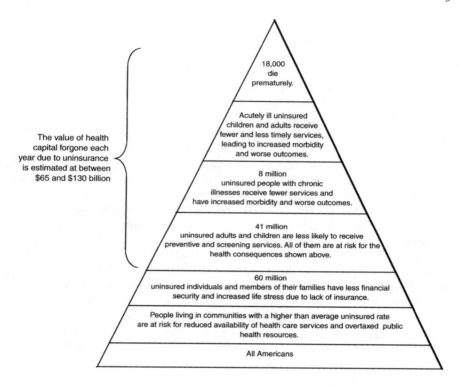

FIGURE ES.1 Consequences of uninsurance.

uninsured for either part of or the entire year is estimated to be $98.9 billion for 2001.

• The best available estimate of the value of uncompensated health care services provided to persons who lack health insurance for some or all of a year is roughly $35 billion annually, about 2.8 percent of total national spending for personal health care services.

The direct costs of uncompensated care provided to uninsured people are largely borne by those who pay taxes. Public support from the federal, state, and local governments accounts for between 75 and 85 percent of the total value of uncompensated care estimated to be provided to uninsured people each year (Hadley and Holahan, 2003a). Public subsidies to hospitals are paid through

• federal Medicaid and Medicare disproportionate share hospital (DSH) payments and other financing mechanisms, and

• state Medicaid DSH payments and other state and local subsidies and budget allocations for hospital care and institutional operating costs.

These subsidies amounted to an estimated $23.6 billion in 2001, approximately the same as the value of hospital bad debts and charity care projected for that year from the American Hospital Association's annual financial survey results. The Committee finds mixed evidence that private payers subsidize uncompensated hospital care. Analysts have proposed that possibly $1.6 to $3 billion annually in hospital revenues from private payers are used to cover hospitals' uncompensated care costs (Hadley and Holahan, 2003a). The Committee concludes that the impact of any such "shifting" of costs to privately insured patients and insurers is unlikely to affect the prices of health care services and insurance premiums.

Even with the considerable federal support for uncompensated care (particularly to hospitals), when states provide health care in kind to medically indigent residents rather than through insurance programs like Medicaid and the State Children's Health Insurance Program, the costs of direct provision fall disproportionately on the local communities where care is provided (IOM, 2003a). Given the lower average incomes of uninsured Americans and the associated socioeconomic profiles of the communities in which rates of uninsurance are higher than average, these communities have relatively little capacity to support the provision of health care services. Financing the health care of those who now lack health insurance through federal or federal and state coverage mechanisms would spread the burden of publicly supported care over a broader tax base than that which supports uncompensated care for those without coverage.

QUALITY OF LIFE AND SECURITY FOR FAMILIES

Uninsured individuals and families bear the burden of increased financial risk and uncertainty as a consequence of being uninsured. Although the estimated monetary value of the potential financial losses that those without coverage bear is relatively small (compared to the full cost of their services) because of uncompensated care, the psychological and behavioral implications of living with financial and health risks and uncertainty may be significant. The Committee estimates that the financial risk borne by those without coverage has an economic cost of $1.6 to $3.2 billion. This would be the value, to those now lacking coverage, of the financial protection provided by health insurance.

Even in families in which all members are insured, the concern about losing coverage remains genuine. One, some, or all members can lose health insurance at some point, because of lifecycle events such as leaving school or retiring or because of economic conditions that result in the loss of income or workplace benefits, such as becoming unemployed or changing jobs. This lack of social and economic security, experienced by virtually all Americans except for those who have gained Medicare coverage on a permanent basis (i.e., those over age 65 or with end-stage renal disease), is truly a hidden cost of our patchwork approach to health insurance.

OTHER COSTS OF UNINSURANCE

Developmental Losses for Children

Uninsured children are at greater risk than children with health insurance of suffering delays in development that may affect their educational achievements and prospects later in life. Good health and meeting developmental milestones in infancy and childhood affect individuals' educational attainment, earning capacity, and long-term health. The Committee's estimate of health capital forgone by uninsured children and adults that was presented earlier subsumes these developmental losses. The Committee includes its review of studies and earlier findings regarding worse health outcomes among uninsured children to provide an empirical underpinning to its approach to estimating health capital losses resulting from the lack of health insurance.

Costs to Public Programs

The Committee considered other costs that are attributable to uninsurance without attempting to quantify them. Although the costs of morbidity and productivity losses associated with individual health conditions have been estimated, there is no body of research with which to investigate these effects as a function of health insurance status in a systematic way. Thus the Committee has identified public program and workforce impacts of health insurance status that can be inferred from related evidence about the effects of health status on disability and productivity and the effects of health insurance on health status, largely based on the Committee's reports *Care Without Coverage* and *Health Insurance Is a Family Matter*.

Based on its findings and conclusions about health outcomes as a function of health insurance status in its earlier reports, the Committee concludes that public programs, including Medicare, Social Security Disability Insurance, and the criminal justice system almost certainly have higher budgetary costs than they would if the U.S. population in its entirety had health insurance up to age 65. It is not possible, however, to estimate the extent to which such program costs are increased as a result of worse health due to lack of health insurance.

As calculated for this study, the value of healthy years of life forgone by those without health insurance does not include any health and longevity impacts that occur after age 65, when Medicare covers virtually the entire population. The Committee's conservative assumption in estimating the value of health lost likely underestimates the health benefits enjoyed by individuals who would gain additional health and longevity after age 65 if they had health insurance continuously prior to that age. It is also likely to underestimate the potentially reduced costs to the Medicare program of financing services for persons with pent-up demand for care or health "deficits" as a result of having been without coverage previously. For example, individuals who have poorly controlled hypertension or diabetes or undetected high cholesterol because of irregular or no medical attention to their condition enter the Medicare program with more comorbidities and worse health status than do persons whose conditions have been treated over time.

Likewise, increasing disability among the working-age population (even as the disability rate has decreased over the past two decades for those older than 65), suggests that health and functional status improvements that health insurance provides could reduce disability insurance claims.

In the case of serious mental illness, for example, there can be substantial spillover costs of uninsurance to society. More than 3 million adults in the United States have either schizophrenia or bipolar disorder (manic-depressive disease), which can involve psychosis and aberrant behavior. Fully 20 percent of the adults with one of these conditions who do not reside in institutions lack health insurance. Although being insured is no guarantee that mental health services are a covered benefit or that one will be treated appropriately for mental health problems, persons with either public or private health insurance are more likely to receive some care for their condition than are those without any coverage. Between 600,000 and 700,000 persons with severe mental illness are jailed each year. Ironically, contact with the criminal justice system increases the chances that someone with a severe mental illness will receive specialty mental health services. The costs of less effective treatment resulting from lack of health insurance likely contribute to the costs of incarcerating people with serious mental illness.

Workforce Participation, Productivity, and Employers

Illness and functional limitations impair people's abilities to work and consequently impose the costs of forgone income and productive effort on those who are sick and disabled, their families, and potentially on their employers as well. The costs for employers of productivity losses on the job for workers with particular illnesses have been increasingly well studied within the past decade. The impact that providing workers with health insurance has on workplace productivity, however, is less well documented. What evidence exists suggests that, although workers' health status may improve as a result of having coverage, individual employers probably do not lose financially, on net, as a result of impaired productivity on the job if they do not currently offer their workers health insurance benefits. Any systemic, regional, or national losses of productivity or productive capacity as a result of uninsurance among nearly one-fifth of the working-age population cannot be measured with the data now available.

Costs for Communities

Not only those who lack coverage but others in their communities may experience reduced access to and availability of primary care, specialty, and hospital services resulting from relatively high rates of uninsurance that imperil the financial stability and viability of health care providers and institutions. Communities that have higher than average rates of uninsurance are more likely to experience reduced availability of hospital-based services and critical community benefits such as emergency services and advanced trauma care (IOM, 2003a; Gaskin and Needleman, 2003; Needleman and Gaskin, 2003).

In addition, population health resources and programs, including disease surveillance, communicable disease control, emergency preparedness, and community immunization levels, have been undermined by the competing demands for public dollars for personal health care services for those without coverage. Because uninsured individuals and families are much less likely than are those who have coverage to have a regular health care provider, they are not well integrated into systems of care. Consequently, population-level disease surveillance and health monitoring is reduced in communities with large uninsured populations.

THE COST OF THE HEALTH CARE THAT UNINSURED PEOPLE WOULD USE IF THEY HAD COVERAGE

In order to evaluate fairly the cost of the better health that uninsured Americans could be expected to achieve if they had health insurance, the Committee reviewed estimates of the value of the additional health services that would be provided to the uninsured once they became insured. **Estimates of the incremental costs of health services that the population that now lacks insurance could be expected to use if they gained coverage range from $34 to $69 billion (in 2001 dollars).** These estimates should not be construed as the costs of any particular plan to reform health care financing to provide health insurance to those now without it. This range of estimates, derived from three independent analyses, assumes no other structural changes in the systems of health services delivery or finance, scope of benefits, or provider payment (Long and Marquis, 1994; Hadley and Holahan, 2003b; Miller et al., 2003). The ultimate cost of any reform will depend on the specific features of the approach taken. These estimated costs amount to 2.8–5.6 percent of national spending for personal health care services in 2001, equivalent to roughly half of the 8.7 percent increase in personal health care spending between 2000 and 2001.

COSTS AND BENEFITS CONSIDERED TOGETHER

Table ES.1 summarizes the Committee's estimates of the amounts and sources of payment for the health care currently provided to uninsured Americans, the

TABLE ES.1 Estimates of Current Annual Cost of Health Care Services for Full- and Part-Year Uninsured Individuals, Projected Incremental Annual Costs of Services If Insured, and Economic Value Gained by Uninsured Individuals If Insured, Annualized

	Billions $, estimated for 2001
Current cost of care for full- and part-year uninsured	98.9
Amount paid out of pocket by full- and part-year uninsured	26.4
Insurance payments (for part-year uninsured only) and workers' compensation	
Private	24.2
Public	13.8
Uncompensated care	34.5
Projected annual costs of additional utilization with coverage	34–69
Benefits of insuring the uninsured	
Aggregate value of health capital forgone by the uninsured, annualized	65–130
Aggregate annual value of risk borne by uninsured	1.6–3.2

SOURCES: Hadley and Holahan, 2003a,b; Vigdor, 2003.

projected cost of the additional health care that the presently uninsured population would receive if insured, and the aggregate, annualized economic value of lost health and financial security that those who lack coverage forgo, despite the substantial health care expenditures made on their behalf.

The next step in the Committee's analysis is to consider the potential benefits of providing the uninsured with coverage in conjunction with the new economic costs of the additional health services that would improve their health. In order to do this, both the average per capita gain in health due to an additional year of health insurance for the uninsured population and the average per capita annual cost of the additional health services that the uninsured population would use if they had coverage must be made comparable. Because the estimate of the value of health gained with an additional year of coverage is calculated as a discounted present value of the gain for a cohort of uninsured people over the course of their lives (with a range of $1,645 to $3,280 as presented earlier), the estimate of the annual cost of the additional health care that the uninsured would use if insured also must be calculated as the present value for an uninsured cohort over the course of their lives.

Using the projected annual cost of the additional utilization by those without coverage from Hadley and Holahan (2003b), the Committee estimated that the discounted present value of the cost of an additional year of health insurance ranges from $1,004 to $1,866, depending on whether the incremental service costs are based on the cost of public or private health insurance. The range of estimated benefits from the incremental coverage ($1,645 to $3,280) is higher than the range of estimated incremental service costs ($1,004 to $1,866) and, for most values within each range, results in a benefit–cost ratio of at least one.

REALIZING SOCIAL VALUES AND IDEALS

Finally, the Committee reflected on several other benefits that our national community and local communities within the United States might gain if health insurance coverage were extended throughout the population. Economic goods that can be valued in monetary terms are not the only kinds of goods that we value having. Providing certain important goods like health care to all members of society has its own value (Walzer, 1983; Coate, 1995). In addressing normative questions, the Committee has attempted to start from values that are widely endorsed throughout American society, such as equality of opportunity, and then to make judgments about whether public policy and economic practices in health care accord with a reasonable characterization of those values. The Committee does not attempt to make a freestanding argument about objective morality but rather claims that collective actions can express or achieve existing social norms and ideals.

Because health care relieves pain and suffering and enhances our ability to function and achieve over the course of a lifetime, making sure that everyone in society has adequate access to this good is a matter of fairness and social decency (Daniels, 1985; Sen, 1993). A commitment to equal opportunity obligates us as a society to ensure that all Americans have sufficient access to health care such that they are not disadvantaged in pursuing the career and other opportunities offered by American society.

Health insurance contributes essentially to obtaining the kind and quality of health care that can express the equality and dignity of every person. Despite the absence of an explicit Constitutional or statutory right to health care (beyond access to emergency care in hospitals, required by the Emergency Medical Treatment and Labor Act), disparities in access to and the quality of health care of the kind that prevail between insured and uninsured Americans contravene widely accepted, democratic cultural and political norms of equal consideration and equal opportunity. The increasing effectiveness of medical interventions in improving health and survival (Cutler and Richardson, 1997; Murphy and Topel, 1999; Heidenreich and McClellan, 2003) make considerations of equity in access to effective care through health insurance more urgent.

Uninsurance in America not only has hidden costs, it represents lost opportunities to more fully realize important social and political ideals that account for our nation's political stability and vitality (Dionne, 1998; NASI, 1999). Extending the social benefit of health insurance would help us make our implicit and explicit democratic political commitments of equal opportunity and mutual concern and respect more meaningful and concrete.

1

Introduction

As a nation, we invest in the health of some (85 percent) of the population by providing tax subsidies for the purchase of private health insurance or direct coverage through Medicare, Medicaid, and the State Children's Health Insurance Program. What does it cost us as a society, in terms of health and social equity, as well as dollars, to leave 15 percent of our population uninsured? This fifth report of the Institute of Medicine (IOM) Committee on the Consequences of Uninsurance examines the implications of uninsurance primarily but not exclusively from the perspective of the national economic costs and financial transfers incurred as a result of our current policies regarding health insurance coverage.

Hidden Costs, Value Lost: Uninsurance in America consolidates information that the Committee has developed over the course of its examination of personal, familial, and community outcomes and considers these findings within the context of the national economy and political culture. In this report, the Committee presents aggregate estimates in monetary terms of

- the costs of health care provided to those who lack health insurance that are borne both by uninsured individuals and their families and by the public and private programs and providers that subsidize uncompensated care and donate services;
- the value of additional years of healthier life that would be gained by those without health insurance in the United States if health insurance coverage were extended to everyone; and
- the cost of the additional health care that would be provided to the uninsured if they gained health insurance.

Hidden Costs, Value Lost attempts to answer another fundamental question: Who ultimately bears the costs consequent to uninsurance within the U.S. population? Understanding who eventually pays for the health care that uninsured people receive and the economic value lost as a consequence of *not* receiving adequate care are important to evaluating alternatives for expanding coverage.

CONTEXT

This report is the fifth in a series of studies that constitute a systematic assessment of the ramifications of failing to include millions of people each year in the predominant organizational form and financing mechanisms for health care services in the United States, private and public health insurance. The Committee has approached its task in a stepwise fashion. It has analyzed the highly complex and interactive health services and insurance sectors and government health and social welfare programs by focusing on different parts of the overall picture in each of its reports to date. Figure 1.1 displays this sequential and cumulative analytic approach as concentric rings spreading out from individual health outcomes, through families and communities, to the social and economic effects of uninsurance in the aggregate, at the national level. This report "slices" through each of these layers and consolidates information about the costs related to each one.

The rest of this section recaps in broad terms the subjects and general conclusions from the previous four reports and notes how their findings are used in this report.

Coverage Matters: Insurance and Health Care (IOM, 2001a), the Committee's introductory report, presented an overview of the dynamics of health insurance coverage in the United States and estimates of the number and characteristics of the population that lacks coverage. It also highlighted discrepancies between the Committee's findings based on empirical research and popular beliefs and understanding of the causes and implications of uninsurance in order to promote greater public awareness of and greater insight into the persistent national problem of uninsurance.

The second report, *Care Without Coverage: Too Little, Too Late* (IOM, 2002a), was a critical review of clinical and epidemiological health outcomes research that evaluated the effect of health insurance status on a variety of general and condition-specific indicators and outcomes for American adults younger than 65. The Committee concluded in this report that health insurance is associated with better health outcomes for adults and with the receipt of appropriate care across a range of preventive, chronic, and acute care services. Adults without health insurance have shorter lives and greater declines in health status over time than those with continuous coverage. *Care Without Coverage* developed illustrative estimates of excess deaths associated with being uninsured for the adult population under age 65, both overall and for several specific diseases. Overall, the Committee estimated that the uninsured adult population under age 65 experiences roughly 18,000

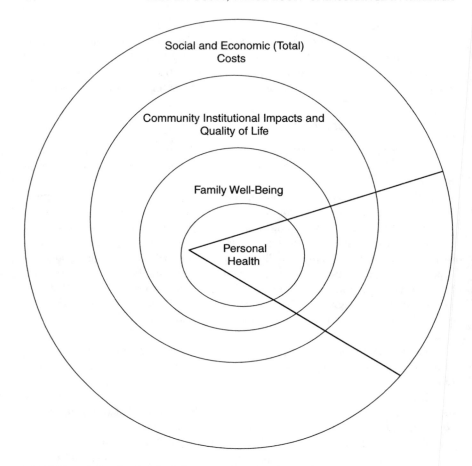

FIGURE 1.1 Levels of analysis for examining the effects of uninsurance.

premature deaths annually that can reasonably be attributed to the lack of coverage and the less adequate health care received as a result (IOM, 2002a). The Committee also developed illustrative estimates for deaths among nonelderly uninsured adults due to hypertension, breast cancer, and HIV/AIDS. The studies and findings of differential health outcomes for insured and uninsured adults contained in the second Committee report are used in this report to estimate the economic value of the healthier years of life forgone due to uninsurance within the U.S. population.

The Committee's third report broadened the focus of analysis to the social and economic unit of the family. *Health Insurance Is a Family Matter* (IOM, 2002b) considers the impact of a lack of health insurance for individuals within a family on the family as a whole, including the financial consequences of burdensome medical expenses, psychosocial stress, and the dependence of children's coverage and health care on their parents' coverage status. The third report also reviewed the extensive body of health outcomes research for pediatric, prenatal, and maternity care as a function of health insurance status. It documented the gains in access to appropriate health care and better health outcomes for children and pregnant women with coverage. The Committee concluded in *Health Insurance Is a Family Matter* that all members of the family face financial risk and may imperil their physical and emotional well-being if anyone in the family lacks coverage. Fully one-fifth of the U.S. population, approximately 60 million people, is affected by the lack of health insurance within their immediate family. The findings and conclusions of the Committee's third report are represented in *Hidden Costs, Value Lost* by the estimates of the value of health forgone due to uninsurance and in the costs of diminished financial security for families and the anxiety and stress that accompany the lack of health insurance within the family.

A *Shared Destiny: Community Effects of Uninsurance* (IOM, 2003a), the Committee's fourth report, adopts yet a broader perspective on the phenomenon of uninsurance within the United States. It looks at how communities are affected by the lack of coverage that some of its members endure, through mechanisms such as the poorer health of uninsured people, their needs and use of health care services and the sources of payment for that care, and the social and economic disparities within communities that are deepened by a lack of health insurance. This report breaks new ground in the analysis of how uninsured populations affect the quality and accessibility of health services within communities generally, and the overall character of communities in terms of health, social cohesiveness, and economic vitality. The Committee concludes in *A Shared Destiny* that high levels of uninsurance within communities disrupt local systems of public health and personal health care and adversely affect the availability and quality of services within the community. Furthermore, the stability and financial viability of community institutions and health care resources are threatened by the amount of uncompensated care that health care practitioners and facilities render. Finally, the national goal of attaining community-wide a high quality of personal health care services across the spectrum of services and providers cannot be met while those without health insurance rely on ad hoc delivery of services.

A *Shared Destiny* identifies several of the costs of uninsured populations that are borne by others. Some of these spillover costs and economic transfers, such as uncompensated or charity care provided when someone without health insurance or the means to pay for care directly is hospitalized, are readily measured in dollars. Other spillover costs of uninsured populations, such as the loss for an urban neighborhood or rural community of a primary care clinic because too many among its clientele have no source of payment for their care, are theoretically quantifiable in monetary terms but the information that would be needed to measure these costs is not available. Still other societal consequences resulting from inequalities manifested in disparate access to health care because of uninsurance within a local community or the national population cannot be represented in monetary terms. The Committee hypothesizes that uninsurance weakens social cohesiveness and exacerbates other social inequalities. Disparities among neighbors and fellow citizens in health insurance status and thus in access to highly valued medical care and attention may erode feelings of social belonging and trust within communities. Thus, with *A Shared Destiny*, the Committee began its investigation of some of the potential spillover costs of uninsurance.

PURPOSE

Hidden Costs, Value Lost continues this examination of the impacts of uninsurance from a national perspective and considers the benefits for American social and political life that could be achieved by guaranteeing health insurance coverage to all throughout their lives. It builds on the evidence presented in the Committee's earlier reports and anticipates the concluding report, which will articulate core principles that derive from these studies and use them to analyze strategies for achieving complete health insurance coverage of the U.S. population. By estimating the resources now devoted to health care for 41 million uninsured Americans, the losses in terms of health and longevity that they experience, and some of the costs and benefits of extending coverage to them, this report provides a baseline against which health insurance reform strategies can be assessed.

The Committee hopes to reach a broad audience—including the voting public, legislators, and other policy makers—with this report, and attempts to present economic and policy research findings and analyses in nontechnical language whenever possible. (A glossary of technical terms is included as Appendix A.) The research and analytic tools of economists and other social scientists, epidemiologists, and public policy analysts are not widely disseminated or well understood by lay audiences. The Committee believes this lack of awareness of the powerful analytic tools of the social and health sciences, and of the information developed by using these tools, fosters a narrow understanding of the costs of having a large uninsured population. By discussing its assumptions, methods, and sources of information, along with its findings and conclusions, the Committee hopes to raise awareness of some of the real costs incurred as a result of widespread uninsurance and to inform policy debates. The analytic approach and estimates of costs presented in the report should be useful to those who are developing their own policy alternatives and strategies.

In preparing this report, the Committee and its Subcommittee on Societal Costs of Uninsured Populations reviewed economic research and policy analysis that offered models for evaluating the costs and benefits of various health interventions. Providing health insurance to those who now lack it can be viewed as one such health-enhancing intervention. Conversely, maintaining a population of 41 million uninsured people can be viewed as a health risk at the population level.

The Committee followed the general approach taken by government agencies that regulate health and safety (e.g., the Food and Drug Administration, the

Department of Transportation, the Environmental Protection Agency, and the Consumer Product Safety Commission) to assess investments in life-saving, health-enhancing, and risk-reducing endeavors. These agencies use an analytic methodology that involves estimating the value of a "statistical" or anonymous life in order to determine if the benefit of a particular risk-reducing or health-enhancing intervention or policy justifies the costs it imposes or entails. The Committee's choice of approach was guided in large part by the highly aggregate nature of the information available on health outcomes dependent on insurance status and its conceptualization of uninsurance as a population-level risk factor. Chapter 2 discusses the Committee's approach further, along with other analytic frameworks, such as those used in studies of the economic costs of discrete illnesses.

The Committee commissioned an analysis by economist Elizabeth Richardson Vigdor to estimate the economic value to those who now lack health insurance of their diminished health and longevity as a result of their lack of coverage. The results of this analysis are described and used in the body of the report, and Vigdor's more technical and complete monograph is included as Appendix B. This analysis is the Committee's major contribution in this report to the quantification of costs of uninsurance.

In addition to presenting quantitative and qualitative information about some of the costs that follow from uninsurance, the Committee reviews several sets of estimates of the costs of providing the additional health care that the uninsured would use once they became insured. This review of the additional costs of providing the benefits of coverage that would reduce morbidity and premature mortality among the uninsured is an essential part of the consideration of the economic and ethical choices to be made concerning universal health insurance coverage.

Finally, in this report the Committee considers important, less tangible aspects of the value of the collective provision of health insurance, whether through public or private mechanisms. The collective, social interests that are at stake when we consider and make choices about health insurance policy in the United States are best demonstrated through examples from our nation's history. These are previewed in the remainder of this section.

Both altruism and justice have been offered as reasons for extending with public dollars health insurance benefits to those who cannot pay for their care or coverage themselves. Altruistic interests in providing access to health care accounted for the establishment of hospitals in the United States, initially by religious and charitable organizations, in the 18th and 19th centuries as places for caring for the poor who were ill and dying. This compassionate motivation was joined with a social ethic of mutual support that became more explicit over the course of the 20th century. By the time of the passage of Medicare and Medicaid in the 1960s, the provision of health benefits to the elderly and to poor families through the mechanism of social insurance was widely understood as a fair and compassionate way to distribute the burdens of ill health and to spread risk across generations and social classes (NASI, 1999). These programs, which now account for 36 percent of national spending for personal health care services, are central features of the social contract in the United States.

Congress enacted Medicare's End-Stage Renal Disease (ESRD) Program in 1972 in recognition that, without such a program, patients dependent on kidney dialysis would die in the near term (Starr, 1982; Bulger et al., 1995). The creation of Medicare benefits for this especially vulnerable group of Americans was perhaps foremost an expression of collective altruism. The ESRD program, however, was enacted without an accurate idea of how costly this expansion of life-preserving benefits would quickly become.[1]

Equity across members of a single society also motivates American social insurance programs. As medical interventions have become more effective in improving health and extending life (Cutler and Richardson, 1999; Murphy and Topel, 1999; Cutler and McClellan, 2001; Heidenreich and McClellan, 2003), the losses associated with not having health insurance also have increased. The Committee documented these losses in *Care Without Coverage* and *Health Insurance Is a Family Matter*. Questions about the equity of access to medical interventions for all members of society regardless of health insurance status have become more urgent as coverage affords access to increasingly effective services (IOM, 2003c).

Recently expanded access to public health insurance illustrates these principles well. The Breast and Cervical Cancer Prevention and Treatment Act of 2000 (P.L. 106–354) allows states to extend Medicaid coverage to women whose disease is identified through a publicly sponsored screening program (a federal program that began in 1990), regardless of meeting other eligibility criteria for Medicaid. This Medicaid option has been picked up by 45 states and the District of Columbia at a historically rapid rate (Miller, 2002a). Federal and state legislators' actions can be understood as a collective response to the fundamental unfairness of life-saving care being beyond the means of most uninsured women, once public resources have been expended to identify the disease. This legislation recognizes the futility of screening for disease if treatment is not available. It also expresses compassion for those with these life-threatening diseases.

ORGANIZATION

Five chapters follow. Chapter 2 presents the analytic context and conceptual grounding for this report. It also articulates the Committee's understanding of the incentives and motivations embedded in private health insurance and public coverage arrangements. Last, it provides a rationale for the particular measures of costs that the Committee adopted.

---

[1]Over the past 30 years, however, the art and science of (and data for) projecting the likely costs of changes in health benefits policies have advanced considerably, and the Committee makes use of these advances in this report.

The third chapter assesses the costs of care now provided to those who lack health insurance and identifies who pays these costs. These include out-of-pocket payments for health care by the uninsured and uncompensated care costs supported by public appropriations and subsidies and by philanthropic support. The chapter also reviews evidence for uncompensated care as a factor contributing to inflation in health care costs and insurance premiums. Last, it considers the distribution of spending across the federal, local, and state governments to support services for uninsured people.

Chapter 4 considers the opportunity costs of extensive uninsurance. The first section presents estimates of the additional value of health and longevity that coverage could provide to those now uninsured. The second section considers the financial risks and other stresses that individuals and families bear when they lack coverage. The remaining four sections discuss in qualitative terms

- impaired developmental outcomes for children,
- the demands placed on Medicare, disability income support, and other public programs,
- workplace productivity and labor force participation, in particular from the employer's standpoint, and
- effects on the availability and quality of health care and on public health.

Chapter 5 provides estimates of the likely increase in health care expenditures that would result from providing health insurance to those who now lack it. This investment, the Committee believes, will lead to the better (i.e., lower) morbidity and mortality experience of Americans and to an array of potential societal benefits summarized in Chapter 4.

In conclusion, Chapter 6 brings together the estimates and analyses from the earlier chapters and considers the cost-effectiveness of the increased services that would likely accompany coverage of those currently uninsured in the context of other investments in health that American society chooses to make. Here the Committee addresses the unquantifiable but critically important contribution that providing health insurance coverage to everyone would make to the fulfillment of values and norms deeply embedded in American history and culture: mutual caring, equal opportunity, and equal respect. Last, it summarizes the Committee's conclusions regarding the national social and economic burdens of uninsurance and the costs and benefits of providing coverage throughout the U.S. population.

2

Costs, Benefits, and Value: Context, Concepts, and Approach

This chapter outlines the Committee's approach to identifying the costs and lost value consequent to uninsurance and to estimating the resources that would be needed to bring the utilization of health care among the uninsured population in the United States in line with that of those with coverage. The Committee builds upon its earlier work. Its findings in previous reports both establish the context for and serve as points of departure for the analysis of costs and benefits presented here. The following are several of the important insights gained from the Committee's earlier work:

- *Health insurance is more than a mechanism for spreading financial risks; it also promotes appropriate use of preventive and routine health care services that otherwise may be underutilized* (IOM, 2002a,b).
- *Uninsurance is not usually voluntary; most individuals and families that lack coverage do so because they do not have a workplace offer or cannot afford the coverage available to them* (IOM, 2001a).
- *The lack of health insurance by some has adverse spillover effects on those with health insurance* (IOM, 2002b, 2003a).
- *The prevalence of uninsurance sits uneasily beside the favorable tax treatment of employment-based health insurance and the health insurance programs of the Social Security Act (Medicare, Medicaid, and the State Children's Health Insurance Program [SCHIP]), which are funded by federal income and payroll taxes and broad-based state taxes* (IOM, 2001a, 2003a).

These aspects of health insurance and the role it plays in the American health care enterprise and the economy more broadly, and its potential impacts on social and political culture, shape the discussion of the costs of uninsurance throughout this report.

This chapter defines and exemplifies the kinds of costs that the Committee considers.[1] Some of these are quantified and expressed in monetary terms, some have not been quantified because the data and analyses needed for quantification are not available, and some have no ready monetary equivalents.

The first section sets out the context for the analysis of costs, benefits, and value presented in the report, including the conceptual framework that has guided the Committee's work in its previous reports. The second section presents definitions and a categorization scheme for the types of costs referred to throughout the report. The third section describes the Committee's approach to determining the costs of uninsurance and the costs and benefits of coverage. Finally, the last section reviews the limitations of the Committee's analysis and of the data and research base used to evaluate these costs and benefits.

ANALYTIC CONTEXT

This section (1) explains the Committee's reasons for adopting the societal perspective in this report and what that perspective entails, (2) reviews the conceptual framework that has guided the Committee's assessment of the consequences of uninsurance, and (3) considers the features of health insurance that account for its value as an economic and social good and thus illuminate the costs incurred when all members of society do not have it.

The Societal Perspective

In this report the Committee explicitly takes a broad societal perspective in assessing the performance of the private and public economic resources devoted to health care, health insurance, and alternative uses for these resources. These resources include family resources, firms' investments, and tax revenues. This perspective dictates that the Committee's calculus take into account costs and outcomes beyond those that accrue to economic actors such as individuals, families, and firms as evaluated by these actors individually (Culyer, 1991; Weinstein and Manning, 1997). Health care is valued highly and widely throughout American society. Providing health care to those who need it not only expresses compassion and norms of mutual assistance, but it is also a form of social and political recognition. In the Committee's analysis, the societal perspective implicitly incorporates an assessment of the fairness of the distribution of these costs and benefits across individuals, as members of one national community, as taxpayers, and as business owners because it accounts for all health effects and costs that flow from a particu-

---

[1]In this chapter, terms used in a technical sense are printed in *italics* the first time they appear, and can be found in the Glossary in Appendix A.

lar intervention (e.g., health insurance coverage) regardless of who would experience these effects.

In adopting the societal perspective, the Committee follows the guidance of the Panel on Cost-Effectiveness in Health and Medicine, a nonfederal panel convened by the U.S. Public Health Service that developed consensus-based recommendations for guiding the conduct of cost-effectiveness analysis in health and medicine. The objective of the Panel was to improve the comparability and quality of studies that inform the allocation of health care resources. The Panel argued for adopting the societal perspective because it represents the public interest rather than the particular interest of any one group within society. It also argued that adopting the societal perspective was a practical choice that provides a benchmark against which more particularistic perspectives (e.g., those of employers or population subgroups such as young adults) can be evaluated:

> If an employer adopts an intervention that reduces the employer's health insurance costs but increases costs for Medicare, or if a public health intervention improves the health of one group but causes unwanted side effects for another, the societal perspective includes both changes. No perspective has a stronger claim to be the basis for comparability across studies (Russell et al., 1996, p. 1174).

Conceptual Framework for Identifying Consequences of Uninsurance

The Committee's investigation, as presented in its previous four reports, has been guided by an overarching conceptual framework introduced in *Coverage Matters* (IOM, 2001a). This conceptual framework adapted a widely applied behavioral model of access to health care, developed by Aday and colleagues (1984) and more recently presented in Andersen and Davidson (2001). In summary, the model posits and illustrates how individual and social factors, that is, both individual and community-level characteristics and resources, affect receipt of health care and how individual, familial, and community health, financial, and social outcomes follow from the extent and nature of the care received. The outcomes, which ultimately result from individual health insurance status and coverage rates within communities, cascade from the individual and family to the community level. Figure 2.1 illustrates the conceptual framework, and the right side of the diagram includes the three main consequences of uninsurance examined in this report:

- The economic costs (worse health, developmental, and functional outcomes for children and adults) that result from their lack of health insurance;
- The impact on family economic stability and psychosocial well-being when any member of a family lacks coverage;
- The spillover effects within communities of relatively high uninsured rates on health care services and institutions, local economies, and population health.

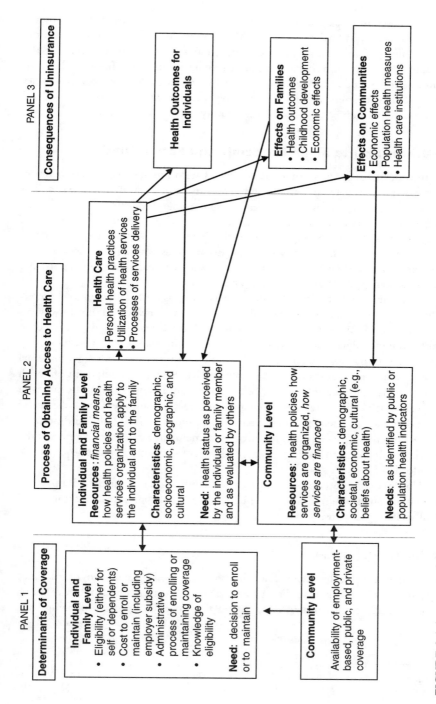

FIGURE 2.1 A conceptual framework for evaluating the consequences of uninsurance—a cascade of effects.

The costs and consequences of uninsurance are, conversely, the potential benefits of universal health coverage. Where possible, the Committee describes the lost value due to uninsurance in monetary terms. The report also considers the lost economic value and social and political opportunities that have not been or cannot be quantified in monetary terms, including the realization of social values and ideals like equality of opportunity, social and political equity, and mutual concern among members of a local community or the national polity.

Health Insurance as an Economic and Social Good

In order to appreciate the costs associated with the absence of health insurance, it is important to understand why and how we, both as consumers and as citizens, value coverage. Americans have long considered health care to be both a market commodity and a social good, a view that has fostered the development of variegated and complex arrangements for the delivery of health care (Fuchs, 1996; IOM, 2001a). This dual identity of health insurance as both a market good and a social good is reflected in the Committee's two-part analysis in this report; the analysis is both positive and empirical, and normative.

Health insurance provides financial protection against uncertain and potentially catastrophic health expenses and also facilitates access to health care services (IOM, 2001a). In the early 20th century in the United States, a private market in health insurance developed concurrently with the increasing cost and increasing effectiveness of medical care and, in the 1960s, continued alongside governmental social insurance programs such as Medicare and Medicaid.[2] The benefits of health insurance (private and public) and charity care are distinct but overlap. Both health insurance and charity care provide financial protection and access to collectively and individually valued health services when individuals fall ill. Additionally, private and public coverage afford enrollees some degree of peace of mind in the knowledge that care that might be needed at some future time will be accessible and affordable.

The following discussion compares and contrasts the features and aspects of value of private health insurance and public coverage through social insurance and social welfare programs.

Private Health Insurance

Private group and individual health insurance are like other kinds of insurance (e.g., fire, accident) in that they protect against financial catastrophes resulting from bad luck; health insurance mitigates the financial burdens of being sick.

---

[2]The Committee's fourth report, *A Shared Destiny,* includes a more extensive history of American health insurance over the 20th century (IOM, 2003a).

Unlike with other kinds of insurance, however, most health insurance policy holders can expect to make claims against their policies.[3] Individuals and policy makers also value health insurance because it facilitates access to services that promote health, such as preventive measures and screening, in addition to those that remedy illness and injury. Health insurance also offers its enrollees the advantages of realizing economies through group purchasing and improving information about health services and providers. Thus health insurance has value beyond that entailed by most other kinds of risk insurance.

Private health insurance, by pooling the risks of many individuals, can improve the *economic efficiency* with which a fixed amount of resources, namely, the dollars that a group of people could devote either to medical care or health insurance, is spent. The *utility* or *welfare* of the individuals contributing to the insurance pool is greater than it would be if each retained their premium dollars and faced uncertain and risky health expenses. Health insurance premiums incorporate a *loading fee*, a charge above the actuarial value of the benefits provided that includes an allowance for risk (the *risk premium*), administrative costs, and profit. The larger the group, the smaller the loading fee per capita, because of economies of scale both in administrative costs and in the risk premium, because the variance in expected expenditures decreases as the size of the group whose risks are pooled increases. Premiums for private health insurance must reflect average spending by enrollees, so in most years, people get back less than the full premium payment, but those with major illness benefit from coverage of expenses that may be well in excess of their annual income.

One feature of insurance that affects the operation and costs of health coverage is *moral hazard*, a term coined by the insurance industry to describe increases in the use of insured goods or services because covered individuals are not directly or fully financially liable when they use services. Physicians and other providers of services also respond to insurance coverage by offering and providing more services than they would otherwise. Low out-of-pocket costs for insured health care result in people getting more care than they would have if they had to pay the full costs out of pocket.

Much of this increased utilization is desirable. Preventive and screening services, for example, are used more frequently and appropriately by the insured than by those without health insurance (IOM, 2002a,b). Insured people are less likely than uninsured people to delay seeking care for potentially serious conditions (Baker et al., 2001). Delayed care is often more expensive and less effective. The differences in use of services between insured and uninsured individuals is reported in Chapter 3, and evaluated in monetary terms in Chapter 5.

Some of the additional medical attention and treatment that insured people

---

[3]This generalization may no longer hold if extremely high-deductible plans continue to increase in the private and group health insurance markets (Christianson et al., 2002).

receive, however, may be worth less than their total costs or even harmful (IOM, 2001b). The increases in premiums due to incurred costs that are not highly valued result in a *welfare loss* for those purchasing the insurance (Currie and Madrian, 1999). Because enrollees would not want or be able to pay the premiums that would result if all care were free and without restrictions, health insurance is structured to limit the use of care through patient cost sharing (deductibles, copayments and coinsurance), provider payment arrangements like capitation, and administrative mechanisms like prior authorization.

Recent work in the theory of demand for health insurance has led to a reconsideration of the extent of welfare losses resulting from "too much" health insurance (de Meza, 1983; Nyman, 1999a,b). This theoretical work assumes that people value certain kinds of (costly) health care more when they are sick than when they are well. Because we do not know with certainty what our health will be in a future time period, we tend to pay a lot to ensure that, if we turn out to need or be able to benefit from such (costly) health care, it is available to us then (Glied and Remler, 2002).

In addition to costs of care following acute crises to apparently healthy people, such as a heart attack or a car crash, other health care costs are predictably larger for some people, such as those with one or more chronic conditions. Insurance is particularly valuable to such people and they are more likely to try to obtain more extensive coverage than those who do not anticipate using the benefits. This phenomenon is called *adverse selection*. Individual insurance is particularly likely to be subject to adverse selection because those who are willing to pay the full premium out of pocket have health-related reasons for valuing it highly. Insurance companies anticipate this adverse selection for individual policies and attempt to limit their liability through medical underwriting, exclusions of preexisting conditions from coverage, high loading, and generally less extensive benefits for premiums (Chollet and Kirk, 1998; Pauly and Percy, 2000).

Insurance offered through large employer groups is less subject to adverse selection because there is a large pool of insured people who have come together for some purpose other than to obtain coverage. Employees are also more likely to elect workplace health insurance because it is tax subsidized and comes with the job rather than because they perceive an immediate need for it. In most large companies, employees with the same type of coverage pay the same out-of-pocket premium. (The full premium price negotiated for the group overall will likely reflect at least the age and gender composition of the workforce and, if available, prior years' claims experience.) When someone (a worker or the worker's dependent) who has group-based health insurance develops a potentially costly health condition, the worker may be particularly reluctant to leave her job because the job-related health insurance has become particularly valuable and health insurance may not be obtainable or affordable either individually or through another employer. This tendency to stay with a job when it is no longer the optimal work situation because of a health benefit that might not be available elsewhere at a comparable price introduces an inefficiency in the labor market referred to as *job lock* (Madrian, 1994).

The private individual and group health insurance markets in the United States fail to offer policies to all who might want coverage, and there are only limited regulatory consumer protections for maintaining private coverage once someone has it. First in 1985, with the Consolidated Omnibus Budget Reconciliation Act (COBRA), and again in 1996 with the Health Insurance Portability and Accountability Act (HIPAA), Congress enacted statutory measures to help individuals who have coverage continue it after leaving or losing their jobs. Still, all Americans, except those who turn 65 and qualify for Medicare on the basis of age or those who have end-stage renal disease (and thus also have Medicare lifelong), are at risk for being without health insurance at some point in their lives (IOM, 2001a, 2002b). While state regulation of health insurance and the creation of high-risk pools in some states have attempted to improve the availability of policies for those in poor health, these efforts are limited and have not resulted in sufficient access to affordable insurance (Chollet, 2000; Nichols, 2000; Pauly and Percy, 2000).[4] Government programs have filled some of the gaps, particularly programs such as Medicare and Medicaid, which provide health care through insurance mechanisms to identified populations with an entitlement to specific services.

Public Coverage

Health benefits are provided publicly through both social insurance and social welfare programs. Social insurance programs typically operate through public taxation and public spending. Social insurance programs can be distinguished from social welfare programs through features such as mandatory contributions, benefits from earmarked sources or funds, qualification for benefits under a uniform set of rules, and a perception by beneficiaries that they have earned or are entitled to benefits (NASI, 1999). In market-based economies, social insurance programs contribute to social stability by providing some degree of economic security by spreading certain kinds of risks broadly across society (Dionne, 1998; NASI, 1999).

The motivations for extending social insurance and social welfare benefits to specific groups within the population or to all members of a society or nation differ by the type of good or benefit provided (e.g., health care or income), among countries (and states within the United States) and by beneficiary group (children, retired persons, citizens). In the United States, the federal government provides health benefits through Medicare and, along with the states, through Medicaid

---

[4]See these and other articles on the individual health insurance market and regulatory efforts in the special issue of *Journal of Health Politics, Policy and Law* devoted to these topics (vol. 25, no.1; 2000).

and SCHIP to people for whom private health insurance markets do not exist or do not work well (the disabled and elderly) or who cannot afford premiums or health services (children and parents in low-income families, low-income disabled and elderly adults).

Medicare was enacted in 1965 to relieve the elderly and their families of the financial burden of catastrophically high medical care expenses, in the face of an inadequate and failing private market for individual health insurance for retirees. Medicaid was enacted at the same time to ensure that women and children receiving income support (and very low-income elderly and disabled persons) had access to needed health care, which included screening, prevention, and treatment of childhood diseases and developmental conditions after 1967. Beginning in the mid-1980s and culminating with the enactment of SCHIP in 1997, a series of expansions in Medicaid income-eligibility standards for pregnant women and children emphasized the public and national interest in and responsibility for investing in healthy starts for infants and children (see IOM, 2002b, for a fuller discussion of these expansions).

In 1994, vaccines for children (VFC) also became an entitlement for uninsured, Medicaid-enrolled, and other lower-income and underinsured children as part of Title 19 of the Social Security Act, a notable broadening of the Medicaid statute (Johnson et al., 2000; Rosenbaum, 2000). The motivation for and commitment to providing public support for children's health coverage include both the recognition by federal and state legislators that children are a particularly vulnerable population who would suffer great harm over their lifetime without adequate health care and that the health and optimal development of children is an investment in the nation's human capital, just as is public investment in their primary and secondary education.

Summary

Whether provided through the private individual and group markets or as public benefits, health insurance coverage is inherently a collective good, valued because it increases individual and collective well-being in a number of distinct ways. It is one aspect of contemporary social and economic life by which we share in each other's fates in important ways and reduce the exposure to health and financial risks that each of us would otherwise face alone.

CONCEPTS OF COST

"Cost" has both everyday and more technical meanings. Without further specification, in some contexts its meaning is ambiguous. In this report, unless otherwise noted, a "cost of uninsurance" refers to an *economic cost*, the value of resources devoted to a given activity measured by their value if deployed elsewhere, also called the *opportunity cost* of the resources (Dranove, 1995). Economic costs can be incurred without explicit payments being made. Economic costs are distinguished from cost or money *transfers*, which do not reflect an increase or decrease in economic cost or value but rather a redistribution of resources between individuals or other economic agents. For example, Social Security Disability Insurance payments to beneficiaries are a transfer of resources from the federal program (from taxpayers' dollars) to entitled and enrolled individuals. This is sometimes referred to as a "program cost," but the transfer payment itself is not an economic cost.

This report categorizes costs under two additional typologies, *health services costs* and *other costs*, and *internal* (private) *costs* and *external* (societal) *costs*. The costs of health care services that those without health insurance use do not, for the most part, represent economic costs attributable to being uninsured. The level of per capita expenditures for those without coverage is important, however, for measuring the difference in health care costs and utilization between otherwise similar insured and uninsured populations. Furthermore, the distribution of these costs among payers and sponsors of uncompensated care is also important. Figure 2.2 presents a matrix of these categories, and locates the particular elements of economic costs and transfers within its cells. Costs that are transfers are noted in the figure. The remainder of the section describes the classifications.

Cost-of-illness studies, which estimate the total value of resources expended as a result of the incidence or prevalence of a particular health condition, typically distinguish direct medical costs incurred from other costs, such as losses of productivity and premature death. The Committee follows this general distinction in the organization of the remaining chapters. Chapter 3 considers the health care services expenditures made on behalf of uninsured individuals. Chapter 4 considers the other, non–health care costs incurred as a result of an uninsured population. Chapter 5 presents estimates of the health care resources that would be needed if the uninsured were to receive the same kind and amount of health care that those with insurance use.

This report also distinguishes economic costs that are borne privately by individuals, families, and particular firms (*internal costs*) from those that "spill over" and affect others in the society or economy (*external costs*). Following Manning and colleagues (1989, 1991), the total social costs of an individual behavior (such as smoking) or a condition (such as having tuberculosis or being uninsured) can be categorized as internal and external costs. Internal costs include the costs of medical services resulting from the behavior or condition for which the individual pays, lost earnings that result from poorer health, and other out-of-pocket expenses incurred as a result of the behavior or condition. The poorer health and reduced longevity associated with being uninsured is an internal cost of uninsurance because it affects the uninsured individual. Conversely, the incremental value of the better health status and longer life expectancy of that same individual if insured is an internal or private benefit of providing health insurance.

External or spillover costs are the costs imposed on others by the behavior or condition. An external cost of an untreated case of tuberculosis, for example, includes the infection of others with the disease. The costs of uncompensated care

	Internal Costs (for individuals, families, and firms)	External Costs (to society)
Health Care Service Costs	• Out-of-pocket expenditures for health care services	• Expenditures for uncompensated care (primarily transfer costs)
Other Costs	• Greater morbidity and premature mortality • Developmental losses for children • Diminished sense of social equality and of self-respect • Family financial uncertainty and stress, depletion of assets (resource and transfer costs) • Lost income of uninsured breadwinner in ill health • Workplace productivity losses (absenteeism, reduced efficiency on the job)	• Diminished quality and availability of personal health services • Diminished public health system capacity • Diminished population health (e.g., higher rates of vaccine-preventable disease) • Higher taxes, budget cuts, loss of other uses for public revenues diverted to uncompensated care (primarily transfer costs) • Higher public program costs connected with worse health (e.g., Medicare, disability payments) (primarily transfer costs) • Diminished workforce productivity • Diminished social capital; unfulfilled social norms of caring, equal opportunity, and mutual respect

FIGURE 2.2 Classification of the costs consequent to uninsurance.

borne by providers of services and taxpayers are external costs (transfers) of an individual's uninsured status. The external costs associated with uninsurance include not only aggregated individual-level costs such as uncompensated care proximately borne by providers, but also community-level costs, such as the impact of relatively high uninsured rates on local hospitals and primary care providers and the local economy generally. The costs discussed in Chapters 3 and 4 include both internal and external (resource and transfer) costs of uninsurance. Chapter 5, which projects the incremental utilization and resources that would be required if those without coverage used services as does the insured population, does not attempt to identify how these incremental costs would be distributed between the uninsured themselves and others.

APPROACH TO ESTIMATING THE COSTS OF UNINSURANCE AND THE COSTS AND BENEFITS OF COVERAGE

The methodological considerations that are important for the analyses presented in this report differ from those of the Committee's earlier work. The Committee established the nature of and, in some cases, estimated the probable magnitude of a number of health, financial, and institutional consequences of uninsurance in the earlier reports. This section outlines the Committee's approach to calculating and aggregating the economic value of these effects, and describes and gives the rationale for the approach taken. Whenever possible, the Committee has relied on consensus recommendations (such as those of the Panel on Cost-Effectiveness in Health and Medicine mentioned earlier) in the treatment and reporting of costs and benefits and on analytic practices in cost–effectiveness and cost–benefit studies in health care and cost-of-illness studies.[5]

The relative merits of cost–effectiveness and cost–benefit analysis continue to be the subject of lively methodological and philosophical debates. The Committee has drawn from each of these approaches to examine the issue of the value of insurance for the uninsured from a variety of perspectives and to gain insight from each.

The remainder of this section describes (1) the analytic structure within which the Committee developed its estimates of the value of health forgone as a result of the lack of coverage and (2) the resources that would be needed to provide the currently uninsured population with the amount and kind of health care that those with either public or private coverage now use. It is important to keep in mind that imputing a monetary value to the reduced health and life expectancy that accompanies being uninsured is a different kind of analytic exercise from the calculation of actual expenditures incurred (or projected to be incurred) by or on behalf of those who lack coverage.

---

[5]For principles for and examples of cost-evaluative studies in health care see Rice (1966); Cooper and Rice (1976); Rice et al. (1985); Scitovsky and Rice (1987); Manning et al. (1991); Rice et al. (1991); Sloan (1995b); Gold et al.(1996b); Russell et al. (1996); USPSTF (1996); Drummond et al. (1997); Messonier et al. (1999), and Glied et al. (2002).

Estimating the Value of Longer Life and Improved Health

As a polity and a society, we make decisions about the economic value of life all the time in evaluating health and safety risks and the costs of reducing those risks. Being uninsured likewise can be thought of in terms of the risks of poorer health and shorter life faced by those without coverage (IOM 2002a,b). The Committee has posed the following question: How much health is lost within the U.S. population due to the lack of universal health insurance coverage? Conversely, what is the value of the increased health across the population that would be gained if those without health insurance coverage were to gain it, across the board? To answer these questions, the Committee adapted a common approach used in government rulemaking on health, safety, and environmental issues to determine the value of the difference in health outcomes, morbidity and mortality, that can be attributed to health insurance status.

Economists have used evidence of actual marketplace transactions that involve implicit tradeoffs between risk and money to estimate the value of a statistical (i.e., not identifiable) life (VSL) (Viscusi and Aldy, 2002). Such estimates have been used by governmental regulatory agencies such as the Environmental Protection Agency (EPA), the Food and Drug Administration, the Consumer Product Safety Commission, and the Department of Transportation. In conducting cost-benefit analyses to guide regulation and investment in health and safety, these agencies, under the guidance of the Office of Management and Budget, have developed their own valuation methodologies and used a variety of approaches (OMB, 2003). The study included as Appendix B reviews these approaches in greater detail and justifies using a mid-range value of a statistical healthy year of life ($160,000) that corresponds to an average lifetime value of $4.8 million (Vigdor, 2003). Box 2.1 illustrates the application of this kind of analysis in the development of EPA regulations that set emissions standards for trucks and buses under the Clean Air Act (USEPA, 2001).

Health Capital and Human Capital

Health capital can be understood as the present value of the stock of health that an individual is expected to have over the course of his or her future lifetime. This concept is derived from the earlier notion of *human capital*, which posits that an individual's stock of knowledge raises his or her productivity in the market sector of the economy and also in the nonmarket or household sector (Becker, 1964; Grossman, 1972; Cutler and Richardson, 1999). Analogous to education in the human capital model, an investment in health care in the health capital model adds to one's stock of health, increasing time spent in a healthier state than otherwise.

Both human capital and health capital are analytic constructs based on the concept of personal utility in welfare economics. Each can be converted into monetary terms. The value of an individual's stock of human capital is often expressed as the discounted present value of future earnings as a function of

BOX 2.1
An Example of Evaluating Costs and Benefits:
Regulations for Clean Air and Vehicle Emissions Standards

Federal agencies are required to evaluate the costs and benefits of regulations that have costs of at least $100 million. This information is part of the regulatory impact analysis that the Environmental Protection Agency (EPA) conducted prior to issuing new vehicle emissions standards.

In 2001, EPA issued air pollution control rules to reduce emissions of particulate matter and nitrogen oxides from new heavy-duty trucks and buses by at least 90 percent below current standard levels by 2030 (USEPA, 2001).[1] These standards require not only engine-based technology changes, but also diesel fuel production requirements to reduce fuel sulfur content by 97 percent. The engine manufacturing and refining changes imposed by the regulation are expected to have an aggregate annual economic cost of just over $3 billion in 2007, rising to $4.2 billion annually by 2030 (all values in 1999 dollars) (USEPA, 2001).

When fully in place (2030), the new standards will reduce emissions of nitrogen oxides, nonmethane hydrocarbons, and particulate matter by a projected 2.6 million tons, 115,000 tons, and 109,000 tons, respectively, each year. The cleaner air that will result from these emissions controls is expected to avoid 8,300 premature deaths among adults aged 30 and older each year, 5,500 cases of chronic bronchitis, and 9,600 hospitalizations for respiratory or cardiovascular reasons. These health outcomes account for over 90 percent of the health and productivity gains of more than $70 billion annually that EPA estimates would be achieved with reduced emissions and improved air quality under the new standards for heavy engines and diesel fuel (USEPA, 2001). EPA used $6.1 million as the value of a statistical life for the purposes of these health benefits estimates.

---

[1]Additional sources: Hubbell (2002); OMB (2003).

educational attainment, something that is easily calculated. Sometimes the value of nonmarket or household production is incorporated into the total value of human capital.

Estimating the value of a healthy life using human capital methods has two major problems. First, people value healthy life years for more reasons than their ability to earn income (Cutler and Richardson, 1997, 1999). Second, this approach values individuals' lives differently depending on their education and income–producing potential, which violates widely held ethical and political principles of valuing the lives of all members of a democratic society alike. Although this second objection could be addressed by imputing the national mean or median human capital estimate to everyone, the first objection cannot be overcome. The Committee judged that the health capital approach better reflected the demonstrated value placed on better health and longer life.

Health capital takes into account people's valuing of their own lives beyond their ability to be productive and earn income over their working lifetime. The health capital approach, however, can be misleading because it is based on workers' or consumers' *revealed preferences* through their choices in the marketplace for small changes in the risks to their health and safety that they face. Although people are willing to pay substantial amounts for small reductions in risk, by buying smoke detectors or bicycle helmets (even if not required to by law), because of limits on their income they would not be able to "scale up" these amounts for slightly better health and safety in a statistical sense to the value equivalent that represents the value of their entire remaining life. It thus appears that people cannot "afford" their own lives, in the sense of being able to "pay" for the value ascribed to life through earnings capacity. At the same time, valuing life at more than earnings capacity has contributed to public policy decision making over the past 30 years and is based on empirical evidence of consumers' implicit *willingness to pay* to reduce risks to life and health. Approaches using revealed preferences (through market transactions) can be contrasted with stated preferences approaches like *contingent valuation*, which is a survey-based approach to eliciting individuals' preferences and priorities, described further below.

Valuing life at more than earnings capacity is consistent with how individuals and society as a whole make decisions. When insured people get seriously sick, they expect their insurance to pay substantial amounts if necessary, to purchase services that can provide a cure or ease their symptoms (de Meza, 1983; Nyman, 1999a,b). These amounts are often more than the insured could afford, sometimes many times more than their income. Pooled across many individuals through insurance, these costs are affordable. Analyzed as costs per life saved or compared to the improved quality of life they purchase, they generate estimates comparable to those used in the health capital analysis we present.

The remainder of this section reviews the metrics of health-related quality of life and quality-adjusted life years, which the Committee has employed in its analysis of health capital. These metrics are frequently used in clinical medical research and public health analysis to evaluate the effectiveness of particular health care interventions.

Valuing Different Health Outcomes

Converting the multiple dimensions of health status into a single metric that reflects the quality of life associated with a particular health profile poses a formidable challenge for economic and policy analysts. Health outcomes can be characterized more or less precisely and specifically. The most basic distinction in states of health is between being alive and being dead. The measure of premature mortality provides information about a determinant of health outcomes in terms of death prior to achieving an expected lifespan. The metric of years of life (YOL) lost converts this all-or-nothing measure of premature deaths into a proportionate measure, but one that is relatively crude. Health has many dimensions: physical, psychological, social, and functional.

One widely accepted scale measure of health status that attempts to build in these dimensions of health is the *quality-adjusted life year* (QALY) (Patrick and Erickson, 1993; Gold et al., 1996a). QALYs combine the length of life and the *health-related quality of life* (HRQL) that can be attributed to a given health state (CDC, 2000). QALY values or weights are derived empirically by researchers from population surveys that elicit individuals' ordering of their preferences for different health states or disease conditions in any of several different ways, including responses to hypothetical time or health–state tradeoffs (Gold et al., 1996a). Developing QALY weights through survey research of this kind is a form of *contingent valuation*, a stated preference technique to establishing value.

Contingent valuation is "a survey-based methodology for eliciting consumers' willingness to pay for benefits from a particular policy, usually expressed as a small change in risk" (Appendix B, p. 137). Because it directly measures the value someone places on the benefit, it most closely approximates the actual measure sought. Studies of contingent valuation can be conducted from different perspectives, such as that of a community (e.g., the average of the values given by a statistically valid population sample) or that of a single individual. The particular perspective adopted determines how the information is interpreted and should be used.

The Committee's Approach to Valuing Health Capital

The version of health capital analysis employed here takes a comprehensive and egalitarian approach to constructing the value of life years in a particular health state by extending the value of life years beyond their potential for income production and by nominally assigning each person the same value for every year of life in perfect health. The Committee has chosen, in the analysis presented in this report, to value each year of life in perfect health at $160,000, in 2001 dollars. This is the median value ascribed to such a healthy year of life in a recent review of contingent valuation studies. The range of values from contingent valuation studies in this review extended from $59,000 to $1,176,000 per year of life (Hirth et al., 2000). Many researchers and policy makers remain reluctant to convert life years and health–related quality of life into monetary terms because they are skeptical that these very different kinds of goods, life and money, can be commensurated. Thus QALYs themselves often serve as the final unit of value (instead of dollars) for studies of the relative cost effectiveness of alternative health interventions. In her commissioned analysis, Elizabeth Richardson Vigdor uses the information about the relative health outcomes of similar people with and without health insurance that the Committee reported in *Care Without Coverage* and *Health Insurance Is a Family Matter* to estimate the value of years of life, and of quality-adjusted years of life (QALYs) that would be gained if the uninsured had coverage over the course of their lives. This analysis is summarized in Chapter 4 and presented in full as Appendix B. Additional methodological issues and choices the Committee made for this analysis are discussed in Chapter 4.

Approach to Estimating Additional Costs from Added Insurance Coverage

The increases in life expectancy and quality of life underlying the health benefits from health insurance estimated in Chapter 4 are the result of increases in health care utilization—more preventive care, more appropriate care, and improvements in access. In Chapter 5, the Committee examines the costs that would result from the additional use of health care induced by insurance. The chapter reports the results of three analyses that compare utilization and expenditures by those with and without health insurance for the full year. Because the uninsured differ from the insured in a number of characteristics that influence health and health care beyond their different insurance status, any analysis of the costs of insuring the uninsured must account for observable differences in health status, age, gender, race, education, and other factors. Each of the three studies reviewed in Chapter 5 make adjustments to account for systematic differences between insured and uninsured populations. The two more current studies also predict the cost of additional services to the uninsured under two different scenarios. The first scenario assumes that the uninsured acquire the patterns of care of those with private health insurance and the second assumes the uninsured have the patterns of care and expenditures of a similar group with public coverage.

These two benchmarks assume that what happens to the uninsured is similar to the experience of the currently insured as a group. If the scope of the benefits package, the levels of cost sharing, the provider payment, or financing of the plans for the uninsured were different from what is now typical, then the cost could differ accordingly. If there were other structural changes in the health care delivery system, then the estimates would need to be adjusted because the projections assume no shifts in the unit costs of health care services after the implementation of universal coverage.

LIMITATIONS OF THE EVALUATION OF COSTS AND BENEFITS RELATED TO COVERAGE

The Committee's analysis in this report rests largely on the findings and conclusions related to health outcomes, family impacts, and community-level effects of uninsurance contained in its previous reports. The strengths and limitations of the evidence base for the particular findings are included in *Care Without Coverage, Health Insurance Is a Family Matter*, and *A Shared Destiny*. The estimates and discussion of costs and benefits presented in this report have additional important limitations and qualifications.

First, the Committee has quantified only some of the costs of uninsurance, and these estimates are based on a single analysis that the Committee commissioned. The Committee believes that its estimation of the health capital forgone takes a justifiedly narrow and conservative approach to quantifying societal costs and probably underestimates the value lost through uninsurance. The potential for economy-wide and employer-specific costs are discussed qualitatively, but are not quantified in monetary terms.

Second, the estimate of the value of health capital that would result from universal coverage is dependent on the value imputed to a QALY through the stated-preference technique of contingent valuation. Although the value the Committee uses is consistent with current practice in many government agencies reflecting implicit tradeoffs between money and safety, this technique and the value ascribed are both subject to development and revision with further study and application. Again, the Committee believes that the analysis presented here makes reasonably cautious and conservative assumptions.

Third, although the estimate of the direct health care costs now incurred by uninsured Americans has been derived from two independent sources and is well documented and based on reasonable assumptions (see Hadley and Holahan, 2003a), it should not be assumed that these costs necessarily would be offset or eliminated by universal coverage. The extent to which a program of universal coverage would "capture" any of these current subsidies and expenditures depends on the specific provisions of the approach adopted.

Fourth, the resource costs projected in Chapter 5 for increasing the utilization of health care services by uninsured Americans to the level of utilization by those who have coverage should not be construed as the cost of any particular program or set of policies resulting in universal health insurance coverage. Furthermore, the costs of such expansions of insurance coverage are likely to be distributed quite differently from the incidence of costs and burdens associated with the status quo. These projections answer a much narrower question than the questions that would need to be addressed in developing cost estimates for any policy reform proposal. The Committee presents these projections in order to compare the value of statistical healthy life years that would be gained by uninsured individuals if they were to acquire lifelong health insurance coverage in terms of the costs of additional services that would allow them to achieve better health.

Finally, this report and the estimates and analyses it contains are initial efforts at developing an integrated and coherent framework for evaluating a variety of economic costs attributable to the lack of health insurance across the U.S. population. It should not be the last word on the subject. Throughout the report, the Committee notes important questions that cannot be answered adequately because of the lack of data or research. Although this report does not explicitly develop an agenda for further research, the limits of what can be said about the costs due to uninsured populations implicitly point to such an agenda.

SUMMARY

This chapter has presented the analytic context, concepts, and approach that the Committee employs in the remainder of the report and acknowledged the limitations of the analysis. The following chapter considers the health care services costs incurred by uninsured Americans and identifies who ultimately bears these costs.

3

Spending on Health Care for Uninsured Americans: How Much, and Who Pays?

This chapter considers estimates of expenditures for health care services used by uninsured Americans, both the out-of-pocket spending of those without insurance and the value of the health care services they use that are uncompensated or donated. Persons without health insurance, on average, spend less for health care out of pocket than do those with health insurance because they use fewer and less costly services. Uninsured families pay for a higher *proportion* of their total health care costs out of pocket than do insured families, however, and are more likely to have high medical expenses relative to income (IOM, 2002b).[1]

The health care services received by uninsured individuals that they do not pay for themselves are picked up or "absorbed" by a number of parties, including:

- practitioners and institutions, both public and private, that serve the uninsured at no charge or reduced charges;
- the federal government, localities, and states that support the operation of hospitals and clinics, both through direct appropriations and implicit subsidies like the Medicare and Medicaid disproportionate share hospital payments; and
- philanthropic donations.

The claim is often made that hospitals and physicians shift the costs of uncompen-

---

[1]The differences in service utilization costs between uninsured and insured individuals reported in this chapter have not been adjusted for differences between the two groups in age composition and family income, which also affect health services use and spending. In contrast, the projections reviewed in Chapter 5 of service use and expenditures for those without insurance if their utilization was the same as for those with coverage do adjust for demographic and socioeconomic factors.

sated care onto the bills of insured patients, and the Committee also considers the evidence for such cost shifting.

The chapter is organized as follows. The first section briefly compares the average overall health expenditures for uninsured and privately insured populations. The following section examines the out-of-pocket spending by the uninsured and the distribution of their out-of-pocket expenses by service. The third section presents estimates developed by Jack Hadley and John Holahan of the Urban Institute of the amount of uncompensated health care services used by people uninsured for part or all of a year. The fourth and last section examines the incidence of the burden of uncompensated care costs across public and private payers, and more specifically how it is shared among the federal, state, and local governments.

UNINSURED PEOPLE USE LESS MEDICAL CARE THAN DO THOSE WITH COVERAGE

Finding: Uninsured children and adults are less likely to incur any health care expenses in a year than their counterparts who have coverage. On average, those without any form of coverage over the course of a year incur health care costs less than half of per capita health care spending for those under age 65 who have coverage.[2]

Uninsured people are both less likely than those with coverage to use any health services in a given year and have lower expenditures for services on average (Taylor et al., 2001). As earlier Committee reports demonstrated, this lower level of utilization is the source of one hidden cost of uninsurance—higher morbidity and mortality as a result of using fewer and less appropriate health care services. The Committee does not mean to imply by this comparison, however, that all of the additional use of services by those with coverage is effective and appropriate, but simply that the greater amounts of services used by insured populations are associated with and contribute to their better health outcomes, relative to those of uninsured populations.

Table 3.1 presents data from the 1996 Medical Expenditure Panel Survey (MEPS), comparing the experience of full-year uninsured and full-year privately insured individuals under age 65 who used any health services of a particular kind in that year.[3] Sixty-two percent of full-year uninsured persons incurred any health care expenses, compared with 89 percent of those with private insurance for the

---

[2]This reflects the statistics reported in Table 3.2 that are not adjusted for differences in the age and sex composition of insured and uninsured populations. It is also consistent with analyses that are adjusted for demographic differences, as illustrated by the statistics in Table 5.3 in Chapter 5.

[3]The 1996 MEPS is a two-year panel of about 22,000 respondents that is nationally representative of the U.S. noninstitutionalized population.

TABLE 3.1 Use of Services by Full-Year Uninsured and Full-Year Privately Insured Individuals Under Age 65, 1996 (percentage with use)

Service	Uninsured	Privately Insured
Any service	62.0	89.0
Inpatient hospital	2.9	4.6
Outpatient hospital	6.2	13.4
Emergency room	11.5	11.0
Office-based physician	41.3	71.3
Office-based nonphysician	13.6	25.8
Prescription medications	40.6	66.1
Dental	20.4	53.1

SOURCE: Taylor et al., 2001. MEPS 1996.

full year (Taylor et al., 2001). Except for emergency room services, which are used comparably by about 11 percent of privately insured and uninsured persons, the proportion of the uninsured population using any other kind of health service is one-half to two-thirds of the proportion of the privately insured population using each type of service.

Persons uninsured for the full year incur total average annual expenses for health care services that are less than two-fifths of those of someone with either full-year private or full-year public coverage. Box 3.1 reviews the Committee's findings from *Health Insurance Is a Family Matter* about the dependence of children's receipt of care on their parents' health insurance status. Efforts to ensure that children have coverage and receive appropriate health care should take into account these interactions within families.

Table 3.2 presents estimated expenditures for full- and part-year uninsured individuals and compares them with those for persons covered the entire year. For 2001, estimated per capita spending for the population under age 65 overall was $2,163.[4] For the full-year uninsured, per capita spending was $923, 43 percent of the overall average and just 37–38 percent of the average for those with any kind of coverage for the entire year. Those with private health insurance for the full year and those with public coverage (Medicaid) for the full year had roughly comparable estimated spending of $2,484 and $2,435, respectively. Those uninsured for part of the year and with either private or public coverage part of the year had estimated per capita expenditures that ranged from $1,331 for those with private coverage for 5 or fewer months to $2,511 for those with public coverage for between 6 and 11 months.

---

[4]This excludes payments for nursing home and long-term hospital care (which are not standard benefits in private health insurance) and disabled and end-stage renal disease Medicare beneficiaries.

BOX 3.1
Health Insurance and Use of Services Within Families

Health insurance status affects families' relationships with health care providers and the delivery system. One way families with uninsured members manage health care expenses is by not using services. The data comparing use of services and spending on health care for insured and uninsured individuals and families demonstrates this vividly. This discussion illustrates the mechanisms by which children with uninsured parents are harmed by the lack of coverage within the family.

Among adults under age 65, 59 percent who were uninsured throughout 1996 did not have a physician office visit that year, twice the 29 percent of those who had private insurance (Taylor et al., 2001). Among children under age 18 who were uninsured throughout 1996, 49 percent did not have a physician office visit, twice the 24 percent of children with private insurance. Among children who had visits, the average number of visits among those who were uninsured was 2.7. Among children with private coverage, the average was 4.2 visits, half again as many as among uninsured children (McCormick et al., 2001).

Children without health insurance are less likely to have a usual source of care than children with health insurance. The parent of a child without health insurance is less likely to have an answer to the question, "Where do I go if my child becomes sick?" An evaluation of a Pennsylvania program to expand health insurance for children found the share of children with a regular source of care increased from 89 percent at baseline to 99 percent at 12 months, and the share with a regular dentist increased from 60 percent to 85 percent (Lave et al., 1998).

Children benefit from the greater access to health care services that health insurance brings only when their parents or guardians act. They acquire health insurance when adults enroll them and receive health care when parents bring them to a provider. The Committee concluded in *Health Insurance Is a Family Matter* that a child whose *parent* has health insurance is more likely to receive care. Children whose parents do not have health insurance are less likely to use health services, even if the child has health insurance (Newacheck and Halfon, 1986; Hanson, 1998; Minkovitz et al., 2002). In one comparison, having an uninsured parent decreased the probability that a child had any visit with a medical provider by 6.5 percent and a well-child visit by 6.7 percent, compared to children whose parent had health insurance (Davidoff et al., 2002).

If all parents had health insurance, a larger share of children could be expected to receive the regular medical attention that is of proven value for children's health and development.

When people who lack insurance do obtain care, it is paid for by a number of parties, including the uninsured themselves. The remainder of this chapter examines who provides and also pays for this care, and the economic implications of uncompensated care burdens on health care providers, payers, governments, and taxpayers.

TABLE 3.2 Total and Per Capita[a] Medical Care Spending, by Insurance Status, 2001 (estimated)

Insurance Status	Total Spending ($ billions)	Per Capita[a] Spending ($)
Private Insurance, Full Year	375.1	2,484
Public Insurance, Full Year	42.5	2,435
Uninsured, Part Year		
Private insurance for 1–5 months	10.4	1,331
Private insurance for 6–11 months	25.9	1,796
Public insurance for 1–5 months	5.0	1,729
Public insurance for 6–11 months	12.0	2,511
Uninsured, Full Year	30.0	923
Total Uninsured (full and part year)	83.1[b]	1,335[b]
Total Population[a,c]	500.9	2,163

[a]Civilian, noninstitutionalized population under age 65, excluding people with any Medicare coverage, nursing home, and long-term hospital care.

[b]No adjustment for MEPS undercount of uncompensated care.

[c]Entries do not sum to total because of rounding.

SOURCE: Hadley and Holahan, 2003a. Pooled data from the 1996, 1997, and 1998 MEPS, projected to 2001 levels.

OUT-OF-POCKET COSTS FOR UNINSURED INDIVIDUALS AND FAMILIES

Finding: People who lack health insurance for an entire year have out-of-pocket expenditures comparable to those of people with private coverage, but they also have much lower family incomes. Out-of-pocket spending for health care by the uninsured is more likely to consume a substantial portion of family income than out-of-pocket spending by those with any kind of insurance coverage.

Families with members who do not have health insurance face substantial financial risks. The nature and consequences of those risks were addressed in the committee's third report, *Health Insurance Is a Family Matter*. While the mean out-of-pocket expenses for someone uninsured for the full year is only slightly higher than for someone privately insured for the full year ($426, compared with $402 in 1996), the average family income of someone without health insurance is substantially lower than that for the privately insured.[5] In 2001, the median annual family

---

[5]These comparisons are not age adjusted. Those without health insurance are disproportionately young adults, whose per capita health spending is lower on average than that of older adults.

income of uninsured persons was between $20,000 and $29,000 and that for those with private coverage was over $50,000 (Fronstin, 2002). In addition, the average for those without insurance includes a higher proportion of families that have not incurred any costs than does the average for those with health insurance, so the expense is spread less evenly across the population. Fifteen percent of families in which all members were without health insurance for all of 1996 had health costs that exceeded 5 percent of their income and 4 percent of uninsured families had expenses that exceeded 20 percent of their annual income (compared with 1 percent of privately insured families). Among uninsured families with incomes of less than 125 percent of the federal poverty line, however, between 8 and 9 percent had health care expenses greater than 20 percent of income (Taylor et al., 2001).

Families with some or all members uninsured for longer than a year are more likely to experience a period in which their medical expenses are substantial. Assuming for simplicity that years in which medical expenses are high are statistically independent (not likely to be true because these expenses are correlated across time), a family with no members insured for 5 years would be slightly more likely than not to have at least one year with health care costs that exceeded 5 percent of its income (Merlis, 2001).

Food, shelter, transportation, and clothing account for 85 percent on average of the expenditures of families without health insurance. With few assets to use up, medical expenses lead to a lower standard of living. For some families, medical costs may mean bankruptcy (IOM, 2002b.) Hospital stays are the most expensive kind of health care service. Because hospitals frequently reduce, or write off as bad debt, charges to uninsured patients, families are spared some of the financial adjustments that would be required to meet the full cost of treatment. Accepting charity care or incurring bad debt exposes families to other kinds of costs. Box 3.2 reviews some of the implications for individuals and families of receiving care for which they cannot pay.

Uninsured individuals pay for a larger share of services received on an ambulatory basis than they do for inpatient care. Figure 3.1 displays the proportion of costs that uninsured individuals pay out of pocket for various kinds of services and the share of total health expenditures represented by each kind of service.

Both the chances of substantial illness and asset levels tend to increase with age. Older persons without health insurance are both more likely to experience illness and have fewer years until retirement to replace assets depleted by the costs of illness. One in every six people ages 51 to 61 participating in the Health and Retirement Survey who were initially uninsured experienced a new diagnosis of cancer, heart disease, or stroke within the next 6 years (Levy, 2002). Those who did not have health insurance had substantially lower levels of wealth than those who did at the start of the study. Median nonhousing wealth totaled $61,000 for those with health insurance and $19,000 for those without health insurance. Liquid assets, such as amounts in checking, savings, or money market accounts, amounted to $7,000 for the median insured person who went on to experience a

BOX 3.2
Charity Care and Bad Debts

A person or family that seeks charity care must submit to probing questions about their financial means, and may feel stigmatized or shamed by having to accept charity. Stigma is one reason those who are eligible for assistance often do not apply (Moffitt, 1983).

If an individual or family does not apply for charity care when the patient obtains hospital services, they receive a bill that asks for payment of the hospital's charges. The amount billed to patients without insurance coverage is not reduced by any "contractual allowances," reductions from the hospital's charges that payers negotiate (or in the case of public payers like Medicaid or Medicare, set unilaterally) (Wielawski, 2000; Lagnado, 2003a,b).

In time, a hospital may write off as bad debt the amount that an uninsured patient does not pay. But between initial receipt of a bill and a bad debt writeoff, the patient and family receive monthly billings that may exceed the family's income. Even if the collection process ends with a hospital or collection agency writing off the unpaid amount, a family faces ongoing consequences. A report by a hospital or other health care provider that a family did not pay for its health care remains part of the family's credit report for up to 7 years (Federal Trade Commission, 1999). A person who while uninsured experienced a costly episode of health care can find that years later his or her or another family member's health care shapes whether he or she obtains credit to buy a house or lease a car or rent an apartment. If a family has a home, it may find that a health care provider has placed a lien on the home to satisfy an unpaid health care bill (Lagnado, 2003a; Schneider, 2003). A lien must be satisfied at the time the property is sold, potentially separating the time a family incurred an expense and its payment by 20 or more years.

These repeat billings and collection efforts on the part of the hospital are dictated by standard hospital accounting and audit practices, which require hospitals to demonstrate efforts to collect before writing off an outstanding account balance as bad debt (Herkimer, 1993; Lagnado, 2003a,b). These repeat billings also add to hospitals' administrative costs.

new diagnosis and just $900 for the median uninsured person who similarly had a new diagnosis (Levy, 2002.)

Public subsidies for coverage make health insurance financially more feasible for lower-income persons and families, yet many who are eligible are not enrolled in public programs or cannot afford to take up workplace offers. Public coverage through Medicaid offers health insurance without paying a premium for those with very low income.[6] State Children's Health Insurance Programs (SCHIPs) and state-only insurance programs may require income-related premiums for families with incomes above the Medicaid or SCHIP full-subsidy level (SCHIP limits

---

[6]*Health Insurance Is a Family Matter* presents state-by-state income eligibility standards for Medicaid and the State Children's Health Insurance Program in Appendix D.

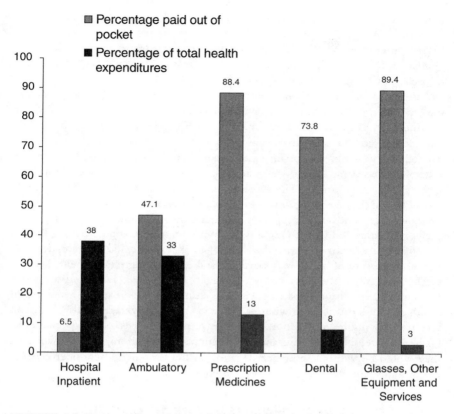

FIGURE 3.1 Share paid out of pocket by uninsured persons under age 65, within each type of service and share of total health expenditures that each type of service represents, 1997.

SOURCE: Agency for Healthcare Research and Quality, 2001. Data from 1997 Medical Expenditure Panel Survey.

cost sharing to less than 5 percent of income). The tax treatment of health insurance allows workers to obtain health insurance without paying income or payroll tax on the premium paid by the employer. Despite Medicaid requiring no premiums and SCHIP relatively modest ones, if any, many who are eligible for these programs are not enrolled. Based on eligibility simulations by the Urban Institute, in 2001 an estimated 5.26 million children were eligible for either SCHIP or Medicaid but not enrolled, and an estimated 3 million lower-income (family income less than 200 percent of the federal poverty level) adults under age 65, both parents and those without children, were eligible for but not enrolled in Medicaid (Schneider, 2002). Among children who are eligible for Medicaid but not enrolled, nearly 85 percent live in families that had some health costs over a one-year period, and 29 percent had out-of-pocket costs that were greater than $500 (Davidoff et al., 2000). Although the reasons why so many children are eligible but not enrolled vary, their lack of coverage entails both health and financial losses within the family (IOM, 2002b).

If people without health insurance were to gain coverage, the change in their out-of-pocket costs for health care would depend both on the scope of benefits of and the cost sharing required by the policy or program they enrolled in, and on any increase in the amount or cost of care they received as a result of being insured. The change in the financial circumstances of persons without health insurance who gained health insurance would also depend on how their care-seeking behavior changed. The Committee's second report, *Care Without Coverage*, addressed the adverse health consequences for persons who do not have health insurance from not obtaining preventive and regular chronic disease care. If the previously uninsured were to use services more frequently, approximating the use patterns of those with coverage, their out-of-pocket costs could increase, depending on the nature of their plan's coverage and cost-sharing requirements because of the increase in their average spending on health care, including insurance premiums. (See Chapter 5 for benchmark estimates of the expected increase in health services costs if those without insurance gained coverage similar to that of the currently insured population.) Whether or not enrollees' out-of-pocket costs for health care, including insurance premium payments, are higher or lower than they would be without insurance depends on the time period considered, their health status, and the extent of any premium subsidy.

UNCOMPENSATED CARE TO UNINSURED PERSONS

Finding: The best available estimate of the value of uncompensated health care services provided to persons who lack health insurance for some or all of a year is roughly $35 billion annually, about 2.8 percent of total national spending for personal health care services.

The Committee's fourth report, *A Shared Destiny*, provided an overview of the level and sources of uncompensated health care in the United States in order to elucidate the mechanism by which uninsurance affected communities, their health care agencies and institutions, and economic resources. This information is also a central component of this report because it bears on how the costs of care received by those without coverage are distributed. Most of the costs of uncompensated care provided to those without coverage do not represent new economic costs attributable to uninsurance per se, but are instead transfers of resources from public and private sources to those receiving health care.

To the extent that individuals who lack coverage receive less effective or more costly health care than do those with coverage, the overall costs of their care will include some amount of true economic costs attributable to the condition of lacking coverage. These economic costs are borne by taxpayers and others that support the provision of uncompensated services, as well as by the out-of-pocket payments of uninsured individuals. Box 3.3 presents studies that have documented and attempted to estimate the relative magnitude of one aspect of inefficient and costly care among uninsured populations—potentially avoidable hospitalizations.

A recent analysis and comprehensive set of estimates of the value of health care services provided to Americans without health insurance were prepared by economists Jack Hadley and John Holahan of the Urban Institute (2003a). They used two independent approaches and sources of data for their estimates of the value of free hospital, physician, and clinic services the uninsured use annually, adjusted to reflect estimated spending in 2001.

The first estimate used pooled data from the 1996, 1997, and 1998 Medical Expenditure Panel Survey (MEPS) of the civilian, noninstitutionalized population to calculate the volume of services provided to individuals who were uninsured for part or all of the year.[7] From this source the authors were able to distinguish between the expenditures on behalf of full- and part-year uninsured. Combining periods without coverage for those uninsured for only part of the year to calculate full-year-equivalent periods of uninsurance and adding these uninsured years to those of individuals uninsured for the full year resulted in an overall average of 45 million person-years of uninsurance for each year, 1996–1998. To offset MEPS' systematic undercounting of uncompensated services by private hospitals and other private facilities and of general government appropriations and payments to hospitals, the authors increased the MEPS-based estimates of care received by the uninsured by 25 percent. This reflects a reconciliation of MEPS-reported health expenditures with the more comprehensive National Health Accounts estimates of the Centers for Medicare and Medicaid Services (Selden et al., 2001).

The authors' estimate for 2001 of the value of uncompensated health care services received by people uninsured for either part or all of a year was $34.5 billion, $24.6 billion of which was for those uninsured for the entire year and $9.9 billion for those uninsured part of the year (see Table 3.3). Free or uncompensated care accounted for 61 percent of the value of services used by those uninsured for the full year and 17 percent of the value of services provided to those uninsured for part of the year.[8] This amount represents 2.8 percent of the projected total personal health care expenditures nationally for 2001 (Hadley and Holahan, 2003a).

---

[7]MEPS is an annual national household survey conducted by the Agency for Healthcare Research and Quality that includes information on health insurance, medical care use, and charges and payments for care received. Household responses about payments for care are corroborated by querying providers.

[8]MEPS imputes the cost of uncompensated care provided by public hospitals and clinics, and the estimate for private hospitals and other private providers was based on an imputation of what the provider would have been paid for that care if rendered to those with private health insurance.

BOX 3.3
Potentially Avoidable Hospitalizations:
Costs of Inefficient Utilization

While uninsured individuals bear the direct costs to health of inappropriate (including inadequate) use of health care services, when care is received too late or in settings such as hospital emergency departments, additional economic costs are created. These economic losses are subsumed in the estimates of both out-of-pocket spending and uncompensated care expenditures for the uninsured.

One avenue by which these costs are introduced is potentially avoidable hospitalization for conditions that, if medical attention is prompt and appropriate, can often be effectively managed on an outpatient basis. Measured across areas or population groups, rates of potentially avoidable hospitalizations not only serve as an indicator of the acuity of illness experienced within a population, these rates also reflect the efficiency with which health care is provided. If some hospitalizations could be avoided with earlier, more appropriate, and less costly care, then some portion of uncompensated care costs could be eliminated. Because uninsured persons themselves pay less than 7 percent of the expenditures for hospital care that they incur, public programs and other sources of support pay the rest (AHRQ, 2001).

Uninsured patients are more likely to experience avoidable hospitalizations than are privately insured patients when measured as the proportion of all hospitalizations (Pappas et al., 1997). Nationally, the proportion of hospitalizations that were potentially avoidable for persons younger than 65 have grown more substantially over the past two decades for uninsured persons than for those with Medicaid or private insurance: from 5.1 to 11.6 percent between 1980 and 1998 for the uninsured, compared with increases for Medicaid enrollees from 7 to 9.8 percent and for those with private insurance from 4.1 to 7.5 percent (Kozak et al., 2001).

Pappas and colleagues (1997) examined rates of hospitalization for diagnoses[1] that they identified as potentially treatable on an outpatient basis (adjusted for age and sex) in relation to median income within ZIP-code areas. They estimated that these conditions accounted for between 3 million and 5 million hospitalizations in 1990 (12 to 19 percent of all hospitalizations in that year, excluding those related to childbirth and for psychiatric conditions). They used the rates of hospitalization for these designated conditions that residents in areas with the highest median household incomes ($40,000 or more) experienced as the baseline rates below which such hospitalizations presumably could not be reduced. The authors then calculated that nearly 30 percent of such hospitalizations (between 844,000 and 1.4 million nationally) could represent excessive prevalence and severity of illness, and poorer access to ambulatory care, within lower-income neighborhoods. Age-adjusted rates of potentially avoidable hospitalizations per 1,000 population were higher for uninsured compared with privately insured groups (4 per 1,000 for the uninsured group and 3 per 1,000 for the privately insured population). Less than 6 percent of the uninsured had household incomes of $40,000 or more, so their experience is reflected almost entirely in the differentially high rates of avoidable hospitalizations. Notably, the differences in rates of hospitalization by income class diminished substantially after age 65, when everyone gained Medicare coverage (Pappas et al., 1997).

---

[1] The diagnoses were pneumonia, cellulitis, asthma, malignant hypertension, congestive heart failure, diabetes, perforated or bleeding ulcer, pyelonephritis, ruptured appendix, hypokalemia, vaccine-preventable conditions, and gangrene.

TABLE 3.3 Medical Care Expenditures[a] and Sources of Payment for People Under Age 65 Uninsured for at least Part of the Year, 2001 ($ billions, estimated)

Source of Payment	Uninsured Full Year[b]	Uninsured Part Year[c]	All Uninsured
Free Care[a]	24.6	9.9	34.5
Other public sources	5.0	1.5	6.5
Other private and unknown sources	8.9	3.4	12.3
In-kind[d]	10.8	5.0	15.8
Out of Pocket	14.1	12.3	26.4
Private Insurance	1.9[e]	22.3	24.2
Public Insurance	0.0	13.8	13.8
All Sources	40.6	58.3	98.9[a]

[a]Adjusted for MEPS undercount of uncompensated care relative to National Health Accounts.
[b]Average of 32.4 million people per year from 1996–1998 MEPS.
[c]Average of 29.9 million people per year from 1996–1998 MEPS.
[d]Estimated from the difference between payments and charges.
[e]Payments by workers' compensation.
SOURCE: Hadley and Holahan, 2003a. Derived from pooled data from the 1996, 1997, and 1998 MEPS projected to 2001 levels.

In their second set of estimates, Hadley and Holahan calculated the value of uncompensated care to the uninsured from private provider surveys (e.g., by the American Hospital Association and the American Medical Association) and public provider budgets and appropriations (for clinics and other government direct care programs, such as Department of Veterans Affairs services). In this calculation, the authors also estimated the proportion of uncompensated or charity care that was provided to uninsured patients by each provider type (e.g., hospitals, clinics, physicians in private practice).

Uncompensated Hospital Care

In 1999, hospitals reported $20.8 billion in expenses for all services to all patients who did not pay their bills in full, an amount representing 6.2 percent of total hospital expenses in that years (MedPAC, 2001).[9] Because hospitals apply

---

[9]This amount represents the sum of charges reported by each hospital as bad debt or charity care, reduced by the hospital's cost-to-charge ratio.

different billing policies for patients in similar circumstances, this amount represents both charity care and bad debt reported by the hospitals in the annual American Hospital Association (AHA) survey. This amount is certainly an overestimate of the uncompensated care costs of the uninsured because some proportion of bad debt is attributable to insured patients who do not pay some part of the hospital bill for which they are responsible—the deductible, coinsurance, or noncovered services. Increasing this 1999 estimate to projected Medicare payment increases by 2001 yields an estimate of $23.6 billion in uncompensated care in the latter year.

Clinics and Direct Care Programs

The Committee's previous report, *A Shared Destiny*, provided an overview of the federal, state, and local governmental programs involved in the direct provision of personal health care services to underserved and vulnerable populations, including those Americans who lack health insurance. Hadley and Holahan (2003a) estimate the value of health care services that the various governmental grant and direct care programs provide to those without health insurance, including

- the community health center and other programs of the federal Bureau of Primary Health Care,
  - Maternal and Child Health clinics and services,
  - National Health Service Corps,
  - HIV/AIDS care,
  - Indian Health Service,
  - Department of Veterans Affairs (VA), and
  - local health departments.

Table 3.4 presents the budgets or expenditures for each of these service categories or providers, an estimate of the proportion of total program clients or expenditures that the uninsured represent, and the authors' resulting estimate of total expenditures on care to the uninsured. The authors note that these separate program appropriation and expenditure figures may double count some expenditures for the uninsured because many clinics and health centers are grantees of multiple federal and state programs. For local health departments, for which client health insurance status is not available, the authors assumed that the same proportion of local public health clinic expenditures were attributable to uninsured users as for Bureau of Primary Health Care programs, 32 percent. As shown in Table 3.4, the estimate of expenditures for care to the uninsured from community health and other providers of direct care is $7.11 billion, of which the VA accounts for more than half of the total.

TABLE 3.4 Estimated Expenditures for Care for the Uninsured, Community Health Care Providers and Government Direct Care Programs, FY2001

Source	Total Expenditures ($ billions)	Uninsured (%)	Total Expenditures on Care to Uninsured ($ billions)
Bureau of Primary Health Care	3.46[a]	31.8[b]	0.84[c]
Maternal and Child Health Bureau	2.45[d]	12.7[e]	0.31
National Health Service Corps	0.65[f]	18.3[b]	0.12[c]
HIV/AIDS Bureau	1.75[g]	39.0[e]	0.68
Indian Health Service	1.86[h]	37.0[i]	0.69
Veterans Affairs	18.5[j]	21.0	3.89
Local Health Departments	1.81[k]	32.0	0.58
Total	30.48		7.11

[a]CY2001 data on medical and other professional health services (excluding dental), "Uniform Data System (UDS) Rollup Report," ftp.hrsa.gov/bphc/pdf/uds.

[b]Self-pay patients' share of total charges.

[c]Net of payments collected from self-pay patients.

[d]FY2000 data on direct medical services, trended forward, "Federal-State Title V Block Grant Partnership Budget," http://www.mchdata.net/reports.

[e]Share of users who were uninsured.

[f]CY2000 data trended forward, "NHSC UDS National Rollup Report."

[g]FY2001 appropriation for Emergency Relief-Part A and Comprehensive Care-Part B, "HRSA FY 2002 Budget," http://newsroom.hrsa.gov/NewsBriefs. Includes $0.24 billion in state spending reported by National Association of State Budget Officers (NASBO), 2001.

[h]FY2001 appropriation for clinical services, http://www.ihs.gov/adminmngrresources/budget. Includes $0.06 billion in state spending from NASBO (2001).

[i]Percent of Native Americans reporting only Indian Health Service or no insurance coverage, calculated from the 1997–1999 Current Population Surveys.

[j]FY2001 appropriation for medical care, excluding nursing home, subacute, and residential care.

[k]NASBO, 2001.

SOURCE: Hadley and Holahan, 2003a.

Physicians

By waiving or reducing their fees to uninsured patients and volunteering their time in free clinics and similar settings, physicians provide a significant amount of charity care. One American Medical Association (AMA) survey reports that physicians provided about equal amounts of reduced-price and free care (Emmons, 1995). Unlike the case with hospitals and publicly supported clinics, physicians and others in individual and small-group practices usually do not receive explicit subsidies for uncompensated care nor do they have the organizational superstructure and capacity of larger providers to absorb and balance the financial burdens of uncompensated care.

The Committee's previous report, *A Shared Destiny*, reviews the several sources of information about physicians' provision of charity care, primarily the American Medical Association's periodic surveys of practicing physicians (Emmons, 1995; Kane, 2002) and the Center for Studying Health System Change's Community Tracking Study (CTS) (Cunningham et al., 1999; Reed et al., 2001; Cunningham, 2002). These two sources provide similar estimates of the proportion of practicing physicians who provide any charity care and quite different estimates of the average amount of charity care provided by those physicians who provide any.[10]   One factor that may contribute to the high estimate from the AMA surveys is that salaried physicians who provide uncompensated care within an institutional setting report it as charity care.

Hadley and Holahan based their estimate of the value of uncompensated care physicians provide to uninsured persons on the midpoint of the range of average weekly hours of charity care reported for the 1994 AMA survey (7.2 hours, Emmons, 1995) and the 1999 CTS estimate. The authors used the earlier AMA survey because it included estimates of physicians' average gross earnings per hour for that year ($105) and a breakdown of charity care into that which was entirely free and that for which physicians reduced their prices. They assumed that all of the free care and one-third of the reduced-price care were provided to uninsured patients. Applying the same estimate of gross hourly earnings (updated to 2001 by the medical care consumer price index) to the hours per week of charity care reported by the AMA and CTS surveys, Hadley and Holahan estimated a range of values from $4.5 to $9.1 billion in physician-provided charity care in 2001. The midpoint of the range is $6.8 billion. As a final adjustment to eliminate the double counting of charity care provided by salaried physicians practicing in teaching hospitals, public clinics and hospitals, and community health centers, the authors used the CTS survey estimate that 25 percent of the time physicians reported as spent providing charity care was as salaried employees to reduce the $6.8 billion to $5.1 billion.

Sum of Provider Budget Estimates of Uncompensated Care

Combining the estimates of uncompensated care reported by hospitals through the AHA survey ($23.6 billion), services to uninsured clients by clinics and community health care providers ($7.1 billion), and charity care by physicians in private practice and as volunteers ($5.1 billion), the overall estimate of uncompensated care provided to uninsured Americans based on providers' financial and

---

[10]The 1999 AMA survey found that 65 percent of responding physicians reported providing some charity care, and those physicians who reported any such care reported an average of 8.8 hours weekly, representing 14.4 percent of their total patient hours (Kane, 2002). The CTS surveys in 1999 and 2001 found that 72 percent of responding physicians reported providing any charity care and in 1999 they reported providing an average of 10.6 hours per *month* (2.65 hours per week) of such care (Reed et al., 2001; Cunningham, 2002).

practice information is $35.8 billion for 2001, $1.3 billion more than the estimate based on the MEPS (Hadley and Holahan, 2003a).

The Committee concludes that $35 billion is a reasonable, "ballpark" estimate of the monetary value of the uncompensated care that uninsured individuals used in 2001. The study's authors derived their estimates from two sets of data sources independently and thoroughly documented and justified the assumptions they made in developing the estimates. Nonetheless, the point estimate of $35 billion is simply the approximate midpoint of a range of values that could be used with equal confidence.

WHO BEARS THE COSTS OF UNCOMPENSATED CARE FOR THOSE WHO LACK COVERAGE?

Finding: Public subsidies to hospitals amounted to an estimated $23.6 billion in 2001, closely matching the cost of uncompensated services that hospitals reported providing. Overall, public support from the federal, state, and local governments accounts for between 75 and 85 percent of the total value of uncompensated care estimated to be provided to uninsured people each year.

Spending for personal health care services and supplies amounted to $1.236 trillion nationally in 2001 (Levit et al., 2003). An estimated $99 billion (8 percent of all personal health care spending) was for the 62 million people estimated to be uninsured for all or part of the year (Hadley and Holahan, 2003a). Of this total, private health insurance paid for an estimated $22.3 billion of the care received by those with some period of uninsurance within the year and public coverage (primarily Medicaid) paid $13.8 billion for services used by the part-year uninsured (Table 3.3). The estimated $35 billion burden of uncompensated care is shared among governments and private sponsors, although ultimately individuals bear the costs of these uncompensated services as taxpayers, providers, employees, and health care consumers.

Table 3.5 summarizes the distribution of funding that Hadley and Holahan estimate is available from public and private sources. The amounts *available* from these sources for uncompensated care exceed the authors' point estimate of $34.5 billion derived from MEPS by $3 to $6 billion annually, as shown in the table.

Federal, state, and local governments support uncompensated care to uninsured Americans and others who cannot pay for the costs of their care, primarily as hospital ($23.6 billion) and clinic services ($7 billion). Sixty percent of governmental support for uncompensated care in hospitals is federal, through Medicare and Medicaid disproportionate share hospital (DSH) payments to general hospitals, a portion of Medicare payments for indirect medical education that supports services to medically indigent patients, and other supplemental Medicaid financing

TABLE 3.5 Sources of Funding Available for Free Care to the Uninsured, 2001 ($ billions)

Provider	Private	Federal	State/Local	Total Government	Total Available for Free Care
Hospitals	2.3–4.6	14.2	9.4	23.6	25.9–28.2
Philanthropy	0.8–1.6				
Private payer surplus	1.5–3.0				
Direct support/ indigent care			7.4	7.4	
Medicare (DSH + IME)		6.6		6.6	
Medicaid (DSH + UPL)		7.6	2.0	9.6	
Clinics	0.1	5.7	1.3	7.0	7.1
Physicians	5.1				5.1
Total	7.5–9.8	19.9	10.7	30.6	38.1–40.4

NOTE: DSH = disproportionate share hospital payments; IME = indirect medical education payments; UPL = upper-payment limit payments.
SOURCE: Hadley and Holahan, 2003a.

such as upper-payment limit (UPL) mechanisms. State and local governmental support for uncompensated hospital care is estimated at $9.4 billion, through a combination of $3.1 billion in tax appropriations for general hospital support (which the Medicare Payment Advisory Committee [MedPAC] treats as funds available for the support of uninsured patients), $4.3 billion in support for indigent care programs, and $2.0 billion in Medicaid DSH and UPL payments (Hadley and Holahan, 2003a).[11]

Although hospitals reported uncompensated care costs in 1999 of $20.8 billion (projected to increase to $23.6 billion in 2001), it is difficult to determine how much of this cost ultimately resides with the hospitals (MedPAC, 2001; Hadley and Hollahan, 2003a). As just discussed, federal, state, and local subsidies of various kinds appear to equal the estimate of hospital uncompensated care costs. Philanthropic support for hospitals in general accounts for between 1 and 3 percent of hospital revenues (Davison, 2001) and, because much of this support is dedicated to other purposes (e.g., capital improvements), only a fraction is available for uncompensated care, estimated to fall in the range of $0.8 to $1.6 billion

---

[11]The authors of this analysis reduced the amount of nominal state DSH and UPL payments based on separate analyses of the proportions of these state contributions that are retained by hospitals. The Committee's previous report, *A Shared Destiny*, contains a more extensive discussion of Medicare and Medicaid DSH payments and policies.

for 2001. Another $1.5 to $3 billion in hospitals' own-source funds (from payments from private payers in excess of hospital costs) may be available to support uncompensated services, according to Hadley and Holahan.

Hospitals had a private payer surplus of $17.4 billion in 1999 (based on AHA and MedPAC reporting). These surplus payments, however, tend to be inversely related to the amount of free care that hospitals provide. A study of urban safety-net hospitals in the mid-1990s found that safety-net hospitals' case loads on average included 10 percent self-pay or charity cases and 20 percent privately insured, whereas among nonsafety-net hospitals, just 4 percent were self-pay or charity cases and 39 percent were privately insured (Gaskin and Hadley, 1999a,b). Thus, those hospitals with private payer surplus revenues (and revenues from sources other than patient care, such as parking fees) are not the hospitals that bear most of the load of uncompensated care. Based on this reasoning, Hadley and Holahan assume that between 10 and 20 percent of these surplus revenues subsidize care to the uninsured. The issue of cross-subsidies of uncompensated care from private payers and the impact of uninsurance on the prices of health care services and insurance are discussed in the following section.

Physicians in private capacities, within their own practices and as volunteers in clinics, are the predominant source of private contributions to uncompensated care for the uninsured, with an estimated $5.1 billion in donated services accounting for 15 percent of the $35 billion total.

Increases in Prices of Health Care Services and Insurance Premiums[12]

> **Finding: There is mixed evidence that uncompensated care is subsidized by private payers. The impact of any such shifting of costs to privately insured patients and insurers is unlikely to be so large as to affect the prices of health care services and insurance premiums.**

Have the 41 million uninsured Americans contributed materially to the rate of increase in medical care prices and insurance premiums through cost shifting? Health care prices and health insurance premiums have increased more rapidly than other prices in the economy for many years. In 2002, medical care prices rose by 4.7 percent, while all prices rose by only 1.6 percent. Since the last benchmarking of the series between 1982 and 1984, overall prices have risen by about 80 percent, while medical care prices have risen by 185 percent (BLS, 2002).

---

[12]The discussion of cross subsidization (cost shifting) in this section focuses only on the relationship between uncompensated care for uninsured patients and private health insurance premiums and providers' charges; it does not address or draw conclusions about the existence or impact of cost shifting between public programs like Medicaid and private insurance payments or premiums.

Health insurance premiums rose by 12.7 percent between 2001 and 2002, the largest increase since 1990 (Kaiser Family Foundation and HRET, 2002). These high rates of increases in medical care prices and health insurance premiums have been attributed to a number of factors, including medical technology advances (e.g., prescription drugs), aging of the population, multiyear insurance underwriting cycles, and, more recently, the loosening of controls on utilization by managed care plans (Strunk et al., 2002).

If people without health insurance paid the full bill when they were hospitalized or used physician services, there would seem to be no reason to believe that they contributed any more to the large increases in medical care prices and insurance premiums than insured persons. Although uninsured patients are not the only people who account for uncompensated care, the estimates presented assume that they are responsible for much of it. It is certainly an overestimate to attribute all hospital bad debt and charity care to uninsured patients, as Hadley and Holahan acknowledge, because patients who have some insurance but cannot or do not pay deductible and coinsurance amounts account for some of this uncompensated care. Of those physicians reporting that they provided charity care, about half of the total was reported as reduced fees, rather than as free care (Emmons, 1995). To reach their final estimate, Hadley and Holahan assumed that all of the free care by physicians and one-third of the reduced price care were provided to uninsured patients. Although 60 to 80 percent of the users of publicly funded clinic services, such as provided by federally qualified community health centers, the VA, and local public health departments are publicly or privately insured, these providers are not likely to be able to shift costs to private payers.

Little information is available for investigating the extent to which private employers and their employees subsidize the care given to uninsured persons through the insurance premiums they pay or the size of this subsidy. Because uninsured patients are disproportionately served by safety-net facilities, which serve relatively low proportions of privately insured patients (Gaskin and Hadley, 1999a,b; Lewin and Altman, 2000; IOM, 2003a), the opportunity for cross-subsidy is limited. Using the example of South Carolina, about seven-eighths of the private subsidies for uninsured care from nongovernmental sources came from philanthropies and other hospital (nonoperating) revenue, while the remaining one-eighth came from surpluses generated from private-pay patients (Conover, 1998).

It is difficult to interpret the changes in hospital pricing because published studies have examined individual hospitals rather than the overall relationships among uncompensated care, high uninsured rates, and pricing trends in the hospital services market overall. If for-profit hospitals are presumed to be profit maximizers (as standard economic theory predicts), they would have little or no opportunity to raise prices to private payers to compensate for providing services to the uninsured (Needleman, 1994; Zwanziger et al, 2000). One analyst argues that there has been little or no cost shifting during the 1990s, despite the potential to do so, because of "price sensitive employers, aggressive insurers, and excess capacity in the hospital industry," which suggests a relative lack of market power on the part of hospitals (Morrisey, 1996). Finally, the total burden of utilization and expenses by uninsured people has remained quite stable over the past decade or so (Taylor et al., 2001). For uncompensated care utilization by the uninsured to affect the rate of increase in service prices and premiums, the proportion of care that was uncompensated would have to be increasing as well.

There is somewhat more evidence for cost shifting among nonprofit hospitals than among for-profit hospitals because of their service mission and their location (Hadley and Feder, 1985; Dranove, 1988; Frank and Salkever, 1991; Morrisey, 1993; Gruber, 1994; Morrisey, 1994; Needleman, 1994; Hadley et al., 1996). Private hospitals have become less able to shift costs as health services markets have become more competitive (Morrisey, 1993; Bamezai et al., 1999; Keeler et al., 1999), although some analysts argue that the ability to shift costs remains substantial (Zwanziger et al., 2000). Some studies have demonstrated that the provision of uncompensated care has declined in response to increased market pressures (Gruber, 1994; Mann et al., 1995).

The concern with cost shifting from the uninsured to the insured population as a phenomenon may be changing to a focus on the transference of the burden of uncompensated care from private hospitals to public institutions due to decreased profitability of hospitals overall (Morrisey, 1996). Instead of shifting costs, private hospitals are cutting costs and reducing uncompensated care (Campbell and Ahern, 1993; Gruber, 1994; Zwanziger et al., 1994; Hadley et al., 1996; Morrisey, 1996; Dranove and White, 1998).

Private subsidies and cost shifting may also take place among community-based providers, particularly in rural areas. Coburn (2002) argues that physicians in private practice are able to provide the 20 to 40 percent of uncompensated care in rural communities that they do because they are supported or subsidized by their community's hospital. For employers in rural areas, the seriousness of the question of cross-subsidy is a function of scale. It is a greater burden in small towns, where there are fewer employers across whom to spread the cross-subsidy when it occurs in the form of higher costs for health care and for health insurance premiums. As a result, there is a competitive disadvantage that accrues to employers who offer more generous or greater subsidies of their employment-based coverage.

The extent to which cost shifting exists and thus the extent to which it influences medical care price increases are probably quite small. As reported in the previous section, the uninsured used an estimated $35 billion in uncompensated care in 2001. Hospitals received an estimated $23.6 billion in government subsidies basically earmarked for the care of the uninsured. Philanthropic support for hospital care to the uninsured has been estimated at another $800 million to $1.6 billion. Hadley and Holahan (2003a) assume that cross-subsidies from private insurance revenues to cover the costs of care provided to uninsured patients amount to 10 to 20 percent of the profit from hospital care provided to privately insured patients ($1.5 to $3 billion). Physician charity care to uninsured patients accounted for 1.6 percent of national spending on physician and clinical services in 2001 (Hadley and Holahan, 2003a; Levit et al., 2003).

The Committee concludes that there is little reason to believe that uncompensated hospital and physician care appreciably inflates the prices that providers charge their private patients.

Comparing Public Financing of Direct Services with Insurance Programs

Finding: The costs of direct provision of health care services to uninsured individuals fall disproportionately on the local communities where they reside.

Most of the costs of care for uninsured Americans are passed down to taxpayers and consumers of health care in the forms of higher taxes and fewer resources available for other public purposes. A high uninsured rate locally may both reflect and contribute to an area's economic challenges because the rate reflects the lack of employment-based coverage. Such coverage is less likely to be available in areas with a lower-waged labor force (IOM, 2001a). The tax burden of funding care for uninsured residents is more concentrated locally than is the burden of Medicaid finance or other insurance-based public programs in which the federal government participates (IOM, 2003a).

As the Committee noted in *A Shared Destiny*, given the differences in scope of public finance arrangements and the range of strategies employed to finance uncompensated care and safety-net arrangements from community to community, there is no generalized, simple relationship between a community's uninsured rate and its tax burden. One would expect an increasing uninsured rate to create pressures to increase taxes and reallocate public funds devoted to other activities, if the legal structures of taxation and spending allow. Thus, a relatively greater or rapidly increasing uninsured rate may result in higher local and state tax burdens than in areas with proportionately fewer uninsured residents. On the other hand, states and localities are constrained in their ability to raise additional revenues through taxes to subsidize care for uninsured persons (Desonia, 2002). States with low per capita income or depressed economies, characteristics that are positively associated with uninsurance, experience even more fiscal stress financing care than do more prosperous states (Holahan, 2002; IOM, 2003a).

During the middle to late 1990s, the fiscal capacity and resources of all levels of government for spending on health programs grew. Starting in 1999, states increasingly have been experiencing hard times, with economic recession, federal cuts to Medicare and Medicaid, and public resistance to raising taxes (Dixon and Cox, 2002; Lutzky et al., 2002). Many states plan to cut Medicaid spending in 2003 and in the coming years (NASBO, 2002; Smith et al., 2002). The consequences of these responses are likely to result simultaneously in lower public funding for health insurance, fewer public funds available for other purposes, and higher taxes.

The entitlement nature of most state government support for health financing means that these programs tend to absorb discretionary revenues (Hovey, 1991). Once funding levels for health entitlement programs have been decided, substantial pressure is placed on the remaining items in state and local budgets, including direct financing of public hospital and clinic services. States' ability to levy taxes and their tax structures constrain revenue increases to support care for uninsured persons. Box 3.4 illustrates the health services funding crisis recently faced by Los Angeles County, a metropolitan area with approximately 8.7 million people under the age of 65, of whom nearly one-third lack any form of coverage.

Medicaid represents 20 percent, on average, of states' budgets, and the financial incentives of the federal match as well as federal program requirements draw state funds away from more discretionary spending on the uninsured and into the Medicaid program (Miller, 2002b).[13] Changes in a state's spending on Medicaid are likely to affect its uninsurance rate and the demand for uncompensated care. Fifty-seven percent of national Medicaid expenditures are paid for by the federal government and 70 percent of SCHIP spending nationally has been paid for by the federal allocation.[14] Health care provided through federally matched insurance programs like Medicaid and SCHIP are supported by a broader public financing base than is direct support for uncompensated care programs, which rely primarily on local or a combination of local and state financing (IOM, 2003a).

SUMMARY

The Committee has sketched the range of costs involved in providing health care services for uninsured people, both those borne out of pocket by the uninsured themselves and uncompensated care costs borne by a variety of public programs, providers of services, philanthropy, and possibly by other payers as well.

The full costs of being uninsured for uninsured individuals themselves, however, are not limited to their own payments for the services that they do receive. Uninsured persons, and children in families with uninsured members, on average use less health care than do insured persons and members of fully insured families. This "lost" utilization is hidden from view, yet it can prove costly in terms of subsequent ill health, disability, and premature death (IOM, 2002a). When uninsured persons do use health services, they and their families bear a disproportion-

---

[13]Forty-four percent of total Medicaid spending is for nursing home and other institutional care services, primarily for those over age 65 and for younger, permanently disabled individuals (HCFA, 2000).

[14]SCHIP estimate based on unpublished analysis of Vic Miller, Federal Funds Information for States, Washington, DC, 2002.

BOX 3.4
Los Angeles County, CA

California is home to the greatest number of uninsured people of any state in the nation. Los Angeles County, with nearly a third of its 8.7 million population under age 65 uninsured, has more uninsured people than do each of 46 states. About three-quarters of the 800,000 patients seen annually through the county public health system are believed to be uninsured. Over the past year, county officials have responded to the prospect of a large projected budget shortfall by 2005 by closing health clinics and hospitals and by laying off health care workers. Financial strains on the county health department's budget, attributable to the sheer number of uninsured persons and their need for health care (which has been only partially met) have pressed the county to reduce its capacity to provide uncompensated care and safety net services. In the face of threatened cuts in emergency medical services and trauma care, Los Angeles voters took the unusual step in November 2002 of approving a property-tax increase, the first property-tax referendum since 1978, to raise about $170 million in additional revenues annually to secure these services.

The economic downturn in the state, mirroring national trends, and rising costs for health care and for health insurance premiums have increased demand for uncompensated care. In the mid-1990s, a 5-year federal Medicaid waiver allowed the county to continue operating its public hospitals and to promote the use of outpatient, primary care rather than hospital emergency departments for nonurgent needs. This waiver was renewed for a second 5 years in 2000. Without the continued support of federal and state dollars, public-sector health care services for both insured and uninsured low-income county residents threaten simply to collapse.

The current fiscal crisis for the county anticipates the end of the Medicaid waiver, which is scheduled to expire in 2005. California's governor has declined to make up the loss of federal funds with state dollars and the state is also likely to cut back on Medicaid eligibility, which will increase the number of uninsured Los Angelenos. Closings within the county to date in response to budget shortfalls include 16 clinics and 2 public hospitals (High Desert in Lancaster, which will reopen as an outpatient clinic, and Rancho Los Amigos National Rehabilitation Center in Downey). Because these two hospitals did not have emergency departments, they were considered less central to the preservation of safety net arrangements in the county.

SOURCES: Brown et al. (2002); Cardenas and Briscoe (2002); Cohn (2002); Riccardi (2002); Riccardi and Ornstein (2002); Rundle (2002); Sanchez (2002); Briscoe and Ornstein (2003); IOM (2003a); Ornstein (2003).

ately higher proportion of the cost of care in relationship to their often lower incomes, in comparison to insured families and their higher incomes, on average. For uninsured persons and families, utilization is more likely to lead to higher out-of-pocket expenditures and greater financial stress (IOM, 2002b).

Health care services used by uninsured people often are uncompensated in part or whole, resulting in costs to providers, communities, and society, as well as being a source of financial stress, anxiety, and possibly shame for recipients. The burden of uncompensated care is distributed widely and unevenly across providers and sponsors, depending on local configurations of health care services and institutions and on the structure of state and local revenue sources (IOM, 2003a).

Uncompensated care costs may beget additional external costs in the forms of higher local taxes to subsidize or reimburse uncompensated care, diversion of public funds from other public programs, and reduced availability of certain kinds of services within communities. These costs are discussed in the following chapter.

BOX 4.1
Organization of Chapter

The Value Lost in Healthy Life Years
- Estimating Health Capital
- Imputing a Value for a Year of Life
- Results

Quality of Life and Security for Families
- The Value of Avoiding Risk and Uncertainty
- Peace of Mind

Developmental Outcomes for Children

Uninsurance and Public Programs
- Savings to Medicare
- Disability Income Support
- Reductions in Justice System Costs for Uninsured Persons With Severe Mental Illness

Workforce Participation, Productivity, and Employers
- Workforce Participation
- Employment-based Health Insurance

Health Systems Impacts
- Access to and Quality of Health Care
- Public Health System Capacity

Summary

4

Other Costs Associated with Uninsurance

In this chapter the Committee considers costs other than the direct costs of health care—opportunity losses—that uninsured individuals, their families, local communities, and the nation bear due to the lack of continuous and permanent health insurance coverage for the entire population. In contrast with the estimates of the costs of medical care provided to those without insurance, the costs considered in this chapter have not, in most cases, been studied systematically. The Committee has developed quantified estimates only for two kinds of internal or private opportunity losses: the worse health attributable to lacking coverage and the financial "exposure" faced by uninsured individuals that would be eliminated by health insurance.

The Committee reserves one important, noneconomic opportunity loss for consideration in Chapter 6. In its conclusion to the report, the Committee examines the implications of extensive uninsurance nationally for American social and political values and ideals, including those of mutual caring and concern, equality of respect among members of a democracy, and equality of opportunity. This normative discussion is cast in terms of the benefits that could be expected if everyone had comparable financial access to care and the security afforded by health insurance.

Box 4.1 provides a roadmap to the organization of the chapter.

Following the schema of consequences of uninsurance that are presented in Figures 2.1 and 2.2, here the Committee relates its findings from previous reports and considers additional information from cost-of-illness and productivity studies to draw qualitative conclusions about certain economic impacts of lacking coverage and of relatively high rates of uninsurance within communities. The first two sections present quantified findings and the last four sections qualitative findings.

The first section focuses on the findings from *Care Without Coverage* and *Health Insurance Is a Family Matter* concerning health and health care deficits among uninsured adults and children and excess morbidity among uninsured adults resulting from a lack of health insurance. The Committee estimates the value of the increased lifespan and better health that uninsured persons could be expected to experience if they had continuous health insurance coverage over the course of their lives. This estimate is based on a commissioned analysis that is included as Appendix B of the report (Vigdor, 2003). The presentation of the qualitative findings notes when this quantified estimate of the probable value of healthier years of life forgone encompasses and subsumes the costs described qualitatively later in the chapter and when it does not.

The second section considers the quality of family life and financial security, building on the Committee's investigation of these issues in *Health Insurance Is a Family Matter*. Here the Committee presents its estimate of the monetary value of the financial risk protection that health insurance would provide to those now without coverage, both per capita and in the aggregate.

The third section reviews findings from *Health Insurance Is a Family Matter* on children's health and developmental outcomes as they depend on receipt of adequate services facilitated by insurance coverage. The fourth section looks at the implications of uninsurance for public program spending, including those that represent economic transfers as well as those that entail real resource costs. The fifth section considers productivity and workforce participation as related to health insurance status, primarily from the perspectives of the employer and the employee. Last, the sixth section summarizes findings from the Committee's fourth report, *A Shared Destiny*, about health system and population health impacts of uninsurance at the community level.

THE VALUE LOST IN HEALTHY LIFE YEARS

Finding: The Committee's best estimate of the aggregate, annualized economic cost of the diminished health and shorter life spans of Americans who lack health insurance is between $65 and $130 billion for each year of health insurance forgone. These are the benefits that could be realized if extension of coverage reduced the morbidity and mortality of uninsured Americans to the levels for individuals who are comparable on measured characteristics and who have private health insurance. These estimated benefits could be either greater or smaller if unmeasured personal characteristics were responsible for part of the measured difference in morbidity and mortality between those with and those without coverage. This estimate does not include spillover losses to society as a whole of the poorer health of the uninsured population. It accounts for the value only to those experiencing poorer health and subsumes the losses to productivity that accrue to uninsured individuals themselves.

The Committee approached placing a value on the difference in health outcomes that health insurance would make for those who lack it using the concept
of *health capital*. As described in Chapter 2, health capital is the value to the
individual of the "stock" of health that he or she can expect to have over the
remaining course of life. Health capital encompasses and subsumes the market-
based valuation of an individual's productive capacity over the years of labor force
participation that is represented by the notion of *human capital*. The capacity to be
economically productive and to earn income is some, but not all, of the reason
that we value good health. In order to account more fully for the value of better
health, the Committee chose to base its estimates on the broader metric of health
capital.

The value ascribed to health capital, the present value of the stock of health
that one will experience over the remainder of one's lifetime, is the value the
individual herself places on life in particular states of health. Most of the benefits
that can be expected to accrue to uninsured individuals themselves if they were to
gain health insurance, including increased productivity and labor force participation, and improved developmental outcomes among children (with whom the
formation of human capital begins), are represented in the single estimate of gains
in health capital. It does include, but goes beyond, the value we attach to being
alive rather than being dead. It does not, however, include the value that others
may ascribe to an individual's particular state of health. The benefits realized by
families, such as greater financial security and less stress and worry about health
care and coverage, may well be additional to those that are accounted for in the
aggregate estimate of gains in healthy life years because these benefits are interpersonal, not individual.

The Committee commissioned an analysis by economist Elizabeth Richardson
Vigdor to estimate the value of diminished health and longevity among the 40-
some million persons who lack health insurance.[1] Vigdor measures health capital
empirically by combining data on length of life, the prevalence of adverse conditions among those alive, and the health–related quality of life conditional on
having these conditions for insured and uninsured populations. She used the
Current Population Survey (CPS) for determining the size and demographic
composition of the uninsured population and the National Health Interview
Survey (NHIS) for morbidity information.

Relative mortality rates for insured and uninsured populations were taken
from the Committee's systematic literature review of health outcomes as a function of health insurance status presented in *Care Without Coverage* and *Health
Insurance Is a Family Matter* (IOM, 2002a, 2002b). Based on its earlier work, the
Committee chose to use a point estimate of a 25 percent greater mortality risk for

---

[1]This analysis used the latest Current Population Survey (CPS) estimates of uninsurance available at
the time, which were for 2000, reported in September 2001 (Fronstin, 2001b). For 2001, CPS
reported increased numbers and age-specific proportions of uninsured Americans (Fronstin, 2002;
Mills, 2002).

uninsured individuals between ages 1 year and 65 years compared with those insured. This value reflects the results of two observational longitudinal studies (Franks et al., 1993; Sorlie et al., 1994) that adjusted for demographic and socio-economic characteristics (and in the former for multiple health status and health behaviors as well). The confidence intervals around the mortality differentials found in these two studies are large; hence the point estimate of 25 percent is uncertain. However, these two studies' results are reinforced by multiple cross-sectional studies of disease and condition-specific mortality rates as a function of health status that are also part of the literature review, and the Committee believes this assumption is reasonable.

Estimating Health Capital

In her analysis, Vigdor uses alternative assumptions that bound the range of likely values of health capital. In the first set of estimates, the years of life (YOL) approach, everyone who is alive is assumed to be in perfect health. Thus the difference in health capital for the insured and the uninsured is due exclusively to the differences between their adjusted mortality rates, as reported previously by the Committee in *Care Without Coverage* (IOM, 2002a).

The second approach incorporates morbidity information to determine qual-ity-adjusted life years (QALYs), but assumes that the insured and uninsured popu-lations have the same disease prevalence and health-related quality of life (HRQL). This approach provides a lower bound of the loss in morbidity-adjusted health capital because, in fact, the uninsured are likely to have additional morbidity as a result of lacking coverage. Vigdor derived HRQL weights empirically from popu-lation-wide prevalence estimates for 15 conditions (from the NHIS and the Sur-veillance, Epidemiology and End Results databases).

The third approach took into account variations in disease prevalence and HRQL by insurance status. Because the uninsured differ from the insured across several characteristics, however, the observed difference in morbidity is unlikely to be entirely caused by lack of health insurance. Even after controlling for differ-ences between the two populations in terms of age, gender, race and ethnicity, and educational attainment, unobserved differences that are correlated with higher morbidity among the uninsured likely remain. Therefore this estimate serves as an upper bound to the possible health gains from insurance. In this upper-bound approach, age and sex-specific prevalence estimates were obtained from the NHIS, controlling for insured status, race, ethnicity, income, urbanicity, and region of the country. In age-sex groups where the insurance status coefficient was not statistically significant at $p = 0.10$, no difference in prevalence by insurance status was assumed for that condition. The HRQL weights were also allowed to vary by insurance status, although most of these interactions were not significant. Notably, being uninsured had a significant negative effect on HRQL even after controlling for other factors. This result is reflected in the health capital estimates as well.

After calculating health capital as a function of insurance status under each set of assumptions, Vigdor determined how much health would be gained if the current population of uninsured individuals had coverage. The analysis assumes that those without coverage acquire the same mix of insurance policies as those currently insured and that the previously uninsured maintain coverage until turning 65 and becoming eligible for Medicare. The coverage scenario presented in this chapter assumes that each individual faces the average probability of being insured each year until reaching age 65. This results in a conservative estimate because it assumes (1) that there is no correlation between current insurance status and insurance status next year, and (2) that the overall rate of uninsurance does not increase in the future. If being uninsured currently increases the probability of being uninsured in the future, and if length of uninsured spell has an adverse impact on health outcomes, this scenario underestimates the potential gains from health insurance.

The actual mortality differential between insured and uninsured individuals could be either less than or greater than the estimated 25 percent, and the economic value estimated for health insurance is approximately proportional to this estimate. If unmeasured personal characteristics account for some of the mortality differential, this would lower the estimate of health capital attributable to health insurance. On the other hand, several disease- and condition-specific outcomes studies, including studies of breast and prostate cancer and HIV infection report higher mortality differentials (Ayanian et al., 1993; Lee-Feldstein et al., 2000; Roetzheim et al., 2000a,b; Goldman et al., 2001).

Imputing a Value for a Year of Life

Each of the benchmark estimates of health capital assumes a value of $160,000 per year of life in perfect health. As noted in Chapter 2, the value of a life year is taken from a survey of the literature by Hirth and colleagues (2000) and is the mean value of the estimates they obtained from a number of contingent valuation studies. *Contingent valuation* is a survey-based methodology that captures the value of intangible benefits (such as the intrinsic value of having good health) and benefits that are not traded in a competitive market. The results from contingent valuation studies are not driven solely by the respondent's ability to pay. Vigdor notes that ascribing a value of $160,000 to a year of life in perfect health corresponds to an average value of $4.8 million for a statistical life, assuming a 3 percent discount rate and a life expectancy at birth of 76 years. This places the $160,000 value in the mid-range of values ($3 to $7 million for a statistical life) used by federal regulatory agencies to evaluate the economic costs and benefits of risk reduction and life-saving interventions (Vigdor, 2003).

In this analysis, contingent valuation measures the entire health benefit to an individual (and thus incorporates gains in productivity or productive capacity that accrue to the individual), but does not capture any external effects that an individual's improved health might have for society. The analysis gives equal value to every life year across people, ages, and time. Thus, by assuming that a year of each person's life is equally valuable, this approach builds in a substantial element of equity.

Following the recommendations of the Panel on Cost–Effectiveness in Health and Medicine (Gold et al., 1996b), the analysis uses a 3 percent annual discount rate for costs and benefits occurring in future years. Tables in Appendix B also present results using 0 and 6 percent annual discount rates, producing a wider range of estimated values.

Results

Table 4.1 presents the summary results of the commissioned analysis. Using the benchmark assumptions just described, the approximate present value of future forgone health to an uninsured 45-year-old male is $10,300 using the YOL approach, and between $8,300 and $12,600 when morbidity is incorporated (QALY approach, upper and lower bounds). For a male newborn, the figures are $7,700 under the years of life method, and $6,600 to $15,600 using the QALY approach. The value of future forgone health to an uninsured 45-year-old female is $7,800 for the YOL method, and between $6,200 and $10,500 once morbidity is incorporated. An uninsured baby girl forgoes health worth $4,600 under the YOL method and $3,900 to $11,600 under the QALY method. The differences in estimates by sex reflect differences in life expectancy and morbidity, not differences in earnings. These numbers add up to a very large aggregate cost across the currently uninsured population of approximately 40 million, with estimates of the total discounted present value of this cohort's forgone health ranging from $250 billion to $500 billion. (See Table B.11 in Appendix B.)

These estimates range over a wide interval and depend critically on the assumptions used in the analysis. It is not possible to select a single set of assumptions to represent the adverse health consequences of uninsurance. The lower-bound number likely underestimates the size of the effect that health insurance status has on health outcomes and the higher-bound number likely overstates this effect.

These estimates can also be construed in terms of the expected gain in value of statistical healthy years *per year of additional insurance provided*. Because health insurance is an investment in future health, and most adverse health outcomes occur at older ages, the benefit per year of insurance provided rises quite sharply with age. In this exercise, the value of future health gains is discounted to the present annual value. The benefit per year of insurance for a 45-year-old male ranges from approximately $3,100 to $4,800 under the different scenarios, while for a 45-year-old woman it ranges from $2,100 to $3,600. In contrast, the health capital gain per year of additional insurance for a newborn boy (discounted to present value at 3 percent per year) ranges from $1,200 to $2,800, and for a newborn girl the gain is between approximately $750 and $2,300.[2] It is important

---

[2]These values are presented in Tables B.9 and B.10 in Appendix B.

to remember that these annualized values are predicated on continuous health insurance coverage. Based on its previous review of studies, the Committee found that health measures and outcomes for those with intermittent coverage are more similar to those for uninsured than to insured counterparts (Schoen and DesRoches, 2000; Baker et al., 2001; IOM, 2002a).

Using the actual age distribution of those who reported being uninsured in 2000, the average value of health capital (i.e., quality-adjusted years of life) that could be gained with a year of insurance for a member of this population ranges from $1,645 to $3,280. (See the next-to-last row in Table 4.1.) Aggregating over the population of uninsured individuals (40 million individuals × $1,645 or $3,280), the annualized value of health capital lost through uninsurance is in the range of $65–$130 billion. (See the last row in Table 4.1.)

QUALITY OF LIFE AND SECURITY FOR FAMILIES

Finding: Uninsured individuals and families bear the burden of increased financial risk and uncertainty as a consequence of being uninsured. Although the estimated monetary value of the potential financial losses that those without coverage bear is relatively small (compared to the full cost of their services) because of uncompensated care, the psychological and behavioral implications of living with financial and health risks and uncertainty may be significant.

Health insurance confers health and financial benefits on families. It also improves their well-being in ways that extend beyond their individual health status and family finances. Having family members insured reduces the extent of tradeoffs that families must make between health care and other uses of their money. Even if all members are healthy today, health insurance reduces the stress and uncertainty about future medical care needs and financial demands that can accompany the lack of coverage. Families in which all members have health insurance do not experience the worries, demands, and indignities that accompany illness without coverage (Kaiser, 2000; Andrulis et al., 2003).

The lower incomes of families who are uninsured further constrain their financial choices. As incomes rise, families have more to spend both on necessities and on discretionary purchases. The lower income among families with uninsured members means the payment for a doctor visit represents a larger share of income than it does for the typical family where all members have health insurance. Gaining health insurance would relieve some of the impact of health expenses on family budgets.

The Value of Avoiding Risk and Uncertainty

Health insurance reduces families' risks and uncertainty regarding future health care costs. People with health insurance benefit from less unpredictability and

TABLE 4.1 Increases in Health Capital with Health Insurance for Those Currently Uninsured, by Sex and Age[a]

	Change in Health Capital Average pr (ins) Until 65[b]			Benefit per Year of Insurance Average pr (ins) Until 65[b]		
	YOL Approach	Lower-Bound QALY Approach	Upper-Bound QALY Approach	YOL Approach	Lower-Bound QALY Approach	Upper-Bound QALY Approach
	(dollars)					
Men						
0	7,716	6,567	15,572	1,408	1,198	2,842
18	10,715	8,942	19,136	1,841	1,536	3,288
25	10,652	8,789	17,680	2,197	1,812	3,646
35	10,581	8,612	15,362	2,952	2,403	4,286
45	10,268	8,271	12,638	3,872	3,119	4,766
55	8,433	6,732	9,075	4,466	3,565	4,806

Women						
0	4,577	3,864	11,646	893	754	2,273
18	5,874	4,826	13,018	1,120	920	2,482
25	6,427	5,241	12,180	1,427	1,164	2,705
35	7,258	5,864	11,528	2,009	1,624	3,191
45	7,772	6,225	10,544	2,661	2,131	3,610
55	7,076	5,618	8,186	3,267	2,594	3,780
Overall average per uninsured person[c]				2,014	1,645	3,280
				(dollars in millions)		
Total for 40 million uninsured				80,560	65,800	131,200

[a]Calculations assume a value of a life year of $160,000 and a real discount rate of 3 percent.
[b]Assumes that uninsured individuals face the average probability of being uninsured until reaching age 65.
[c]Calculated by summing the average difference in health capital by age and sex over all uninsured people under age 65 in the United States in 2000.
SOURCE: Vigdor, 2003.

variability in their out-of-pocket spending for health care. Lower variability itself is a benefit to people who do not like to face financial risks. Those who are "risk averse" care both about the expected cost of a risky event as well as about how variable those expected costs are. The value of the reduction in the risk of financial loss that health insurance provides is calculable empirically (Buchanan et al., 1991). The Subcommittee on the Societal Costs of Uninsured Populations followed the methodology of Buchanan and colleagues to construct an estimate of the value of the risk borne by the uninsured.[3] The insurance value of coverage was estimated by applying a constant relative risk aversion parameter (0.00024) to the reduction in the variance of out-of-pocket spending obtained through insurance coverage.[4] While risk reduction is one consideration in valuing health benefits, it turns out to have a small value for those without health insurance because of the kinds of out-of-pocket costs the uninsured actually pay. (See the discussion in Chapter 3 and Figure 3.1 on out-of-pocket costs among uninsured individuals.)

There is much more variance in the total expenses incurred by persons without health insurance than there is in their out-of-pocket payments. In the sample of respondents to the Medical Expenditure Panel Survey (MEPS), the highest total annual health expense observed for an uninsured individual was nearly $500,000. The highest amount reported paid out of pocket by an uninsured individual, however, was $26,000 (although less than 1 percent of those without insurance spent $5,000 or more).[5] If buffering mechanisms such as charity care, bad-debt writeoffs, and bankruptcy did not exist, and each uninsured person was compelled to pay for the health care he or she used (through loans, for example), the per capita value of the risk reduction from having health insurance would be more than $2,100. Because out-of-pocket expenses for the uninsured show less variation than their total expenses, the value of the reduction in variance is proportionately lower. The predominant source of variation, inpatient costs, is not being paid out of pocket by uninsured individuals. They tend, instead, to pay out of pocket for the smaller elements, and inpatient costs are borne by a combination of public and charitable support and absorbed as hospital bad debt. In effect, a large share of the overall "financial exposure" has been shifted to those who ultimately pay for uncompensated care. For this reason, the estimated value of the risk that uninsured individuals bear (and that they would not have if insured) is between $40 and $80. This modest amount represents an annual aggregate cost borne by families with uninsured members of $1.6 to $3.2 billion.

---

[3]Calculations by Sherry Glied, Columbia University, from merged MEPS files for 1996, 1997 and 1998 prepared by Jack Hadley, Urban Institute.

[4]This value represents the midpoint of the range identified by Szpiro (1986) and is comparable to the estimate used by Manning and Marquis (1996).

[5]These annual expenses measured by MEPS do not include fees and interest charges that may be added by collection agencies for late payment. See Lagnado (2003a) for a recent account of such cumulative billings.

This finding of the relatively small value of the reduction in financial risk that health insurance would bring to those who lack it helps to explain why some individuals who could afford insurance or who are eligible for public coverage but not enrolled forgo it. The "cost" of the extra financial risk that such individuals bear may be outweighed by the value of personal resources (money, time and effort, personal dignity) that is conserved by not purchasing health insurance or applying for public program benefits.

Peace of Mind

Even for families that have health insurance now, the prospect of not having health insurance in the future can be a source of anxiety and uncertainty. While the annual estimate of the number of uninsured Americans is more than 41 million, a study of insurance status over a longer time (from the 1996 to 1997 MEPS panel) found that 80.2 million people experienced some period of time without health insurance over that 2-year period (Short, 2001.) For many persons who currently have health insurance, the prospect of losing it is a very real fear (Ehrenreich, 1989; Rubin, 1994; Sullivan et al., 2000; Kaiser Family Foundation, 2003). Box 4.2 describes federal legislation over the past 15 years that has attempted to address the problem of loss of coverage. Some have referred to such provisions as "uninsurance insurance."

If health insurance were universal and effectively permanent, as Medicare now is for those over age 65, not only would those who now live without it have the added security of knowing that, at the point of needing it, health care is both accessible and not ruinous financially, but those with health insurance today would not have to worry about losing it tomorrow. The impermanence of health insurance coverage not only exacts costs in terms of disruptions in care and exposure to financial risks, it distorts personal choices about employment (including those about retirement and changing jobs), affects whether children participate in school sports (both schools and parents may prohibit uninsured children from playing), and amplifies the distress of unemployment and impoverishment. It is difficult for Americans to imagine how major life choices might be affected if maintaining coverage or anticipating its loss were not something to be considered in weighing important personal and family decisions.

DEVELOPMENTAL OUTCOMES FOR CHILDREN

Finding: Uninsured children are at greater risk than are children with health insurance of suffering delays in development that may affect their achievements and opportunities in later life.

Development in infancy and childhood shapes individuals' opportunities and prospects in later life. The health and health care of infants and children are investments that affect their future life chances, just as education does. The dimin-

BOX 4.2
Federal Initiatives to Prevent the Loss of Coverage

Congress responded to the demands for more certainty of future coverage for those currently insured with several pieces of legislation, as follows:

• The Consolidated Omnibus Reconciliation Act of 1985 (COBRA) requires firms employing more than 20 employees that provide health benefits to make health insurance coverage available to former employees for up to 18 months following departure, and to those losing dependent status for up to 36 months, at full cost to the former employee or dependent.
• The Health Insurance Portability and Accountability Act of 1996 (HIPAA) protects the ability of workers to obtain health insurance when they move from one job to another by prohibiting insurers from excluding coverage for preexisting conditions for individuals who have been insured continuously over the previous 12 months.
• Most recently, in August 2002, Congress enacted a health insurance tax credit for eligible workers as part of the Trade Adjustment Assistance Reform Act. This provision provides for an advanceable, refundable tax credit of 65 percent of the cost of health insurance for laid-off workers and their dependents who are qualified for Trade Adjustment Assistance.

Although each of these programs is limited in scope or impact, they represent policy initiatives to increase the continuity and security of health insurance coverage among workers and their families.

ished developmental outcomes of uninsured children are captured by the estimates of health capital forgone presented later in this chapter. The following discussion illustrates the mechanisms by which this loss of value occurs.

The Committee concluded in *Health Insurance Is a Family Matter* that children who do not have health insurance have less access to health care and use appropriate, recommended medical and dental care less than do children who have coverage. As a result, uninsured children often receive care late in the development of a health problem or do not receive any attention for problems that could be resolved or ameliorated with prompt attention (IOM, 2002b).

In 2000, about 7.6 percent of all newborns had low birthweight (Martin et al., 2002). Uninsured newborns are more likely than insured newborns to have low birthweight. Health insurance expansions accompanied by enhanced prenatal services have shown some efficacy in reducing low birthweight, although expanded coverage alone may not be effective (IOM, 2002b).

One study of 8,000 children ages 6 to 15 participating in the Child Health Supplement of the NHIS that adjusted for sex, race, education of the head of household, poverty status, and geographic region found that children that were low weights (< 2,500 grams) at birth were 50 percent more likely to be enrolled in special education classes than were children with higher birthweights (Chaikind and Corman, 1991). The authors of this study estimated that the incremental effect of low birthweight on special education costs amounted to $370 million in 1990.

Less access to care and use of fewer services could follow many paths in reducing children's future chances. In the most severe cases, health insurance provides access to care that prevents premature death. Coarctation of the aorta, a relatively common congenital cardiovascular malformation that can be treated with surgery or medical management, is one condition for which outcomes have been found to differ starkly for insured and uninsured infants. One study reported that infants with this condition who did not have health insurance coverage were more likely to die, in part but not solely due to a failure to identify the condition timely (33 percent compared with 3.8 percent of children with any kind of health insurance) (Kuehl et al., 2000).

For many more children, the connections between health insurance and life chances relate to their ability to achieve normal developmental milestones and to benefit from schooling. A path can be traced from lack of health insurance to a child not fulfilling his or her academic potential. Some pieces of the chain of evidence have been established. There is a body of evidence that show a relationship among illness, school absence, and learning (Wolfe, 1985). Extensive research literatures have developed around a number of common and treatable childhood conditions, including iron deficiency anemia, dental disease, otitis media (ear infection), asthma, and attention deficit hyperactivity disorder (IOM, 2002b). The Committee concluded, based on research that relates improved health outcomes to receipt of treatment and on studies demonstrating that private or public health insurance increase the likelihood of receipt of care for children, that providing health insurance to children would improve health outcomes for conditions critical to their normal development and opportunities for success in school (IOM, 2002b).

Asthma is the most common chronic illness among U.S. children, affecting roughly 5 million under the age of 18 nationally (CDC, 1996). It accounts for between 3.6 and 11.8 million lost school days every year (Smith et al., 1997; Weiss et al., 2000). For children with poorly controlled asthma, absences may lead to poor performance in school. In time, the child could be reading below grade level and beginning to experience frustration that culminates in a decision to drop out of high school or a decision not to pursue higher education. In an evaluation of a health insurance expansion in New York State prior to the establishment of the State Children's Health Insurance Program (SCHIP), parents of children with asthma reported that their child's severity level and quality of care for the condition had improved following enrollment in the program, and about half of the surveyed parents reported that their child's overall health had improved (Szilagyi et al., 2000).

Although the discrete contribution of uninsurance to poorer health among children and their diminished academic achievement as a result cannot be measured, these costs should not be ignored. These worse outcomes have long-term implications for the productive capacity of the American workforce, which is discussed later in this chapter.

UNINSURANCE AND PUBLIC PROGRAMS

Finding: Public programs, including Medicare, Social Security Disability Insurance, and the criminal justice system almost certainly have higher budgetary (transfer and economic) costs than they would if the U.S. population in its entirety had health insurance up to age 65. It is not possible, however, to estimate the extent to which such program costs are increased as a result of worse health due to lack of health insurance.

This section explores the potential for savings due to improved health outcomes to accrue to public programs such as Medicare, disability income support programs, and the criminal justice system, if those who now lack health insurance were to gain continuous coverage. We assume spending implications for the Medicare program of the increases in longevity beyond age 65 that would result from health gains among the currently uninsured population are negligible. Recent studies of the impact of improved health on Medicare expenditures have found that healthier people have similar discounted costs over their remaining lifetime to sicker people because the savings from reduced expenditures with good health in the years before death and from postponing the high costs associated with death are large enough to pay for medical care in the additional years (Singer and Manton, 1998). Likewise, the Committee has not included in its estimates of increased health capital changes beyond age 65.

Some of the potential budgetary savings, such as reduced income support payments resulting from lower rates of disability, represent changes in the transfer of resources (i.e., from taxpayers, to the Social Security Disability Insurance [SSDI] program, to disabled beneficiaries) rather than the conservation of economic resources. Other potential savings, however, such as a reduction in crimes, prosecution, and incarceration of uninsured people with severe mental illnesses whose symptoms might be better controlled if they had coverage and appropriate care, represent resources conserved (i.e., costs avoided), and thus reduced societal economic costs.

Savings to Medicare

The projections presented at the beginning of this chapter of improved longevity and health status among the uninsured do not take into account any benefits of insuring the uninsured that might extend past age 65 and the acquisition of Medicare coverage (Vigdor, 2003). This is a conservative assumption, one that most likely underestimates both the health benefits enjoyed by the individuals who gain additional years and health-related quality of life after age 65 and the potential savings to the Medicare program of uninsured individuals entering the program in poorer health and with health care deficits that demand costly "catch up" services. The question of whether uninsured adults incur such "catch up" costs upon gaining Medicare at age 65 is one that researchers and health policy analysts have speculated about, but one that has not yet been subjected to systematic analysis. The Committee hypothesizes that, based on the evidence that it has considered of

- health and functional status declines in late middle age among those who are uninsured or who lose coverage (Baker et al., 2001), and of
- the greater disease severity found among uninsured persons with end-stage renal disease (ESRD) who enter the Medicare program (Obrador et al., 1999; Kausz et al., 2000),

uninsured persons gaining Medicare coverage at age 65 use health care services more intensively and incur program costs higher than they would have had they been continuously insured prior to age 65. This question is one that merits further investigation. One obstacle to such research that has stymied researchers so far is the absence of any information about prior health insurance status in Medicare beneficiary records and data files. While it is relatively straightforward to analyze utilization of and expenditures for services by Medicare beneficiaries with the Medicare Current Beneficiary Survey, a cohort analysis comparing beneficiaries aging into Medicare who did and did not have health insurance prior to age 65 requires a reliable source of information about previous insurance status.

The Committee suggests that the Department of Health and Human Services undertake such research into the excess program costs that uninsurance imposes on the Medicare program. Such an analysis could possibly be conducted by matching existing data sets such as the National Health Interview Survey and the Current Beneficiary Survey.

Disability Income Support

In 2001, the SSDI Program paid benefits to 6.2 million people. Disability insurance payments to disabled workers and their dependents amounted to $60 billion (SSA, 2002). Disabled workers account for approximately 85 percent of disability insurance beneficiaries (others are widow[er]s and adult children). The average age of a disabled worker receiving SSDI payments is 51. About one out of seven low-income SSDI beneficiaries also receive Supplemental Security Income (SSI), which is primarily federally funded.[6] Unlike SSDI, SSI does not require that its beneficiaries previously participated in the labor force.

---

[6]See Box 4.3 for the Social Security Act definition of disability, which applies to both SSDI and SSI.

Although the rate of disability among those over age 65 has declined over the past several decades (Manton et al., 1997; Freedman and Martin, 1998), the rate among the working-age population has increased. Lakdawalla and colleagues constructed a model using National Health Interview Survey (NHIS) data from 1970, 1978, 1984, 1990, and 1996 that produced age-specific estimates of disability prevalence with a smoothing technique that allowed them to avoid the problem of small sample sizes within each age band. Between 1984 and 1996, the rate of disability reported in the NHIS, defined in terms of needing help with personal care or other routine needs, has increased nearly 40 percent among those in their 40s, from 2 percent of the population to nearly 3 percent (Lakdawalla et al., 2001).[7] This increase has coincided with the increasing prevalence of asthma and diabetes among younger Americans. The researchers found that the increase in asthma prevalence alone was enough to account for the change in reported disability. Between 1990 and 1996, the proportion of people in the NHIS who report that their health status was good, fair or poor (in contrast to very good or excellent) grew significantly for people under age 50, remained constant for those between 50 and 60, and decreased for those older than 60. The authors also present an alternative but compatible hypothesis to explain increasing rates of reported disability: changing incentives for disability insurance claims.

The Committee has not attempted to calculate what proportion of disability income support payments might be avoided with universal health insurance coverage of the population under age 65. Based both on the evidence of worse health outcomes among uninsured adults presented in *Care Without Coverage* and on the divergent trends in disability rates among younger (under age 65) as compared with older Americans within the past few decades, the Committee concludes that some portion of the disability insurance claims would be eliminated if the nearly one out of every five working age adults without health insurance had continuous coverage.

Reductions in Justice System Costs for Uninsured Persons with Severe Mental Illness

About 1 percent or 2 million adults in the United States have schizophrenia, a serious and chronic mental illness whose symptoms may include psychosis, and another 0.7 percent or 1.4 million adults have bipolar disorder (also referred to as manic-depressive disease), also a chronic mental illness that may involve psychotic symptoms (Narrow et al., 2002). Fully 20 percent of noninstitutionalized adults with these severe illnesses lack health insurance (McAlpine and Mechanic, 2000). Although having health insurance does not guarantee that mental health services are covered, persons with either public or private insurance are more likely to receive some kind of care for their condition than are those without coverage

---

[7]The NHIS excludes people living in institutions, who are the most disabled.

(Rabinowitz et al., 1998, 2001; Cooper-Patrick et al., 1999; McAlpine and Mechanic, 2000; Wang et al., 2000). People with severe mental illnesses are particularly vulnerable to losing coverage, either when they can no longer work or because maintaining enrollment in Medicaid presents major challenges, given their reduced capacity to navigate complex administrative procedures (Sturm and Wells, 2000; IOM, 2002a).

One of the consequences of the inadequate treatment of persons with severe mental illness is their disproportionate and potentially avoidable involvement with the criminal justice system (Arons, 2000; President's New Freedom Commission on Mental Health, 2002). In mid-1998, according to surveys conducted by the Department of Justice, more than 280,000 mentally ill persons were incarcerated in U.S. prisons and jails, 16 percent of state prison and local jail inmates, and 7 percent of federal prison inmates (Ditton, 1999). More than half a million probationers (16 percent) also reported a mental condition or an overnight stay in a mental hospital. Altogether, between 600,000 and 700,000 persons with severe mental illnesses are jailed each year, primarily for nonviolent offenses (Bazelon Center for Mental Health Law, 2003). An evaluation of the societal costs of schizophrenia based on 1991 data and dollars calculated that approximately $2 billion was spent on jailing, prosecuting, and imprisoning schizophrenic offenders in that year, about 10 percent of the estimated cost of treatment-related services provided to persons with schizophrenia in that year (Wyatt et al., 1995). Ironically, contact with the criminal justice system increases the chances that someone with a severe mental illness will receive specialty mental health care services (McAlpine and Mechanic, 2000).

A position statement of the Bazelon Center for Mental Health Law on criminalization of people with mental illnesses argues as follows:

> Perversely, the drift of people with mental illnesses into criminal justice has benefited public mental health systems by shifting their financial burden for "hard to serve" groups to the budgets of state corrections departments. As a result, taxpayers' resources are wasted on expensive and counterproductive incarceration instead of financing more appropriate and effective community mental health and supportive services (2003, p. 2).

Although health insurance coverage alone will not remedy the inadequacies of treatment of those who have severe mental illness, continuous and permanent health insurance coverage would improve the chances that persons with severe mental illness receive appropriate treatment that maintains their ability to function and reduces symptoms that lead to arrest.

WORKFORCE PARTICIPATION, PRODUCTIVITY, AND EMPLOYERS

Finding: Individual employers who do not currently provide health insurance benefits to their employees are unlikely to be economi-

cally worse off—taking the cost of providing insurance into account—as a result. Any systemic, regional, or national losses of productivity or productive capacity as a result of uninsurance among almost one-fifth of the working-age population cannot be measured with the data now available.

This section considers one aspect of the value of health to individuals: its impact on work and productivity. Although the information necessary to measure the impact of uninsurance on these indicators is not available, the Committee presents analyses that have evaluated discrete aspects of the multiple connections among the workplace, health insurance, health, and productivity to illuminate the decisions made about health insurance and the workplace by both employers and employees. Almost two-thirds (65.6 percent in 2001) of Americans under age 65 have health insurance through their own or a family member's job (Fronstin 2002). Although the Committee has for the most part adopted the societal perspective in this report, the motivations of and incentives facing employers and employees are important for understanding labor market outcomes involving health insurance and for evaluating alternative policy reforms for the financing and organization of health insurance coverage.

The first section considers workforce participation and the productive capacity of the workforce overall as it is related to health and functional status. The second section considers evidence relating to incentives for employers to offer health insurance to their workforce.

Workforce Participation

Illness and *functional limitations* impair people's abilities to work and consequently impose the costs of forgone income and productive effort on those who are sick or disabled, their families, and potentially on their employers as well.[8] In 1994, among the 159 million adults aged 18–64, 78.6 percent were in the labor force. That is, they were employed, just laid off, or actively looking for work. Among those without any *activity limitation*, 83 percent were in the labor force. Of those with any activity limitation, however, only 52 percent were in the labor force (1994 NHIS, reported in Kraus et al., 1996). Box 4.3 presents estimates of the population affected by functional limitations and work disabilities.

The lack of health insurance among 18.5 percent of U.S. residents aged 18–64, almost one out of every five, is one factor contributing to the burden of disease, functional limitations, and reduced health status of those without coverage. The extent to which the lack of coverage contributes to workforce participa-

---

[8]See Janet Currie and Brigitte Madrian's article, "Health, Health Insurance and the Labor Market" (1999) for a review of research examining the impact of health status on earnings, productivity and participation in the work force.

BOX 4.3
Estimates of Functional Limitations and Work Disability

The size of the U.S. working-age population that is disabled or has health problems that limit their performance of work can be estimated only over a fairly wide range of values because of the various definitions of disability and health and functional limitations that are used in different national surveys and analyses of program and economic data.

The most restrictive definition of the disabled, working-age population is people who receive benefits from either Social Security Disability Insurance or Supplemental Security Income.[1] In 2001, 8.8 million persons between the ages of 18 and 65, 5 percent of the working-age population, received benefits from one or both of these programs (SSA, 2002).

An alternative source of national data is the Current Population Survey (CPS), which estimates, from self-reports of work limitations, the proportion of working-age people who are unable to work or who work restricted hours or for limited periods within the year for reasons of health at 7.6 percent of the working-age population in 1988, or 11.1 million people (Haveman et al., 1995).

A broader measure of the economic impact of functional limitations and disabilities is that of *lost earnings capability,* which reflects losses in the productive capability of the workforce. Haveman and colleagues (1995) define this as the difference between the actual earnings capability of the working-age population and what the earnings capability of the population would be in the absence of health and disability limitations. This broader measure, unlike the calculation of lost earnings in most cost-of-illness studies, is not influenced by individual preferences to work and also accounts for the impact of functional limitations on wage rates (in addition to changes in the amount of time at work). The authors used alternative sources of information to identify those working-age adults who could be characterized as having potential earnings losses for health-related reasons (those reporting through the CPS that they had work limitations due to health problems or that they received disability payments from a public program and, separately, responses to the Survey of Income and Program Participation [SIPP] on labor force participation and health status and functional limitations). Depending on how health problems and disabilities were defined (e.g., whether fair or poor health, or number of limitations in *activities of daily living* are used), the SIPP yielded estimates of the population with health limitations that range from 8.5 million (7 percent of the working-age population) to 24 million people (nearly 20 percent of the same population.)

---

[1] The Social Security Act defines disability for adults as the inability to engage in any substantial gainful activity because of a medically determinable physical or mental impairment that can be expected to result in death or that has lasted or is expected to last for at least 12 months and is of such severity that not only is the individual unable to perform his or her previous work, but cannot (considering age, education, and work experience) engage in any other kind of substantial gainful work in the national economy (Wunderlich et al., 2002).

tion, however, has not been studied directly. Conversely, although better health status is associated with higher incomes and longer working lives, the contribution that health insurance coverage makes to workplace productivity has not been well documented.

Although estimates of the prevalence of work disability vary widely depending on both its definition and measurement, the overall economic losses to the U.S. economy are substantial across the entire range of estimates. For a period in the mid-1980s, Haveman and colleagues estimated that the economic loss in earnings capability and productivity for the U.S. working-age population fell within a range of from $131 billion annually for a narrowly defined health-limited and disabled population (7 percent of the working-age population) to $285 billion annually for a more broadly defined population with health limitations (including up to 20 percent of the working-age population). These amounts represent a loss of about 5 to 10 percent of the potential earnings capacity of the entire U.S. working-age population (Haveman et al., 1995).

Whether and how employers or the economy at large captures any of the benefits of increased worker productivity due to improved health (in addition to the benefits reaped by individual workers) is another question that cannot be resolved with research to date. In international comparisons of economic productivity, Bloom and colleagues (2001) conducted a cross-sectional study of national economic performance as a function of population health. They hypothesized that the positive individual productivity impacts of education and good health could have positive spillover effects on the productivity of coworkers. The econometric model estimated the presence and size of any externalities. Comparing life expectancies (a proxy for health status in this study) among countries, the authors concluded that relative longevity has a positive and substantial effect on aggregate output and economic growth, with a one-year improvement in life expectancy contributing to a 4-percent increase in aggregate national output. Although this study tells us nothing about impacts of health insurance coverage per se, it suggests that not only direct but also spillover productivity effects can be investigated.

Employment-based Health Insurance

This section explores the economic implications for employers of the decision to offer employees health insurance as a benefit of employment. As discussed in Box 4.4, most economists conclude that employees as a group ultimately bear the cost of employer contributions to health insurance premiums through reduced cash wages. Federal and state tax subsidies, however, make it relatively more attractive for employees to receive compensation as health benefits than as wages and thus serve to encourage employers to include health insurance as a benefit of employment.

Employer offers of health insurance benefits to employees need not be all or nothing; employers may legally limit the offer of benefits to employees who work a minimum number of hours per week and to those who have been employed for

BOX 4.4
The Incidence of the Employer Premium Contribution

Standard economic theory posits that employers do not, in most instances, bear the costs of premiums paid for their employees' health insurance, but rather that employers reduce cash wages dollar-for-dollar (adjusted for tax treatment) for any premium payments made on behalf of their employees (Pauly, 1997; Currie and Madrian, 1999). Employees often benefit from having their pretax earnings decreased because they get health insurance at an advantageous group rate and because their wages after taxes fall by only a fraction of the pretax reduction. On average, the marginal federal tax rate on wage income is about 26 percent and the Social Security tax is 15.3 percent up to $87,000 annual earned income in 2003 (or 7.65 percent if the employee share is excluded).[1,2] State income tax for all but the 9 states without one adds another 3 to 10 percent.[2]

For each $100 decrease in pretax wages associated with health insurance, then, the average employee only sees a decline in after-tax earnings of between $50 and $60. For workers with lower incomes and thus lower marginal tax rates, this decline in after-tax income is smaller and the subsidy is smaller. For workers with higher wages and higher marginal rates, the decline is larger and the subsidy is larger. Because many of the taxes are flat, have caps, or are regressive, the overall progressivity is less than indicated here. The distribution of benefits across workers within a firm depends on how the costs of health insurance are allocated among the workers, as well as on the workers' marginal tax rates.

---

[1]This includes the 2.9 percent (1.45 percent excluding the employee share) Medicare tax, which is not capped.
[2]NBER TAXSIM models for 1999 and 2000. See Feenberg and Coutts (1993) and http://www.nber.org/~taxsim.

a minimum length of time such as 6 months or a year. They may not, however, discriminate among classes of workers with respect to offering health insurance benefits by characteristics such as level of compensation (Farber and Levy, 2000; Christensen et al., 2002).

Could employers who do not offer health insurance benefits to any of their employees improve their profitability if they did so? (The same question could be asked of employers that exclude certain groups of employees, such as part–time workers or recent hires, but the calculus of the employer's advantage would have different parameters in the marginal case.) Are there benefits that accrue to the particular employers who do offer health insurance that make the costs of doing so worthwhile? More narrowly, is there empirical evidence of such benefits? Would these benefits accrue to other employers that currently do not offer health insurance if they were to provide health benefits? Box 4.5 describes recent trends in employment–sponsored health insurance.

BOX 4.5
Recent Trends in Employer Health Insurance Coverage

Even though the number of firms offering health insurance to at least some of their workers has increased in recent years, the proportion of workers with an offer of coverage has decreased. Between 1979 and 1998, the proportion of workers with insurance provided by their own employer fell from 66 percent to 54 percent (Medoff et al., 2001). This decline accompanied a shift in that 20-year period from manufacturing jobs to service jobs and from large employers to small employers, who in either case are less likely to offer insurance to their employees. Shifts in industry and occupation accounted for about 30 percent of the decline in employment-based coverage. The rest was the result of a widespread drop in coverage in nearly all industries. See Figure 4.1 for changes in employment-based coverage over time.

The decline in coverage among wage earners is not distributed uniformly across the labor force, however. Over the period 1979–1998, the percentage of private-sector workers aged 21–64 with insurance from their own employer fell from 72 to 60 percent.[1] The percentage of workers with such insurance in the highest income quintile fell from 90 to 80 percent. The percentage of workers with such insurance in the lowest 20 percent of the wage distribution fell from 42 to 26 percent. As posited by economic theory, the decline in the insurance status among workers is larger for the low-wage workers whose productivity increases are likely to be smaller than the increase in premiums.

Several studies have confirmed that declining take-up rates of employment-based coverage are a major component of overall declines in coverage (Cooper and Schone, 1997; Farber and Levy, 2000; Cutler, 2002). Examining the change in employment-based coverage over the past decade, David Cutler (2002) found that the proportion of the U.S. population under age 65 with such coverage fell from 71 percent in 1987 to 68 percent in 2000, while the proportion of the same population that was uninsured increased by 3 percentage points or 7.2 million persons. While the share of workers in firms offering insurance to at least some of its workers remained roughly constant between 1988 and 2001 at about 80 percent, and the eligibility for coverage in firms offering benefits declined only slightly from 93 to 91 percent over the same period, the take-up rate among eligible workers declined from 88 to 85 percent. Among full-time, full-year male workers, for whom offers of and eligibility for coverage are higher than for other workers, the take-up rate among those eligible declined even more over this period, from 94 to 90 percent. Cutler's analysis attributes 61 percent of decline in workers' coverage from their own employer to changes in take-up and the remainder to changes in eligibility. Among full-time male workers, changes in take-up accounted for 80 percent of the decline in own-employer coverage. Using data from employer surveys over this period to model the change in take-up rates as a function of the health insurance premium price faced by the employee, Cutler concluded that nearly all of the decrease in the take-up of insurance coverage between 1988 and 2001 could be attributed to increases in employee share of premiums over this same period.

---

[1]This calculation does not take into account those with health insurance through a family member's employment benefit.

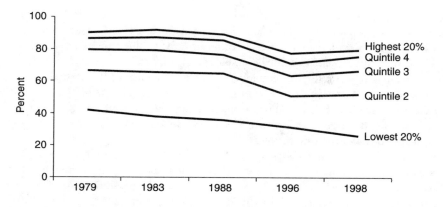

FIGURE 4.1 Percent of private-sector employees with insurance from own employer, by hourly wage quintile, 1979–1998.
NOTE: In 1998, the lowest 20 percent earned less than $7 per hour and the highest 20 percent earned more than $21 per hour.
SOURCE: Medoff et al., 2001. Data from the Current Population Surveys: May 1979, 1983, 1988; March 1996, 1999.

In their review of the history of health insurance in the United States, Currie and Madrian (1999) observe the following:

> . . . the genesis of employer-provided health insurance is rooted in employment-based programs implemented precisely because health impacts labor market activity and labor market activity impacts health (p. 3365).

Although employees have reasons to want health insurance as part of their compensation package and employers also have reasons to provide this workplace benefit, the extent to which employers realize tangible financial benefit from having an insured workforce is not well documented. Two recent surveys of health services and economics research identify the possible reasons that employers might be willing to accept higher production costs in order to provide health insurance to their employees and review the evidence for this proposition (Buchmueller, 2000; O'Brien, 2003). These review articles encompass and expand on much of the discussion that follows.

Having health insurance as part of the offered wage may help employers to attract employees more easily. However, employment situations that provide health insurance benefits may attract workers in relatively worse health or those with sick dependents, which can increase an employer's group premium rate. Still, even healthy employees may value health insurance at more than the forgone wages. Second, health insurance may also help employers to retain workers once they are recruited, although insurance may not be more effective in retaining employees than the equivalent wage (Gruber and Madrian, 2001). Because changing jobs often entails an interruption in or loss of coverage during which the employee or his family may be financially exposed to uninsured health expenses, an aversion to this risk may help keep workers in a firm. This phenomenon, called *job lock*, may or may not benefit the employer. If it increases retention of valued workers, it is positive for the employer. On the other hand, if an employer is unable to attract a desired worker from another firm because of the preferred set of health insurance benefits offered by the current employer, the recruiting employer may feel disadvantaged, and offering benefits can be viewed as providing an advantage to the current employer.

Health insurance may enhance worker effort and productivity because workers may feel that insurance is part of the package that makes a job a desirable one. Employees may work harder if they believe it would be difficult to find an equivalent or better paying job that included health insurance. Health insurance, then, may be considered an employer investment in employees along with education and training, services offered to employees, and general workplace environment for the purpose of maintaining morale and retaining workers. As Buchmueller notes, however, a particular employer will not necessarily reap the benefits of her investment in the better health consequent to offering health insurance to employees; to the extent the worker has the ability to move between employers, another employer may benefit from the worker's enhanced productivity. If long-term health gains can be realized from having health insurance, the benefits would only accrue to the employer if employees were retained for a number of years. Employers that experience relatively high turnover in their workforce would likely continue to do so even if they offered health insurance coverage (Buchmueller, 2000).

Employer Surveys

Employer surveys and business management literature reveal that employers believe that health insurance contributes positively to firm performance. Three-quarters of small employers that offer health benefits reported in one national survey that these benefits had a positive effect on recruitment, on employee retention, or on employee attitudes and performance. About two-thirds believed that health benefits contributed to better employee health, and more than half reported that the benefits helped reduce absenteeism (Fronstin and Helman, 2000).

The Employee Benefit Research Institute and the Consumer Health Education Council recently conducted a Web-based, nonrepresentative survey of 800 firms of all sizes (representing 3 million full- and part-time workers) to determine employer attitudes and policies regarding workplace health benefits (Christensen et al., 2002). Virtually all respondents (97 percent) represented firms that offered health insurance to full-time employees and a third of them to part-time employees. Eighty percent of the respondents identified health benefits as "extremely" or "very important" in recruiting and retaining workers. Forty percent thought that such benefits were extremely or very important for improving worker productivity.

Health Benefits and Workplace Productivity Studies

Although employers who offer health benefits view them positively, the evidence for improved employee health and productivity as a result of health insurance is limited and mixed. Studies of absenteeism rarely include health insurance as an explanatory variable and provide little support for the notion that absenteeism is decreased by health insurance. One simulation study indicates that physician visits and work absences substitute for each other. That is, ill workers have fewer days absent if they receive medical attention, which requires taking time off from work, and they are more likely to receive medical attention if they have health insurance. Health insurance coverage and sick leave benefits together, however, increase both the number of workers taking sick days and the number of sick days taken (Gilleskie, 1998). Thus, having health insurance cannot be shown to reduce absenteeism.

Studies have demonstrated that impaired health is related to absenteeism and reduced productivity (Chirikos and Nestel, 1985; Greenberg et al., 1995; Berndt et al., 1997; Bound et al., 1999; Druss et al., 2001; Fronstin and Holtmann, 2000; Blau and Gilleskie, 2001; Kessler et al., 2001a,b; Ramsey et al., 2002). Particular health care interventions have been demonstrated to make a difference for individual labor market outcomes, including labor force participation, hours worked, and earnings. Studies have shown that people in poor health or with specific illnesses (e.g., arthritis, depression or other psychological disorders, asthma, or chronic backache) work less and earn less than people in good health (Bartel and Taubman, 1986; Mitchell and Butler, 1986; Mitchell and Burkhauser, 1990; Berndt et al., 1997; Ettner et al., 1997; Greenberg et al., 1999; Kessler et al., 1999; Berndt et al., 2000; Birnbaum et al., 2002). Other studies have found that workers in poor health are more likely to quit work or retire early than are workers in better health (Diamond and Hausman, 1984; NAAS, 2000). Still, the measurement of workplace productivity in relation to health and as a function of particular health interventions is a relatively young field.

Greenberg and colleagues (1995) suggest that employers can take either a narrow view of illness-related costs in the workplace or a much broader view. In the former case, employers focus only on their out-of-pocket costs related to illness and health care, including employer health insurance premium contributions, employer contributions to the Medicare trust fund, workers' compensation and temporary disability insurance, and in-house health services. In the latter case, adopting a broader view, employers take into account indirect costs related to their decisions about health care. These indirect costs include productivity effects, in terms of both performance on the job and health-related absences. These authors propose a model to estimate the value of employee productivity lost to illness rates, based on both the prevalence of the illness in the workforce (the impairment rate) and the annual percentage of work time affected by the illness. Obviously, both of these factors vary by the illness in question. Particular employers also must consider the wage profiles of the employees affected in order to calculate their specific costs.

A number of management tools for the measurement of workplace productivity are currently under development (Lynch and Riedel, 2001). Experts in the field of health and productivity management stress the importance of focusing analyses relatively narrowly on particular health conditions and job performance requirements and criteria if these tools are to be useful to managers. Although this field of inquiry is promising, it has little to contribute at this time to informing an employer's decision to offer workers health insurance benefits.

The benefits of having healthier workers may include reductions in other labor costs, especially long-term and short-term disability insurance rates and workers compensation costs. Studies of workers compensation and health insurance fail to show significant reductions in these related costs, however (Card and McCall, 1996; Buchmueller, 2000). Experience rating of workers compensation premiums for large firms might show small reductions, but virtually all those firms offer health insurance to at least some of their employees anyway. Small firms that do not offer health insurance are also not paying workers compensation premiums that vary with their own employees' claims experience.

The Small Group Market

The practices and policies of insurers that sell in the small group market also figure in the decisions of some firms to offer health insurance. These insurers require firms perceived as having higher than average medical risk to pay higher premiums, relative to the value of the coverage purchased. Nearly every state has enacted legislation to curb the more extreme of these practices. These reforms have neither resulted in the increase in coverage of workers hoped for by the reformers, nor in the decrease feared by the critics of those reforms. Overall, the impacts of reform legislation have not been large. One reason for this may be that small employers are not aware of the reforms and may continue to have a distorted impression of the barriers to their offering insurance (Fronstin and Helman, 2000; Mulkey and Yegian, 2001). Education of small employers might help to expand coverage, although its potential impact is limited.

Many small employers are also employers of relatively low-waged workers. The cost of health insurance benefits represents a proportionately larger share of low-waged workers' total compensation package than it does for higher-waged workers. Both the employers of low-waged workers and low-waged workers themselves may be reluctant to trade off take-home pay for health benefits (Hadley and Reschovsky, 2002).

Summary

Evidence shows that, other things being equal, having health insurance improves the health of working-age Americans (Hadley, 2002; IOM, 2002a). Nonetheless, the information available does not lead to the conclusion that any productivity benefits accruing to individual employers of insured workers are sufficient to induce them to offer health insurance when offering it increases their payroll costs. Worker demand for health insurance is the primary determinant of whether or not a firm offers it (Buchmueller, 2000; Christensen et al., 2002). Those employers that provide this workplace benefit have demonstrated the value that they ascribe to it through their action. The "business case" probably cannot be made, however, for the group of employers that now do not offer it to any workers, predominantly smaller and lower-wage firms. It is unlikely that additional small employers can be induced to offer health insurance to their workers without additional public subsidies.

HEALTH SYSTEMS IMPACTS

Finding: Not only those who lack coverage but others in their communities may experience reduced access to and availability of primary care and hospital services resulting from relatively high rates of uninsurance that imperil the financial viability of health care providers and institutions. In addition, population health resources and programs, including disease surveillance, communicable disease control, emergency preparedness, and community immunization levels, have been undermined by the competing demands for public dollars for personal health care services for those without coverage.

Uninsurance throughout the United States at its present level (16.5 percent of the population below the age of 65) has deleterious effects on the financial stability of health care providers and institutions and may affect the availability and quality of health care services not only to those who lack coverage but also to others who share common health care facilities and community resources (IOM, 2003a). Although extensive insurance coverage has led to excess capacity in the health care system over the past three decades, this trend has recently been countered by its converse. In this section, the Committee summarizes its findings, presented in *A Shared Destiny: Community Effects of Uninsurance*, regarding two aspects of health care services that are adversely affected by uninsurance: the availability and quality of personal health care services within communities and the ability of public health agencies to perform their core mission of protecting population health.

Access to and Quality of Health Care

As discussed in Chapter 3, health care practitioners and institutions provide substantial amounts of uncompensated care to uninsured patients. The cost of this care is ultimately borne by providers themselves as bad debt and donated services, local, state, and federal taxpayers; and, to a much lesser extent, organized philanthropy. Where support and subsidies for care provided to uninsured patients is not adequate, physicians, clinics and hospitals may cut back or withdraw services from areas with large uninsured populations, affecting access to and quality of care to local residents more broadly. *A Shared Destiny* assesses available evidence about what happens, and lays out the Committee's hypotheses about what reasonably can be expected to happen within communities when one factor, the local rate of uninsurance, is relatively high or rising. This section reviews the findings from that report and suggests how health insurance coverage for the whole population could improve the availability and quality of health care within communities.

The effects of uninsurance at the community level are components for assembling the national picture of spillover costs. These effects are often easier to detect locally than nationally, where the aggregation of information averages out marked local variation in the organization, financing, and delivery of health care. One key causal pathway by which uninsurance affects communities is lower provider revenues resulting from the combination of less use of services by the uninsured compared with that of insured persons and the costs of uncompensated care that providers incur when uninsured patients receive services for which they cannot pay.

Uninsurance may affect the availability of health services within communities. In an effort to avoid the burden of uncompensated care or to minimize its impact on the financial bottom line, health care providers may cut back on services, reduce staffing, relocate, or close. Already overcrowded hospital emergency departments may be further strained as they increasingly serve as the provider of first and last resort for uninsured patients. Physicians' offices or even hospitals may relocate away from areas of towns or entire communities that have concentrations of uninsured persons. Especially for institutions that serve a high proportion of uninsured patients such as center-city community hospitals or academic medical centers, a large or growing number of uninsured persons seeking health care may "tip" a hospital's or clinic's financial margin from positive to negative.

The quality of care for both uninsured and insured persons may be adversely affected by uninsurance within the community. The IOM Committee on the Quality of Health Care in America describes the goals for health care in the United States as a systematic approach to care that is safe, effective, patient centered, timely, efficient, and equitable for all Americans, irrespective of insurance status (IOM, 2001b). While the Committee's second and third reports, *Care Without Coverage* and *Health Insurance Is a Family Matter*, have documented the lesser effectiveness of health care received by the uninsured, its fourth report considers how high uninsured rates undermine the capacity of health care institutions to provide high-quality care more generally. *A Shared Destiny* documents reduced availability within the community to clinic-based primary care, specialty services, and hospital-based care, particularly emergency medical services and trauma care, in areas with relatively large uninsured populations (Gaskin and Needleman, 2003; Needleman and Gaskin, 2003).

Reduced access to primary care increases the demand for services by both insured and uninsured persons in already overcrowded hospital emergency departments (EDs) (Derlet, 1992; Grumbach et al., 1993; Baker et al., 1994; Billings et al., 2000). In 1986, the Emergency Medical Treatment and Labor Act (EMTALA), which was conceived to counter the practice of hospitals turning away or inappropriately transferring patients who did not have the means to pay for their care, established a right to medical screening and stabilization and hospitalization, if necessary, for all patients presenting to EDs for treatment regardless of ability to pay (Bitterman, 2002). Thus hospital EDs may be one of the few health care providers to whom uninsured patients can turn when they seek routine or urgent, as well as emergency care.

Large metropolitan areas and multicounty rural areas depend on highly specialized and resource-intensive care provided by trauma centers affiliated with EDs. The lack of adequate financing for the emergent care of uninsured ED and trauma patients risks diminished access for all residents of a region. In many urban and rural areas, hospital emergency departments are often filled beyond capacity, affecting all who rely on them (Richards et al., 2000; Derlet et al., 2001; Lewin Group, 2002).

Relatively high uninsured rates are associated with the lessened availability of on-call specialty services to hospital emergency departments and the decreased ability of primary care providers to obtain specialty referrals for patients who are members of medically underserved groups (Asplin and Knopp, 2001; Bitterman, 2002). One strategic response of some hospitals to such cost pressures has been to eliminate specialty services with relatively high levels of uncompensated care, such as burn units, trauma care, pediatric and neonatal intensive care, emergency psychiatric inpatient services, and HIV/AIDS care (Gaskin, 1999; Commonwealth Fund Task Force on Academic Health Centers, 2001). In rural areas, all residents may experience lessened access to specialty care (as with primary care) if providers leave the community because of financially unviable practice conditions (Ormond et al., 2000).

The health sector is a critical component of many local economies, particularly in rural areas, where hospitals serve as social, historic, and civic anchors, as well as economic engines. A high uninsured rate and the corresponding burden of uncompensated care on the local health care system may reduce the economic base of the community. The economic role of local hospitals is particularly influential in rural areas (Cordes et al., 1999; Colgan, 2002). Rural hospital closings result in the loss of community physicians and the jobs and tax revenues that private practices generate (Hartley and Lapping, 2000; Doeksen et al., 1997). Public financing, particularly through Medicare and Medicaid, is also especially important for the rural health services infrastructure (Cordes, 1998). Universal health insurance coverage could be expected to reinforce the health services infrastructure similarly because it would provide a stable source of revenues for providers and one that corresponds to the size of the population served.

Public Health System Capacity

The sheer number of uninsured persons in an area adds to the community burden of disease and disability. Uninsured children and adults have diminished health status and greater likelihood of premature mortality, in part because they receive less timely and appropriate care. Geographic differences in self-reported health status across the states and across urban, suburban, and nonmetropolitan communities are negatively correlated with the local uninsured rate, suggesting unmet health needs (Cunningham and Ginsburg, 2001; Holahan, 2002).

Areas with higher uninsured rates and correspondingly higher burdens of disease place relatively greater demands on the population-based public health services that health departments provide, because uninsured residents are more likely to rely on these services (e.g., immunization and well-baby clinics, treatment for sexually transmitted and other communicable diseases) than are residents with public or private health insurance (IOM, 2003b). Health departments in communities with higher uninsured rates, however, are also likely to face higher demands to provide personal health services to uninsured persons, in their role as providers of last resort. Budgets for population-based public health, including disease and immunization surveillance, emergency preparedness, environmental health, and restaurant inspections, which benefit all members of a community, can be squeezed by demands on health departments to provide or pay for safety-net services for uninsured persons, adversely affecting the capacity to deliver public health services to the community (IOM, 1988, 2003b). In many parts of the country, health department officials have expressed their perceptions of being caught between the increasing demand and need for care of growing numbers of uninsured persons and diminished budgets (Goldberg, 1998; Lewin and Altman, 2000). Some health departments have tried to address the unmet health needs of sizable or growing uninsured populations by shifting discretionary funds toward the delivery of health services at the expense of population-based public health programs (IOM, 2003a,b).

One result of the cutting back in population-based public health activities is the risk of higher incidence and prevalence of vaccine-preventable and communicable diseases, especially in areas where health departments have been chronically short of funding. Communicable disease control is a core health department function that helps prevent the spread of disease through the screening, tracing and notification, and for some diseases, treatment, of persons with whom an infected individual has come into contact. For example, underimmunization increases the vulnerability of entire communities to outbreaks of diseases such as measles, pertussis (whooping cough), and rubella (IOM, 2000). Both categorical immunization efforts and public and private health insurance that provide these services to their enrollees are needed to ensure adequate levels of immunization among children and adults (DeBuono, 2000; Fairbrother et al., 2000; Sisk, 2000). Uninsured children and adults are both the primary clientele of health department immunization programs and substantially tax the capacity of these public agencies to serve them.

To give another example, tuberculosis (TB) is a preventable and treatable contagious disease whose spread may be exacerbated by community uninsurance. In past years linked with HIV/AIDS, substance abuse, and life in institutional settings (e.g., homeless shelters, prisons), TB more recently has been associated with low-income, foreign-born communities in urban areas, along the southwestern U.S. border, and in other medically underserved communities with high uninsured rates (Geiter, 2000; CDC, 2001; Kershaw, 2002). Timely diagnosis and appropriate treatment are integral to stemming the transmission of TB. Inadequate access to primary and follow-up care has contributed to the increase in drug-resistant tuberculosis, which poses a public health threat (CDC, 1999). Screening for TB, contact tracing, notification, and oversight of the daily medical treatment that the disease requires are all part of the communicable disease control activities carried out by health departments. The diversion of resources from communicable disease control to the provision of personal health care services to uninsured and other medically indigent residents has been cited by health department officials as likely to result in increased numbers of persons with tuberculosis (Geiter, 2000).

The diversion of resources from public and population health activities to personal health care for uninsured persons is particularly dangerous because this frequently occurs without explicit public knowledge or endorsement, but rather as the result of ad hoc resource management decisions within state and local health departments (Fairbrother et al., 2000; IOM, 2003b). Providing health insurance to those who now lack it will certainly require public resources in addition to those that health departments spend on personal health care for the same populations. Financing the personal health care of uninsured Americans through insurance mechanisms instead of as direct services would, however, make public resource allocations and programmatic tradeoffs more transparent than they are at present.

SUMMARY

In this chapter the Committee has examined a variety of internal (private) and external (societal) economic implications of the lack of insurance within the United States. Many of these cannot be quantified. The Committee has undertaken an innovative approach to gauging the probable magnitude of the opportunity costs associated with uninsurance within the American populace. By estimating the monetary value of the diminished health and longevity among uninsured children and adults, consistent with the practices of federal agencies that make policy choices about investments in health and safety, the Committee has exposed some of the hidden costs of uninsurance.

 The following chapter presents estimates of the resources that would be needed to increase the health services utilization of uninsured children and adults to the levels used by their insured counterparts. These estimates of resource demands will be used in the concluding chapter, along with the estimates of the value of forgone healthy life years presented in this chapter, to consider the cost-effectiveness of providing health insurance to those currently uninsured.

5

The Cost of the Additional Care That the Uninsured Would Use If They Had Insurance Coverage

Providing health insurance would increase the life expectancy and reduce the morbidity of those who now lack it. In *Care Without Coverage*, the Committee concluded that those without coverage have higher morbidity and decreased life expectancy as a result of being uninsured. Insurance improves the health and well-being of the insured by increasing access to preventive services, timely care, and medical treatment. This chapter presents benchmark estimates of the additional monetary cost of the health care that those without coverage would be expected to use if they had coverage. The more timely care, better prevention, and better access to health services are the mechanisms by which insurance improves the health and well-being of the insured.

Here the Committee considers estimates of the costs of the additional care that would be provided if everyone in the United States had continuous health insurance coverage. The costs of this "additional care," the difference between the amount of health care services that the uninsured actually use and what they might be expected to use if they had coverage, are new economic costs of expanding coverage to the entire U.S. population. The Committee reviews and compares the results from one earlier and two recent statistical analyses of differences in utilization and expenditures among those who are uninsured, have private health insurance, and have public coverage, adjusting for observable differences among these populations. These analyses help predict the new costs (at the societal level) of the additional services that those who are now uninsured would use if they gained health insurance. The cost projections do not speak to the distribution of new costs among taxpayers, enrollees, and other payers nor do they make any assumptions about redistribution of present cost burdens for care provided to the uninsured among payers and providers of that care. Each set of projections of the increase in costs is predicated on there being no major structural changes or reforms in the way health care is financed and delivered. The forecasts also assume no major differences in the mix of plans that would cover the uninsured from those which now cover the privately or publicly insured populations, in terms of scope of benefits, extent of coverage (levels of deductibles, copayments, stop losses, and other cost-sharing elements), or utilization review and other care management practices.

In addition, the estimates that follow assume that the current capacity of the health care system is sufficient to meet the increased demand without generating additional inflation in health care prices. This assumption may not hold in those localities with particularly large uninsured populations and limited health care delivery resources. In any case, estimates of inflation in health care prices would depend on the particular features of a proposed health care reform, including any explicit cost control elements. The possible alternatives are too numerous to be considered in this report.

In what follows, the Committee presents results from the studies by Long and Marquis (1994), by Miller, Banthin, and Moeller (2003), and by Hadley and Holahan (2003b). We do not review the older literature on comparisons of alternative health plans because the estimates depend on very specific features and are usually targeted at the cost of the entire reform proposal, not just the increase in cost for covering those currently uninsured. Typically, the latter is much smaller than the former. We also do not review studies of the effects of cost sharing on demand for health services because there are a number of reviews in the literature that evaluate the response to out-of-pocket costs; see Zweifel and Manning (2000) for one of the most recent.

LONG AND MARQUIS ESTIMATES, 1994

Stephen Long and Susan Marquis (1994) predicted the additional ambulatory and hospital care that the population without health insurance could be expected to use if they had health insurance. Their work was based on data from the middle to late 1980s from three nationally representative surveys: the National Medical Expenditure Survey (NMES), the Survey of Income and Program Participation (SIPP), and the Health Interview Survey (HIS). Based on their estimates of differences in use, they predicted the utilization experience that uninsured people would be expected to have if they were in a typical employment-based plan. The 1987 NMES provided the uninsured population sample, updated by the Census Bureau's Current Population Survey (CPS) to account for changes in the size and mix in the uninsured population between 1987 and 1992. The authors termed the difference in utilization for this standard population in the uninsured and insured states as the "access gap" attributable to lacking coverage. The model assumed that other aspects of health care financing and delivery, such as the mix of prepaid and fee-for-service health plans, cost-sharing provisions, and scope of benefits, remained unchanged. The model assumed no changes in unit prices for services as a result of the increased coverage or any cost-containment efforts.

Long and Marquis reported that uninsured adults have approximately 60 percent of the outpatient visits and 70 percent of the hospital days annually as they would if they had been insured. Uninsured children were estimated to use ambulatory services at about 70 percent of the rate that they would have if insured, and to use hospital days at 80 percent of the insured level. Adults and children in fair or poor health had a greater "access gap" than those with good or excellent health (i.e., with health insurance coverage they could be expected to increase their use of services relatively more than those in better baseline health).

Long and Marquis estimated that the incremental cost of ambulatory and hospital inpatient services to the population gaining health insurance would amount to $20 billion in 1993 dollars (about $ 28.6 billion in 2001 dollars), nearly a 50 percent increase in the spending for this population (the uninsured) for these services. This amount represented 2.2 percent of total national spending for health care in 1993. Adjusting the estimates for the difference in the number of uninsured in 2001 and in 1993, the estimate grows to $35 billion, assuming no differences in the mix of demographic, health, and socioeconomic characteristics of the uninsured between the late 1980s and 2001.

MILLER, BANTHIN, AND MOELLER ESTIMATES

Edward Miller, Jessica Banthin, and John Moeller (2003), economists at the Agency for Healthcare Research and Quality (AHRQ), used more recent data to develop estimates of the annual cost of expanding coverage to all of the currently uninsured updated to 2002. Their model estimates reflect the health status, utilization, and expenditures of respondents in the 1996, 1997, and 1998 Medical Expenditure Panel Survey (MEPS). In order to produce current cost estimates, the sample population weights from the 3 years were adjusted to those of the March 2002 CPS, and 1996, 1997, and 1998 expenditures were calibrated by type of service and source of payment to the 2002 National Health Accounts to reflect the growth in expenditures between the sample year and 2002. This pooled MEPS sample produced estimates of roughly 34 million persons under age 65 uninsured for the entire year and 31 million additional persons uninsured for some part of the year.

Because the uninsured, privately insured, and publicly insured differ in many characteristics beyond their insurance status, the authors adjusted differences in the estimated costs of services for differences in their age, race, sex, proportion of women of child-bearing age, family income and size, education, region, urbanicity, disability, health and decedent status, body mass index, and number of chronic conditions. They used a standard set of models that are employed to deal with the very skewed nature of expenditure data in order to make their estimates robust to extreme cases (Duan et al., 1983).

The authors developed alternative models to produce upper- and lower-bound estimates of the incremental service costs of expanding coverage to the uninsured. The lower-bound model was based on the experience of those who lacked health insurance for a full year and were not eligible for either private or public insurance. To study this case, they limited the "uninsured" sample to respondents who were uninsured for the full year, who had no offer of workplace coverage, and who were not eligible for Medicaid. The authors used the experience of this subgroup that did not have an opportunity to obtain coverage to minimize the correlation of unobserved differences in the propensity to use health care services with actual health insurance status. The authors reasoned that, because the population of uninsured individuals who had an offer of or eligibility for coverage includes individuals who are least likely to use health care (and thus forgo an opportunity to take up coverage), averaging in their utilization experience with that of the "insured" group reduces the difference between the utilization of the uninsured group and the insured group. This makes the estimated *incremental* costs of insuring the uninsured less than they would be otherwise. Those uninsured without an offer of or eligibility for coverage accounted for just one-third (32 percent) of all persons who were uninsured for all or part of the year. The remaining uninsured were included in either a private insurance (group or individual) or Medicaid category if they had that coverage for at least one month or if they had an offer of workplace coverage or qualified for but were not enrolled in Medicaid. In order to predict the incremental expenditures under universal private or public health insurance, the authors "scaled up" the projected expenditures for the subgroup of uninsured without an offer of or eligibility for coverage to account for the entire population of individuals uninsured for part or all of a year.

The second model providing an upper-bound estimate of the increased utilization under universal coverage used as the "uninsured" group all of those individuals who were uninsured for any time during the year regardless of their eligibility or ineligibility for private or Medicaid coverage. Their predicted utilization was based on the experience of only those individuals covered *for the full year* by either private group insurance or Medicaid, thus maximizing the differences in service use and costs between the model's uninsured and insured groups. From these models, the authors estimated the cost of expanding coverage to each of four subgroups of the uninsured: full-year uninsured, who either had or did not have an offer or eligibility for coverage, and part-year uninsured, who either had coverage for less than 6 months or for 6 through 11 months.

Expenditures for those uninsured for part of the year only, who started off with much higher annual health care spending, increased much less over the baseline, ranging from a 3 percent *decrease* in spending for those uninsured for less than 6 months assuming Medicaid coverage, to a 58 percent increase in baseline spending for those uninsured 6 months or more, assuming private coverage. Providing private coverage to those who currently are not eligible for either public or private coverage would increase their per capita annual expenditures by 205 percent (by $1,911 in 2002 dollars) of their baseline (uninsured) expenditures of $934. Alternatively, expanding Medicaid coverage to include these uninsured

TABLE 5.1 Simulated Medical Spending per Uninsured Person: Two Alternative Benchmarks by Length of Time Uninsured and Existence of an Offer or Eligibility for Coverage (2002 dollars)

Baseline Insurance Status	Baseline	Simulated Spending	
		"Average" Private Group Coverage	"Average" Medicaid
All Uninsured	$1,217	$2,302 (89%)[a]	$1,962 (61%)
Part-Year Uninsured			
< 6 months	$1,779	$2,028 (14%)	$1,732 (-3%)
≥ 6 months	$1,350	$2,128 (58%)	$1,815 (35%)
Full-Year Uninsured			
With offer or eligibility	$778	$1,978 (154%)	$1,685 (117%)
No offer or eligibility	$934	$2,844 (205%)	$2,421 (159%)

[a]Percentage increase from baseline spending level.
SOURCE: Miller et al., 2003. Data from 1996, 1997, and 1998 MEPS.

individuals would increase per capita expenditures somewhat less (by about 160 percent or $1,487 in 2002 dollars) over baseline expenditures. See Table 5.1 for the results for each of the "uninsured" subgroups: ineligible, eligible but not covered, covered for less than 6 months, and covered for 6 months or more.

Table 5.2 shows the projected expenditure increases in the aggregate for the four subgroups of the uninsured and overall. The estimated *incremental* health expenditures for all groups of the uninsured, assuming a pattern of utilization and spending that matched the average of all group private insurance, range from $44.9 to $57.4 billion for 2002 and, assuming utilization and spending comparable to the national average per capita Medicaid experience, range from $35.1 to $38.1 billion. These estimates deduct the estimated value of in-kind uncompensated care (that is, uncompensated care for which no revenue support stream can be identified) provided to the uninsured of $13.5 billion under the private plan alternative and of $10.6 billion under the Medicaid alternative.

Miller and colleagues also estimated a range of values for the new costs that would be associated with administering the newly insured health services. They base their estimates on national health account estimates of the percentages of public and private health expenditures spent on insurance administration (4.5 and 8.3 percent, respectively). Administrative costs for the incremental services that the uninsured would use with health insurance range from $3 billion based on a Medicaid expansion to $9–$10 billion with an expansion based on private coverage.

TABLE 5.2 Simulated Incremental Spending for All Uninsured: Two Alternative Benchmarks (2002 dollars, in billions)

	Simulated Spending	
	"Average" Private Group Coverage	"Average" Medicaid
All Uninsured		
Lower bound	$44.9[a]	$35.1[b]
Upper bound	$57.4[a]	$38.1[b]

[a]Incremental medical spending includes a reduction of an estimated $13.5 billion in in-kind uncompensated care.

[b]Incremental medical spending includes a reduction of an estimated $10.6 billion in in-kind uncompensated care.

SOURCE: Miller et al., 2003. Data from 1996, 1997, and 1998 MEPS.

HADLEY AND HOLAHAN ESTIMATES

Jack Hadley and John Holahan (2003b), economists at The Urban Institute, conducted a similar analysis using somewhat different modeling and working assumptions. These authors used the same 3-year pooled sample of MEPS respondents for 1996–1998 to simulate the costs of coverage for the uninsured as they had used to estimate actual health expenditures for the uninsured (as described in Chapter 3). The larger sample from pooling 3 years of data allowed them to examine the effects for children and adults separately; some of the literature suggests that patterns of utilization for children and adults respond differently to cost sharing (Valdez et al., 1986; Newhouse et al., 1993). Hadley and Holahan made adjustments to the MEPS data comparable to those the AHRQ economists had made. They inflated the expenditures to 2001 levels and adjusted for undercounting of uncompensated care in MEPS using National Health Accounts statistics.

Unlike the analysis by Miller and colleagues, Hadley and Holahan limited their sample of privately insured people to those with family incomes less than 400 percent of the federal poverty line. Thus, they assumed that the uninsured's response to insurance will be the same as that for other low- to moderate-income individuals. They used a similar set of covariates to adjust for observable differences between the insured and uninsured. Their statistical model was based on the generalized linear model version of the two-part model (introduced by Blough et al., 1999). They treated an individual as uninsured if he or she was uninsured for any part of the year and they explicitly controlled for the fraction of the year without insurance. Thus, they made no distinctions based on being eligible for but not taking up public or private coverage.

Hadley and Holahan considered two different scenarios for health insurance coverage for the currently uninsured. In the first, they assumed that the uninsured would be covered by the same mix of private health insurance plans as those of low- to moderate-income people with private insurance coverage for the full year. In the second, they assumed that the uninsured would have the same experience as people with public insurance coverage (e.g., Medicaid or the State Children's Health Insurance Program) for the full year. In both cases, the estimation and the predictions assumed that observable differences, other than insurance status, did not change. For each alternative, they pooled the data from the uninsured with either the publicly insured or the privately insured to estimate the parameters of the model, but they did not pool all three groups simultaneously. This analysis accounted for the length of time those who were uninsured during the year had any public or private insurance coverage, demographic characteristics (including age, race, sex), education, family income relative to poverty, marital status, and census region, and health-related characteristics including health status, mental health status, functional status, acute and chronic conditions, and whether the respondent died or was institutionalized during the year.

Table 5.3 presents the per capita spending projected for the uninsured in 2001 assuming that they had either the same mix of private insurance policies or the same mix of public insurance coverage as their insured counterparts. Based on their estimates, Hadley and Holahan predict that per capita expenditures for adults uninsured for a full year would increase to 265 percent of their baseline amount (from $1,158 annually to $3,069) modeled on private group coverage utilization and spending experience, and would increase to 209 percent of baseline (to

TABLE 5.3 Simulated Medical Spending per Uninsured Person: Two Alternative Benchmarks, by Age and Baseline Insurance Status (2001 dollars)

Age and Baseline Insurance Status	Baseline[a] (Actual)	Simulated Spending	
		"Average" Private Coverage	"Average" Public Coverage
All Uninsured	$1,383	$2,676	$2,121
Full-year uninsured	989	2,650	2,068
Part-year uninsured	1,813	2,705	2,178
Uninsured Adults	$1,644	$3,187	$2,568
Full-year uninsured	1,158	3,069	2,419
Part-year uninsured	2,240	3,331	2,751
Uninsured Children (<18)	$733	$1,408	$1,008
Full-year uninsured	475	1,374	996
Part-year uninsured	943	1,434	1,016

[a]Does not include value of uncompensated care.
SOURCE: Hadley and Holahan, 2003b. Data from 1996, 1997, and 1998 MEPS.

TABLE 5.4 Simulated Total Spending: Two Alternative Benchmarks by Baseline Insurance Status (2001 dollars, billions)

Baseline Insurance Status	Baseline Spending[a]	Simulated Spending			
		"Average" Private Coverage		"Average" Public Coverage	
		Total	Change in Spending, $ (%)	Total	Change in Spending, $ (%)
All Uninsured	$98.9	$167.6	$68.7 (69.5)	$132.8	$33.9 (34.3)
Full-year uninsured	40.6	86.7	46.1 (113.5)	67.6	27.0 (66.5)
Part-year uninsured	58.3	80.9	22.6 (38.8)	65.2	6.9 (11.8)

[a]Includes value of uncompensated care.
SOURCE: Hadley and Holahan, 2003b. Data from 1996, 1997, and 1998 MEPS.

$2,419) modeled on average national Medicaid experience. Likewise, for children who are uninsured for the full year, spending would more than double from $475 per capita to between $996 and $1,374 per capita, depending on whether utilization and spending is modeled on Medicaid or private group insurance. Although the baseline estimates of per capita spending are not adjusted to include the value of uncompensated care (which is undercounted in MEPS), the authors adjusted the *total* baseline cost estimate for medical care used by the uninsured to take into account uncompensated care.

The projected increases in spending for children and adults who are uninsured only part of the year are smaller. They range from an 8 percent increase for part-year uninsured children based on Medicaid experience to a 49 percent increase for adults uninsured for part of the year if they had the average private group experience.

Overall, health care expenditures for individuals uninsured for any amount of time during the year are projected to increase to $132.8 billion, 134 percent of the baseline of $98.9 billion in 2001, if their utilization and spending followed the experience of those with Medicaid coverage, and to $167.6 billion, 170 percent of baseline, if at average private group insurance levels.

If we consider the *increased* (i.e., new economic) costs over the uninsured alternative rather than the total cost of additional benefits to the uninsured under universal coverage, then the increase in health care spending would be $33.9 billion for the public alternative and $68.7 billion if the private plan alternative is used (see Table 5.4). Hadley and Holahan note that their estimates can vary by as much as 10 to 20 percent based on issues of sample and model specification.

COMPARING RESULTS

Finding: Estimates of the cost of the additional health care that would be provided to the uninsured once they became insured range from $34 to $69 billion per year, assuming no structural changes in the systems of health care financing or delivery, average scope of benefits, or provider payment. This incremental cost of services amounts to 2.8 to 5.6 percent of national spending for personal health care services in 2001.

These three studies provide a range of estimates of what additional health care services for the uninsured will cost when they become insured. Adjusting the Long and Marquis estimates for differences in the cost of medical care between 1993 and 2001, and prorating the expenses for the larger number of uninsured in 2001, the Long and Marquis estimate amounts to about $35 billion per year. The Long and Marquis estimates are based on differences in visit rates and hospital days per capita, assuming that there are no differences in the cost per visit or the cost per inpatient day between the insured and uninsured.

The two studies that used much more current data from the MEPS differed from the earlier analysis by Marquis and Long in that they looked directly at health care expenditures (including uncompensated care) rather than estimating costs from differences in outpatient and inpatient use rates. Thus the two MEPS-based studies allow for the possibility of differences in intensity of treatment per encounter, a possibility ruled out by the Long and Marquis approach.

Although the details of the two MEPS studies differed in important aspects, the range of estimates from the two both suggest that the cost of providing those now uninsured with the extra health services used by those with coverage could range from about $34 billion to about $69 billion (Hadley and Holahan, 2003b; Miller et al., 2003). Locating a more specific estimate within that range would depend on whether the new coverage was like current public insurance plans or current private insurance plans. The range of estimates largely reflects differences between the expanded coverage through private and public plans, which in turn reflects significant differences in provider payment rates between private and public health plans, on average (Hadley and Holahan, 2003b; Miller et al., 2003).

The differences among the sets of estimates are quite small and may be due to differences in statistical modeling. Long and Marquis used separate two-part models for inpatient and outpatient care to allow for differences in responses to insurance status. Hadley and Holahan used a similar two-part model and the AHRQ economists used a four-part model. Although no attempt has been made to find how much of the difference is due to differences in model specification, Hadley and Holahan note that their own results could change by as much as 10–20 percent based on alternative specifications.

CONCLUSION

This chapter has addressed the cost implications of expanding coverage to those without insurance. This is the correlate to the costs of uninsurance: What might it cost society to provide health insurance coverage to the roughly 41 million Americans who lack it? A precise answer to this question would require specifying many features of the proposed scheme for universal health coverage, including the administrative framework, the scope of benefits covered, the level of cost sharing, the level of provider payments for covered services, and the mechanism that would finance the insurance coverage (e.g., general revenues, payroll tax, employer mandate). Different choices in each of these areas could dramatically change the estimates of the costs of providing universal coverage. The Committee's objective here is not, however, to provide a precise estimate of the net new costs of covering the uninsured population. Rather, it is to provide a range of the likely new real resource costs, based on the best evidence to date, of extending to the uninsured coverage similar to that of individuals who now have public or private health insurance.

These estimates should be treated as benchmarks. The Committee presents a range of estimates of the projected costs of covering those now uninsured that are plausible, generic, and illustrative. The incremental service costs are based on the costs of the coverage that accounts for the differences in morbidity and mortality between otherwise similar insured and uninsured Americans (IOM, 2002a,b).

If these benchmarks are appropriate, then the evidence suggests that the costs of the additional health care that would be provided to the uninsured once they become insured will be on the order of $34 to $69 billion a year, assuming no other major changes in scope of benefits, provider payment, or the structure of the health care financing and delivery systems. This amounts to a 2.8 to 5.6 percent increase in spending for personal health care services for 2001. It is equivalent to between one-third and two-thirds of the 8.7 percent growth in national expenditures for personal health care services between 2000 and 2001 (Levit et al., 2003).

6

Social and Economic Costs of Uninsurance in Context

In the previous chapters of *Hidden Costs, Value Lost*, the Committee

*   developed an analytic structure for examining the societal economic impacts of uninsurance,
*   reviewed estimates of the costs of health care that those who lack coverage now use and identified the parties bearing these costs,
*   estimated the expected gain in health capital that insuring the uninsured would achieve,
*   considered additional, unquantified costs that uninsurance imposes on uninsured individuals and families, and society at large, and
*   presented estimates of the costs of the additional health care that the uninsured could be expected to use if they gained coverage.

This concluding chapter brings these various elements of costs consequent to uninsurance together, along with the anticipated costs and benefits of expanded coverage. Consolidating this information allows the Committee to consider whether allocating scarce social resources to expanding coverage to the more than 41 million uninsured Americans is worthwhile, and how it compares with other investments our society already makes in health- and life-enhancing services and interventions.

The Committee has also reserved for this final chapter an important discussion of the nonmaterial consequences of our nation's policies regarding health insurance and access to health care. It is difficult to make claims about what our national tolerance of uninsurance is costing us ethically and politically because health insurance and even health care have never been recognized as rights of citizenship or social membership that apply universally in the United States. Thus the Committee asks the converse question: What do we as a nation stand to gain by ensuring that all Americans have health insurance coverage? The Committee concludes that adopting a policy of universal health insurance coverage would be a societal expression of values and norms that are deeply, if sometimes obscurely, embedded in American culture and history.[1]

Box 6.1 at the end of the chapter consolidates the Committee findings from previous chapters as well as this one.

SUMMARIZING COSTS AND COMPARING INVESTMENTS IN HEALTH

Conclusion: The estimated benefits in terms of the value of healthy life years gained by providing coverage to those currently uninsured are likely greater than the incremental societal costs of the additional health care services that they would receive if insured. The cost-effectiveness of the additional health care that the uninsured population would use with coverage is comparable to that of many other health-enhancing and life-extending interventions.

In its reports and analyses so far, the Committee has thought about and depicted the relationships among the various hypothesized and documented consequences of uninsurance in terms of a series of concentric circles, broadening outward, as in Figure 1.1. Because the Committee has considered health insurance primarily as it facilitates the receipt of health care by individuals, the health consequences for individuals are at the center of the circle. Immediately "ringing" the circle of uninsured individuals are their family members, a greater number of persons than the uninsured themselves who are at risk for adverse health, psychosocial, and economic impacts related to the uninsured status of a family member. One ring further out from families represents the communities in which uninsured persons and their families reside. Communities with higher-than-average uninsured rates comprise a larger population than that of the families that have at least one uninsured member. Residents of these communities may experience reduced access to health services even when they are insured themselves. Finally, ringing the communities is American society overall, where all members who pay taxes, purchase goods and services, and benefit from the presence of an educated and

---

[1]See *Habits of the Heart: Individualism and Commitment in American Life* by Robert Bellah and colleagues (1985). Through in-depth interviewing and qualitative analysis, these social scientists explore Americans' articulations of cultural and ethical values related to civic and political life. They conclude that, while the values of freedom of action and self-reliance were readily invoked by respondents, collective responsibility and mutual concern among neighbors and fellow citizens were also deeply held values that guided conduct, as described by respondents, but were not as clearly articulated.

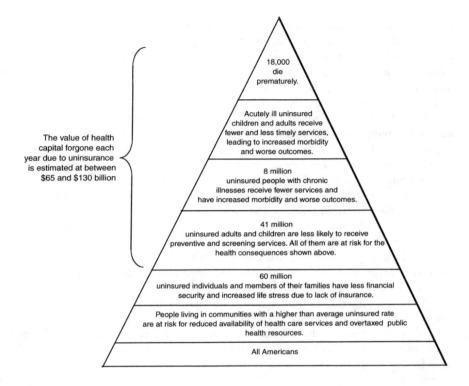

The value of health capital forgone each year due to uninsurance is estimated at between $65 and $130 billion

18,000 die prematurely.

Acutely ill uninsured children and adults receive fewer and less timely services, leading to increased morbidity and worse outcomes.

8 million uninsured people with chronic illnesses receive fewer services and have increased morbidity and worse outcomes.

41 million uninsured adults and children are less likely to receive preventive and screening services. All of them are at risk for the health consequences shown above.

60 million uninsured individuals and members of their families have less financial security and increased life stress due to lack of insurance.

People living in communities with a higher than average uninsured rate are at risk for reduced availability of health care services and overtaxed public health resources.

All Americans

FIGURE 6.1 Consequences of uninsurance.

productive workforce are likely to experience the adverse consequences of uninsurance socially and economically, even those who live in communities with relatively few uninsured persons.

Figure 6.1 presents a wedge sliced out of the concentric circles just described. This slice or pyramid helps visualize the numbers of people affected in different ways by uninsurance. It illustrates the ever greater numbers of Americans adversely affected at each ring or band from the cross-section of the circle. The tip or smallest band indicates the number of uninsured individuals who die prematurely because of their uninsured status, an estimate from the Committee's second report, *Care Without Coverage*. The next two bands add in the number of acutely and chronically ill persons under age 65 who receive less adequate and effective care because of their lack of coverage, as documented in the Committee's second report and its third report, *Health Insurance Is a Family Matter*. Yet the uninsured people who fall ill or suffer injury are only some of the over 41 million persons who lack coverage, all of whom are at risk for adverse health and economic consequences. The 41 million uninsured persons are members of families, leading to an estimated total of 60 million persons who also bear some of the adverse financial, psychosocial, and utilization effects of lack of coverage within the family. The 60 million members of families with at least one uninsured person are in turn residents and members of communities that may experience spillover effects of a relatively large uninsured population. Whether through residence in a community with a disproportionately large or growing uninsured population, or as a taxpayer and citizen, uninsurance touches the lives of all 284 million Americans.

Table 6.1 lists the elements of costs related to uninsurance that were examined in Chapters 3 and 4 and presents estimates for a few of them: expenditures for uncompensated care, forgone health capital, and the risk borne by uninsured people. Even though these are all expressed in monetary terms, they are not simply additive. The cost of uncompensated care provided to uninsured patients, a transfer, is meaningful only in terms of who is bearing this cost—ultimately, primarily taxpayers at all levels of government. (The cost of covering the uninsured will undoubtedly require additional transfers from taxpayers to those newly covered.) Both the value of the stock of health that those without coverage forgo as a result and the burden of financial risk that they are exposed to represent economic opportunity costs or losses to uninsured individuals themselves. These quantified values reflect only some of the very real costs of uninsurance.

Table 6.2 presents in summary form estimates of the current costs of care for the uninsured and projected costs and benefits of coverage. The annual incremental cost of the services the current uninsured population would use if health insurance coverage were universal cannot be compared directly with the annualized present value of the cumulative future benefits of coverage because they are expressed in different metrics.

The final step in the Committee's analysis of economic costs is to consider the potential benefits of providing the uninsured with coverage *together* with the incremental costs of the additional health services that would improve their health. In order to do this, both the average per capita gain in health due to an additional year of health insurance for the uninsured population and the average per capita annual cost of the additional health services that the uninsured population would use if they had coverage must be made consistent with each other. The estimate of the value of health gained with an additional year of coverage is calculated as a discounted present value of the gain for a cohort of uninsured people over the course of their lives (with a range of $1,645 to $3,280, as presented in Table 4.1), and thus the estimate of the cost, for each additional year of insurance, of the additional health care that the uninsured would use if insured must be calculated as the present value for an uninsured cohort over the course of their lives.

The Committee calculated the present value of incremental costs for an uninsured population of the current size and demographic composition based on the Hadley and Holahan (2003b; see Chapter 5) analysis of projected incremental health care costs using a 3 percent discount rate. The cost per additional year of health insurance provided to the otherwise uninsured is the expected lifetime increase in service costs with continuous coverage up to age 65, divided by the additional years of coverage provided over the lifetime. The estimated range of per capita costs for the incremental services calculated in this fashion is $1,004 to $1,866, depending on whether the incremental service costs are calculated based on public or private health insurance expenditures.[2] The estimated benefits ($1,645–$3,280, from Table 4.1) fall in a higher range than the estimated incremental, societal costs ($1,004–$1,866). Because not all of the care that the insured population use is likely to be effective and contributing to their better health outcomes (i.e., some insured care is wasteful and even harmful [IOM, 2001b]), the comparative value of the estimated health benefit achieved with these incremental services, which represent both effective and marginal or ineffective care, is even more notable.

Another way to help judge whether investing in health insurance for the uninsured is "worth it" to Americans as a society is to compare this investment with other investments in health that we do make. Table 6.3 arrays cost-effectiveness ratios, with the costs of adopting the intervention expressed in terms of the cost for each additional quality-adjusted life year (QALY) gained, for selected life-saving and health-improving measures. This array includes the Committee's estimate for the intervention of providing continuous health insurance across the population in boldface type. Dual passenger airbags in autos (compared with airbags on the driver side only), for example, has a cost for every quality-adjusted life year gained of $75,000. Compared to an annual clinical breast exam, an annual mammography for women between ages 55 and 65 carries a cost of $186,000 for every QALY gained. Among women ages 20 to 75, the cost of every additional QALY gained with annual Pap smears (compared with one every 2 years) is $2 million (Graham, 1999).

The Committee calculated the incremental cost per QALY gained by insuring the uninsured by dividing the incremental cost per additional year of insurance provided by the change in QALYs per additional year of insurance provided (see Table 6.4). The change in QALYs per additional year of insurance provided is the total lifetime increase in QALYs from gaining insurance, divided by the number of years of insurance provided over the remaining lifespan. The expected lifetime gain in QALYs is the expected gain in health capital divided by the imputed value of a life year ($160,000).

Converting the Committee's benefit–cost figures for the health value gained relative to the incremental cost of additional health services with coverage yields an incremental cost per QALY of between $50,000 and $180,000. This range reflects two different upper and lower bounds: one is the difference between the cost based on public versus private coverage and the other the high- and low-bound assumptions about differences in the underlying health status of demographically similar insured and uninsured populations. Providing health insurance

---

[2]Calculations made by Committee consultant Elizabeth Vigdor.

TABLE 6.1 Costs of Uninsurance, Estimated (Annual) and Hypothesized

Who Is Affected	Consequence	Units	Value per Unit	Total Estimate
Internal Costs				
Individuals	Morbidity Premature mortality	Disease prevalence rates Decreased life expectancy QALYs	$160,000/year of life in perfect health	$65–$130 billion (Forgone benefits of coverage)
Families	Developmental losses for children	Educational attainment		(Subsumed in health capital)
	Interactive health effects	Differential coverage and utilization effects for children by parental coverage status		(Subsumed in health capital)
	Stress and financial uncertainty	Value of risk borne by uninsured individual	$40–$80 annually per uninsured individual	$1.6–$3.2 billion (Forgone benefits of coverage)
	Depletion of assets	Assets; bankruptcy		(Transfer)
Firms	Time lost from work; reduced productivity on the job	Absenteeism Value of lost production	Unknown	

External Costs

Communities	Uncompensated care: Diverted public resources or additional taxes to pay for care to uninsured	Local tax burdens for uncompensated care Allocational decisions for public budgets Losses from inefficient care for the uninsured	$35 billion (Current expenditures; primarily transfers)
	Diminished quality, availability of health services	Community-wide unavailability of specialty services	Unknown
	Diminished population health, costs to other public programs	Immunization rates; contagious disease rates; disability rates	Unknown
Nation	Workforce productivity	Labor force participation	Unknown
	Unrealized social norms	Disability rates	Not quantifiable

TABLE 6.2 Estimates of Current Annual Cost of Health Care Services for Full- and Part-Year Uninsured Individuals, Projected Incremental Annual Costs of Services If Insured, and Economic Value Gained by Uninsured Individuals If Insured, Annualized

	Billions $, estimated for 2001
Current cost of care for full- and part-year uninsured	98.9
Amount paid out of pocket by full- and part-year uninsured	26.4
Insurance payments (for part-year uninsured only) and workers' compensation	
Private	24.2
Public	13.8
Uncompensated care	34.5
Projected annual costs of additional utilization with coverage	34–69
Benefits of insuring the uninsured	
Aggregate value of health capital forgone by the uninsured, annualized	65–130
Aggregate annual value of risk borne by uninsured	1.6–3.2

SOURCES: Hadley and Holahan, 2003a,b; Vigdor, 2003.

to those who now lack it is likely to be at least as cost-effective in enhancing health and longevity as some other common health care practices.

The final section of the chapter presents the Committee's reflections on the ethical and political significance of health insurance within American society. Claims about cultural values and implicit social norms are particularly likely to be challenged as lacking adequate empirical grounding; nonetheless, the Committee believes it would be irresponsible to remain silent on normative issues and attempts to articulate American cultural and political normative underpinnings and their implications for the health policy choices Americans now face. That some of the benefits of expanding health insurance coverage to the entire population are not quantifiable makes them no less important to our strength and integrity as a democratic national community.

REALIZING SOCIAL VALUES AND IDEALS

Conclusion: Health insurance contributes essentially to obtaining the kind and quality of health care that can express the equality and

TABLE 6.3 Cost-Effectiveness Ratios for Selected Life-Saving Measures[a]

Intervention	Comparator	Target Population	Cost per QALY Saved[a]
Annual colorectal screening	No screening	People 50–75	$22,000
Frontal airbags with manual belts	Manual belts (50% use)	Drivers of passenger cars	$30,000
Radon mitigation in homes	No testing or mitigation	Home residents with radon levels above 20 pCi/liter	$71,000
Dual passenger airbags	Driver side only	Front right passenger	$75,000
Coronary angioplasty	No revascularization	Patients with mild angina and one-vessel disease	$136,000
Universal coverage	**16.5% uninsured population under age 65**	**Currently uninsured**	**$50,000–$180,000**
Annual mammography	Annual clinical breast exam	Women ages 55–65	$186,000
Annual mammography	Annual clinical breast exam	Women ages 40–50	$297,000
Methylene chloride exposure limit of 25 ppm	Limit of 500 ppm	Workers exposed to methylene chloride	$235,000
Solvent-detergent to eliminate AIDS virus and other infectious diseases	No solvent-detergent	Patients undergoing plasma transfusion	$384,000
Screening to prevent HIV transmission to patients	Universal precautions	Health care workers in acute care setting	$606,000
Annual Pap smear	Pap smear every 2 years	Women ages 20–75	$2,000,000
Lap/shoulder belts (9% use)	No restraints	Rear-center seats of cars	$3,000,000

[a]All dollars have been adjusted to 2001 dollars by the medical care price index.
SOURCES: Graham, 1999; Estimate for universal coverage is by the Committee.

TABLE 6.4 Incremental Cost-Effectiveness Analysis of Continuous Health Insurance Coverage for the Uninsured (Estimates for 2001)

	Average change in cost per additional year of insurance, $	Average gain in health capital per additional year of insurance, $	Average gain in health capital per additional year of insurance, QALYs	Incremental cost/QALY, $
Private coverage	1,866			
YOL		2,014	0.013	148,257
QALY lower bound		1,645	0.010	181,489
QALY upper bound		3,280	0.020	91,018
Public coverage	1,004			
YOL		2,014	0.013	79,769
QALY lower bound		1,645	0.010	97,650
QALY upper bound		3,280	0.020	48,972

SOURCES: Committee estimates, from Vigdor, 2003, Hadley and Holahan, 2003b.

dignity of every person. Despite the absence of an explicit Constitutional or statutory right to health care (except for emergency care in hospitals), disparities in access to and the quality of health care of the kind that prevail between insured and uninsured Americans contravene widely accepted democratic cultural and political norms of equal consideration and equal opportunity.

Any kind of accounting of societal costs and benefits from the investment of economic resources in a policy like universal health insurance relies on some kind of unit of value: money, years of life, QALYs, or personal utility.[3] Health care is valued for its contribution to personal health. Likewise, health insurance is valued instrumentally because it facilitates receipt of health care, an additional step removed from health itself. We value health insurance in part because it gives us access to services from which we expect to benefit, even for services far beyond our means to pay out of income and personal savings (de Meza, 1983; Nyman, 1999a,b). Because of the value of health and longevity is not something that we (in American society in the 21st century) readily trade off against other goods that can be purchased in the market place, there is good reason to account for it separately (Culyer, 1991; Weinstein and Manning, 1997).

In addition to the aggregate of costs and benefits calculated for individual lives, collective experiences and circumstances also depend on societal choices about health care and the distribution of health insurance coverage among members of society. In the following discussion, the Committee reviews some of these irreducibly collective implications of policy choices about health care and health insurance in American society. It also considers whether the failure to enact a national policy that guarantees everyone health benefits undermines the Committee's conclusion that equity in access to health care is an important expression of central democratic values of equality of opportunity and mutual respect.

Altruism, Mutual Concern, and Health Care

Americans share a somewhat vague consensus that everyone should be able to obtain at least some forms and amount of health care under certain circumstances. Just how much health care, paid for by whom, and under what circumstances are contended.

In *A Shared Destiny*, the Committee reviewed the history of collective provision of health care in the United States, beginning with hospital charities in the 18th and 19th centuries to care for the poor and, by the middle of the 20th century, instituting public health insurance programs for particularly vulnerable

---

[3]The economic concept of *utility* reflects the ordering of a single person's preferences for alternative outcomes or states of the world.

groups including the elderly, very low-income mothers and children, and the disabled. Despite numerous amendments to and expansions of the original Medicare and Medicaid statutes enacted in the mid-1960s, and greater state and federal regulation of commercial health insurance and employment-based health benefits to allow Americans to secure and maintain insurance coverage and financial access to health care, as a society we have stopped short of guaranteeing the benefits of health insurance to everyone and have tolerated endemic uninsurance.

Some argue that the growth of public provision in care and coverage "crowds out" charitable provision, depriving some of the opportunity to express their altruistic interests by donating to others (Epstein, 1997). On the other hand, some economists have argued that, because so many consider health care to be a good that should be provided to (at least some) people on the basis of need and not ability to pay, personal health care is actually a special kind of public good, a *merit good* (Musgrave, 1959, Fuchs, 1996). The externalities or spillover effects of providing merit goods are not material, but psychological. They are the utility or satisfaction one gets from knowing that others obtain the good one wants them to have. By providing health care or coverage through public provision, taxpayers benefit from knowing that others are receiving needed care, that suffering is reduced, or that families are not becoming impoverished by medical bills (Coate, 1995).

Experimental studies of distributional choices in health care suggest that people favor equity of some form in this arena.[4] Egalitarian distributive choices in experimental settings have been demonstrated for goods, including health care, to which the notion of need, rather than that of taste or preference, applies (Yaari and Bar-Hillel, 1984). Presented with the hypothetical scenario in which respondents were asked to allocate a fixed amount of pain medication between two people, identical in all respects, including level of pain—except that one could not metabolize the pain medication as well as the other, more than three-quarters of the respondents chose to allocate the medication so as to equalize the pain experienced by each of the individuals (Kahneman and Varey, 1991).

Compassionate attitudes and expectations of mutual trust and concern among neighbors and fellow citizens are not static. They interact with and develop in response to particular features of civic life and the reasonable expectations that members of a society have regarding the collective provision of important social goods, such as health care. The strength and resiliency of communities as social, political and economic entities depend in part on intangible social resources sometimes referred to as *social capital*. Social capital is reflected in the extent of civic engagement, in the expression of norms of reciprocity among members of a community, and in the degree of trust among people who are social strangers.

In *A Shared Destiny*, the Committee considered the implications that differential access to health care based on insurance status might have for social cohesive-

---

[4]See Hurley, 2000, for a brief overview of this literature.

ness and social capital. Because this relationship had not been explored in empirical studies, the Committee only formulated hypotheses about the possible interactions between uninsurance and social capital. Widespread uninsurance within a community may erode residents' beliefs or confidence in their ability to take care of themselves or those they care about because of the real or perceived barriers to obtaining care. Conversely, the security or guarantee of financial access to needed care that health insurance offers may enhance the sense of both individual and collective efficacy (Lochner et al., 1999).

Conditions for Achieving Equality of Opportunity and Democratic Equality

Just what the essential equality among members of a democratic society consists of is contested in American political life. Nonetheless, equality in some sense stands with freedom of individual action as a bedrock value of our way of life. Two kinds of equality, however, are particularly fundamental and widely shared: equality of opportunity and equality of respect. The guarantee of health care or the provision of health insurance throughout society can make a unique contribution to the more complete realization of these values.

The state of our health affects what we can do or be in life (Sen, 1993). Building on John Rawls' (1971) highly influential and more generally constructed theory of justice, political philosopher Norman Daniels (1985) developed an account of the special priority that we place on meeting the health care needs of ourselves and of others. When compared with the priority we give to having a dinner out and a movie, for example, health care is more important because it is necessary for maintaining normal functioning as human beings. The normal functioning of people in a particular society reflects a certain range of opportunities and ambitions that members of that society generally consider open to them. Poor health or disability reduces the range of opportunities and life choices open to us, while health care can restore to us a wider range of opportunities and reasonable plans for life than we might have without it. Because equality of opportunity to realize our own life plans and ambitions is a widely shared American ideal, Daniels' account is particularly helpful as a way to explain and to justify giving health care and, derivatively, health insurance coverage, a special place in collective provision.

A second set of arguments for equality in the distribution of some kinds of highly valued goods (such as health care) draws on another widely shared ideal in American culture, that of democratic or political equality. Also following Rawls' original argument, Elizabeth Anderson (1999) proposes that the ultimate goal of equal access to certain valued goods is "to create a community in which people stand in relations of equality to others" (p. 289). Such goods must be made available in ways that express respect for each member of society and not shame or demean those who receive the valued goods. Obtaining health care from public clinics and under charitable arrangements is better than having no access to health care, but for those with no alternatives because of the lack of financial means, it can be a degrading experience that conveys a sense of one's social inferiority and political ineffectuality.

When a highly valued social good like health care or health insurance is not available to all members of society, it belies nominal claims that everyone is deemed to have equal political and social worth (Walzer, 1983). Conversely, ensuring that all in society have the means to obtain health care on comparable terms expresses equality of concern and respect and thus can encourage and reinforce participation in social and political activities. Yet it is clear that we have repeatedly chosen *not* to act to expand health insurance coverage to all. Is this because of a conflict of political and ethical principles, a difference in the interpretation of basic principles, or a failure to recognize what is at stake in the policy choice we have and have not made?

Have We Chosen the Status Quo as a Matter of Principle?

Libertarians, those who place the highest priority on freedom of individual action and personal control over resources and property, believe the state that governs least governs best. Thus, the social contract among a group of equals committed first and foremost to liberty would be a "night-watchman state," a minimal government that provides for mutual physical security and little else, according to political philosopher Robert Nozick (1974). The night-watchman state is not, however, an accurate characterization of the nature of the social contract that has developed over more than two centuries in the United States, as described in Chapters 1 and 2 with respect to the provision of health care and health insurance.

Hospitals were initially established by communities, both through voluntary associations and as public institutions, as collective resources and expressions of compassion and altruistic concern for the most unfortunate members in society, those who were both sick and impoverished (IOM, 2003a). Medical science progressed rapidly over the course of the 20th century, the value and cost of health care and hospital services rose commensurately with advances in efficacy, and both private and public (social) insurance schemes were established to make these increasingly valuable services within the reach of everyone. The federal tax subsidy for workplace health benefits amounts to between $120 and $160 billion for fiscal year 2003 (Burman, 2003; see also Sheils et al., 1999).

Medicare, Medicaid, and the State Children's Health Insurance Program enjoy widespread public support and approval (NASI, 1999). Three-quarters of Americans responding in recent nationally representative opinion polls identified increasing the number of Americans covered by health insurance as a "very important" goal for Congress and the President (Kaiser Family Foundation, 2003). Surveys in both 1993 and 2000 found that more than 80 percent of respondents agreed with the statement that health care should be provided equally to everyone, with more than half agreeing "completely" or "strongly." Two-thirds agreed with the statement that the federal government should guarantee health insurance coverage for every American (Kaiser Family Foundation, 2003). A February 2003 opinion poll with a national sample of 1,200 asked adults whether they would be willing to pay more in higher insurance premiums or taxes to increase the number of Americans with health insurance. Fifty-two percent said that they would and 42 percent responded that they would not be willing to pay more (Kaiser Family Foundation, 2003). When these same respondents were asked in a separate question whether they would be willing to pay a specific amount more in premiums or taxes each month, the results were somewhat more positive. Forty-six percent said that they would be willing to pay $50 more monthly and 12 percent were willing to pay $30 extra monthly to increase the number of insured Americans.

Despite popular opinion favoring coverage expansions, over the past 30 years national efforts at health care reform extensive enough to provide coverage to everyone—to close the gap of the 15 to 20 percent of the American population without it at any given time over this period—have failed repeatedly. Does this mean that the values of equity, compassion, and mutual respect are not deeply held across American society or that equity in access to valuable health care is not important to the realization of these values?

The Committee concludes that these are not the correct conclusions to draw from our policy inaction at the national level. We believe instead that as a society and as a polity, Americans have failed to recognize just how important equitable access to care and coverage has become in honoring long-held ethical and political commitments. Comprehensive health reform has failed for reasons other than to reject the goal of universal coverage (Vladeck, 2003). The Committee believes that the United States has chronic, endemic uninsurance by default rather than by explicit choice.

CONCLUSION

This report and the work of the Committee on the Consequences of Uninsurance not only provide information about the costs resulting from the lack of coverage and some of the costs and benefits of expanding it to everyone, it also presents us with an ethical dilemma. In light of the information and analyses that the Committee has developed about choices we have not made as a society, as well as those that we have made to invest heavily in health care, we cannot excuse the unfairness and insufficient compassion with which our society deploys its considerable health care resources and expertise. Providing all members of American society with health insurance coverage would contribute to the realization of democratic ideals of equality of opportunity and mutual concern and respect. By tolerating a society in which a significant minority lacks the health care and coverage that most Americans enjoy, we are missing opportunities to become more fully the nation we claim to be.

BOX 6.1
Findings and Conclusions

Spending on Health Care for Uninsured Americans

3.1 Uninsured children and adults are less likely to incur any health care expenses in a year and, on average, incur health care costs well below half of average health care spending by all those under age 65.

3.2 People who lack health insurance for an entire year have out-of-pocket expenditures comparable to those of people with private coverage, but they also have much lower family incomes. Out-of-pocket spending for health care by the uninsured is more likely to consume a substantial portion of family income than out-of-pocket spending by those with any kind of insurance coverage.

3.3 The total cost of health care services used by individuals who are uninsured for either part of or the entire year is estimated to be $98.9 billion for 2001.

3.4 The best available estimate of the value of uncompensated health care services provided to persons who lack health insurance for some or all of a year is roughly $35 billion annually, about 2.8 percent of total national spending for personal health care services.

3.5 Public subsidies to hospitals amounted to an estimated $23.6 billion in 2001, closely matching the cost of uncompensated services that hospitals reported providing. Overall, public support from the federal, state, and local governments accounts for between 75 and 85 percent of the total value of uncompensated care estimated to be provided to uninsured people each year.

3.6 There is mixed evidence that private payers subsidize uncompensated care. The impact of any such shifting of costs to privately insured patients and insurers is unlikely to be so large as to affect the prices of health care services and insurance premiums.

3.7 The costs of direct provision of health care services to uninsured individuals fall disproportionately on the local communities where they reside.

Other Costs Associated with Uninsurance

4.1 The Committee's best estimate of the aggregate, annualized cost of the diminished health and shorter life spans of Americans who lack health insurance is between $65 and $130 billion for each year of health insurance forgone. These are the benefits that could be realized if extension of coverage reduced the morbidity and mortality of uninsured Americans to the levels for individuals who are comparable on measured characteristics and who have private health insurance. These estimated benefits could be either greater or smaller if unmeasured personal characteristics were responsible for part of the measured difference in morbidity and mortality between those with and those without coverage. This estimate does not include spillover losses to society as a whole of the poorer health of the uninsured population. It accounts for the value only to those experiencing poorer health and subsumes the losses to productivity that accrue to uninsured individuals themselves.

4.2 Uninsured individuals and families bear the burden of increased financial risk and uncertainty as a consequence of being uninsured. Although the estimated monetary value of the potential financial losses that those without coverage bear is relatively small (compared to the full cost of their services) because of charity care, the psychological and behavioral implications of living with financial and health risks and uncertainty may be significant.

4.3 Uninsured children are at greater risk than are children with health insurance of suffering delays in development that may affect their achievements and opportunities in later life.

4.4 Public programs, including Medicare, Social Security Disability Insurance, and the criminal justice system almost certainly have higher budgetary (transfer and economic) costs than they would if the U.S. population in its entirety had health insurance up to age 65. It is not possible, however, to estimate the extent to which such program costs are increased as a result of worse health due to lack of health insurance.

4.5 Individual employers who do not currently provide health insurance benefits to their employees are unlikely to be economically worse off, on net, as a result. Any systemic, regional, or national losses of productivity or productive capacity as a result of uninsurance among almost one-fifth of the working-age population cannot be measured with the data now available.

4.6 Not only those who lack coverage, but others in their communities as well, may experience reduced access to and availability of primary care and hospital services resulting from relatively high rates of uninsurance that imperil the financial viability of health care providers and institutions. In addition, population health resources and programs, including disease surveillance, communicable disease control, emergency preparedness, and community immunization levels, have been undermined by the competing demands for public dollars for personal health care services for those without coverage.

Additional Costs of Care If Uninsured Gained Coverage

5.1 Estimates of the cost of the additional health care that would be provided to the uninsured once they became insured range from $34 to $69 billion per year, assuming no structural changes in the systems of health care financing or delivery, average scope of benefits, or provider payment. This incremental cost of services amounts to 2.8 to 5.6 percent of national spending for personal health care services in 2001.

BOX 6.1 *Continued*

Social and Economic Costs in Context

Conclusion 1: The estimated benefits in terms of the value of healthy life years gained by providing coverage to those currently uninsured are likely greater than the incremental societal costs of the additional health care services that they would receive if insured. The cost-effectiveness of the additional health care that the uninsured population would use with coverage is comparable to that of many other health-enhancing and life-extending interventions.

Conclusion 2: Health insurance contributes essentially to obtaining the kind and quality of health care that can express the equality and dignity of every person. Despite the absence of an explicit Constitutional or statutory right to health care (except for emergency care in hospitals), disparities in access to and the quality of health care of the kind that prevail between insured and uninsured Americans contravene widely accepted democratic cultural and political norms of equal consideration and equal opportunity.

A

Glossary

Activities of Daily Living (ADLs) Defined by the National Health Interview Survey (NHIS) as bathing, dressing, eating, and getting around the home.

Activity Limitation The NHIS classifies individuals' activity limitations due to a chronic health condition according to four categories: (1) unable to perform a major activity; (2) able to perform the major activity but limited in kind or amount; (3) not limited in the major activity but limited in the kind or amount of other activities; (4) not limited in any way. A major activity is play (for children under 5); attending school (for those 5–17); working or keeping house (for persons 18–69); and the capacity for independent living (for persons 70 and older).

Adverse Selection The disproportionate enrollment of individuals with poorer than average health expectations in certain health plans.

Capital (physical, private, human) *Physical capital* is land and the stock of products set aside to support future production and consumption. In the national income and product accounts, *private capital* consists of business inventories, producers' durable equipment, and residential and nonresidential structures. *Human capital* is the education, training, work experience, and other attributes that enhance the ability of the labor force to produce goods and services.

Contingent Valuation (CV) A method for estimating the monetary value or willingness to pay for an intervention or policy that reduces risk or enhances health, utility, or longevity based on responses to survey questions about hypothetical choices.

Cost (direct, indirect)   *Direct costs* include the value of all goods, services, and other resources that are consumed in the provision of an intervention or in dealing with the side effects or other current and future consequences linked to it. These costs are often thought of as involving—or potentially involving—a monetary transaction. *Indirect costs* refer to productivity gains or losses related to illness or death (Luce, 1996, pp. 178–179).

Cost, Economic Cost   The amount paid or payable for the acquisition of materials, property, or services. Economic cost is defined as the minimum payment necessary to keep a resource in its present employment.

Cost, External   Costs not directly assumed by the entity that owns and operates a product or service.

Cost, Internal or Private   A direct effect, either positive or negative, on profit or welfare arising from a person's or institution's activity.

Cost, Productivity   Costs that are associated with morbidity and mortality, excluding the intrinsic value of health (Luce, 1996, p. 178).

Cost–Benefit Analysis   Comparison of benefits measured in terms of monetary value and costs of a medical intervention in order to determine whether it is worth doing (Sloan, 1995a, p. 3).

Cost–Effectiveness Analysis   Measurement of benefits in terms of some standard of clinical outcome or effectiveness, such as mortality rates, years of added life, or quality-adjusted life years compared to the costs of a medical intervention to establish whether or not the intervention is merited (Sloan, 1995a, p. 3).

Disability   A general term referring to any long- or short-term reduction of a person's activity as a result of an acute or chronic condition.

Efficiency, Economic   The "right" goods are being produced.

Efficiency, Technical   *Technical efficiency* is achieved when, for a given output, the amount of inputs used is minimized or when, for a given combination of inputs, the output is maximized (Culyer, 1991, p. 66).

Entitlement   A legal obligation on the federal government to make payments to a person, business, or unit of government that meets the criteria set in law. Congress generally controls entitlement programs by setting eligibility criteria and benefit or payment rules—not by providing budget authority in the appropriation act (CBO, 2002).

Equity Equity concerns fairness and justice, the idea of balancing legitimate, competing claims of individuals in society in a way that is seen as impartial or disinterested. Distributional equity, which concerns the fair distribution of some good or service of interest, has been the dominant equity concern both of normative economic analysis and of health policy makers (Hurley, 2000).

Fiscal Policy The government's choice of tax and spending program that influences the amount of growth in government debt as well as the level, composition, and distribution of national output and income (CBO, 2002).

Functional Limitation Difficulty in performing any of the following activities: (1) reading newspaper print (with corrective lenses, if used); (2) hearing normal conversation (using aids, if used); (3) speaking understandably; (4) lifting or carrying 10 pounds; (5) walking a quarter mile without resting; (6) climbing a flight of stairs without resting; (7) getting around outside; (8) getting around inside; (9) getting out of bed. These criteria are used to report functional limitations in the Survey of Income and Program Participation (SIPP).

Gross Domestic Product (GDP) The total market value of goods and services produced domestically during a given period. The components of GDP are consumption (both household and government), gross investment (both private and government), and net exports (CBO, 2002).

Health Capital The present value of a person's lifetime health (Cutler and Richardson, 1997, from Grossman, 1972).

Health-Related Quality of Life (HRQL) A measure of those aspects of overall quality of life that can be clearly shown to affect health, either physical or mental. On the individual level, this includes physical and mental health perceptions and their correlates, including health risks and conditions, functional status, social support, and socioeconomic status. Normally scaled so that death = 0 and excellent health = 1 (CDC, 2000).

Human Capital The education, training, work experience, and other attributes that enhance the ability of the labor force to produce goods and services.

Instrumental Activities of Daily Living (IADLs) Used by the National Health Interview Survey (NHIS) to determine need for assistance. IADLs include performing household chores, doing necessary business, shopping, and getting around for other purposes.

Job Lock A distortion in job mobility attributed to employer-provided health insurance when employees keep jobs they would rather leave for fear of losing coverage (from Madrian, 1994).

Loading Fee   The amount added to the actuarial value of the covered benefit (i.e., to the expected or average amounts payable to the insured) to cover all additional administrative costs and contingencies of issuing the policy, including any profit for the insurer.

Lost Earnings Capability   The difference between the actual earning capability of the working age population and what this capability would be in the absence of health and disability limitations. This measure takes into account the effect of functional limitations on wage rates in addition to the amount of time worked (Haveman et al., 1995).

Merit Good   A concept describing situations where the social evaluation of a commodity derives not simply from the standard of consumer autonomy, but implies that individual preferences are either neglected or supplemented by other considerations for the community as a whole. Thus, the common interests and values of the community may give rise to shared needs that individuals feel obliged to support as a member of that community (Musgrave, 1959).

Moral Hazard   The incentive for people to seek more care when they have health insurance (Cutler and Zeckhauser, 2000).

National Income   Total income earned by U.S. residents from all sources, including employee compensation (wages, salaries, benefits, and employers' contributions to social insurance programs), corporate profits, net interest, rental income, and proprietors' income (CBO, 2002).

Nominal Value   The nominal level of income or spending measured in current dollars (CBO, 2002).

Opportunity Cost   The value of resources devoted to a given activity measured by their value if deployed elsewhere.

Present Value   A single number that expresses a flow of current and future income (or payments) in terms of an equivalent lump sum received (or paid) today (CBO, 2002).

Productivity   The amount of output (what is produced) per unit of input (labor, equipment, capital) used.

Public Good   A good that all individuals can consume despite not having contributed to its production, and if one individual consumes the good, utilization by others is not reduced.

Quality-Adjusted Life Year (QALY) A measure of health outcomes used to combine mortality and morbidity effects of an intervention. It is calculated by assigning a health-related quality of life weight ranging from 0 to 1 to each period of time. The number of quality-adjusted life years represents the number of healthy years of life that are valued equivalently to the actual health outcome. A weight of 1 translates to perfect health and a weight of 0 translates to a health state deemed equivalent to death (Garber et al., 1996, p. 29).

Risk Responsibility for paying for or otherwise providing a level of health care services based on unpredictable need for these services (Academy for Health Services Research and Health Policy, 2000).

Risk Premium The additional return that investors require to hold assets whose returns are more variable than those of riskless assets. The risk can arise from many sources, such as the possibility of default (in the case of corporate or municipal debt), the volatility of earnings (in the case of corporate equities), or changes in interest rates (CBO, 2002). The *risk premium* is that part of an insurance policy premium that accounts for the riskiness of the policy to the issuer—see *Loading Fee*.

Social Capital A research construct with either or both cognitive and social structural elements that refers to the stocks of resources available through social relationships, as measured by indicators such as civic engagement, norms of reciprocity, and interpersonal trust (Macinko and Starfield, 2001).

Social Cohesion The degree of perceived or operationalized social connectedness or integration among a group of people, sometimes measured as social capital (Kawachi and Kennedy, 1997).

Spillover Effect A direct effect, either positive or negative, on a person's or institution's profit or welfare developing as a byproduct of some other person's or firm's activity. Also referred to as an economic externality.

Transfer, Transfer Payment Payments made to an individual or organization for which no current or future goods or services are required in return. Federal transfer payments include welfare, Social Security, and unemployment benefits (CBO, 2002).

Uncertainty When the likelihood of future events is indefinite or incalculable.

Utility   The capacity of a commodity or a service to satisfy human wants. Satisfaction and utility are generally interchangeable terms. *Marginal utility* is the satisfaction gained through consumption of a single additional unit of any consumption good.

Value of a Statistical Life (VSL)   A measure of how much wealth people are willing to forgo for a small reduction in mortality risk. The total amount that a large group of people would pay to avoid one expected fatality among them, not the amount one person would pay to avoid certain death.

Welfare Gain or Loss   The change in total or net human satisfaction or utility occurring through any action by a consumer, a producer, or a government. The difference between the benefit derived from the action and the cost of the action is the gain or loss.

Willingness to Pay (WTP)   Either demonstrated (revealed) preference through market transactions or stated preference in survey responses of the maximum amount consumers would be willing to pay for a program or intervention.

B

Coverage Does Matter: The Value of Health Forgone by the Uninsured

Elizabeth Richardson Vigdor

In the United States, 16.5 percent of the nonelderly population lacks health insurance (Fronstin, 2002). This translates into approximately 41 million people who are exposed to the potential risks of being uninsured. This problem has not attenuated over time. In fact, the uninsured proportion of the population has been on a generally upward trend for more than 10 years (Fronstin, 2002).[1] There has long been concern in the policy world about the cost to society of this phenomenon. Health insurance is a key component of access to timely and effective medical care. Without the latter, individuals may end up consuming unnecessarily costly medical care at a later date, and productivity may be adversely affected if individuals are unable to work. One factor that is often overlooked, however, is the cost of forgone health experienced by the uninsured individuals. This paper examines the loss in health capital—the imputed dollar value of health that individuals will have over their remaining lifetimes—that accrues to society from this lack of health insurance.

To measure this, I apply a variation of the methodology previously developed by Cutler and Richardson (1997) to measure "health capital," following Grossman (1972). This measure combines several different dimensions of health to estimate the present value of the stock of present and future quality-adjusted life years. This analysis measures health capital empirically, using data on the length of life, the

---

[1] At the time this analysis was conducted, the latest Current Population Survey estimates of insurance coverage were for calendar year 2000. Henceforth, this paper refers to those data, as presented in Fronstin (2001b).

prevalence of various health conditions, and the quality of life conditional on having those conditions. I estimate the average health capital of the insured and the uninsured first assuming perfect health, then incorporating morbidity. I calculate a lower-bound estimate of morbidity-adjusted health capital assuming no difference in morbidity between the two groups, and an upper-bound estimate using observed cross-sectional differences in morbidity. I then estimate the amount of health capital lost by not insuring the uninsured. I examine this under two scenarios. One assumes that everyone who is uninsured today will remain so until age 65, and another assumes that the uninsured face the average probability of being uninsured in a given year.

Using benchmark assumptions of a 3 percent discount rate and a $160,000 value of a life year, I estimate that the value of future forgone health to an uninsured 45-year-old is between $7,800 and $83,000 using the years of life (YOL) approach, and between $6,000 and $102,000 using the quality-adjusted life year (QALY) approach. The value of future forgone health to an uninsured infant is between $4,600 and $50,000 with the years of life approach, and between $3,800 and $98,000 when morbidity is incorporated. These numbers add up to an extremely large social cost. Reasonable, conservative estimates of the total cost to society of forgone health are between $250 billion and $3.3 trillion, depending on the assumptions about lifetime insurance status. If health insurance were extended to the currently uninsured population, the average gain in healthier years of life would be between $1,600 and $4,400 per additional year of coverage provided.

WHOSE HEALTH LOSS ARE WE MEASURING?

This analysis addresses the question of how much health is lost due to a lack of universal insurance coverage. Another way to frame that question is to ask how much health would be gained if we were to suddenly provide coverage to the uninsured. In order to do this, there are several steps that one must take. First, one must identify the population of interest. Second, one must determine the precise intervention to be undertaken. Many individuals transition in and out of insurance, remaining uninsured for only a short spell. Others remain uninsured for a long time. Clearly, the impact of granting universal coverage will have a very different impact on the two groups. Similarly, there is a difference between insuring someone for the rest of their life and giving them insurance for a short period of time, such as a year. Indeed, there are an infinite number of permutations for such an intervention when one considers timing, degree of coverage, cost-sharing arrangements, and so on. Next, we need to determine the differences in the underlying components of health capital that arise from being uninsured. Finally, we must calculate health capital before and after the intervention, and sum the difference over the relevant population.

TABLE B.1. Percentage of Population
Uninsured by Age Category, 2000

	Male	Female
Under 18	11.6	11.6
18–24	30.1	24.4
25–34	23.9	18.9
35–44	16.9	14.3
45–54	12.0	12.1
55–64	12.0	15.2

SOURCE: Fronstin, 2001b.

Identifying the Population

The population comprises the uninsured from ages 0 to 64 in 2000 as estimated by the March Current Population Survey (CPS) (Fronstin, 2001b). The March CPS health insurance questions refer back to the previous year. If people are answering the questions correctly, the Fronstin estimates represent people who were uninsured for the whole year.[2] The percentage of the population without health insurance by age category is presented in Table B.1. Men are more likely to be uninsured than women until about age 45, at which point women have a higher likelihood of lacking insurance. For both men and women, one is most likely to be uninsured between ages 18 and 24. Nearly 30 percent of men and a quarter of women in this age group did not have health insurance in 2000.

I use the estimates from Fronstin to determine the size and age distribution of the population of interest, multiplying the proportion of individuals without insurance at a given age by the sex- and year of age-specific population for 2000 (CPS, 2001). I assume that the age-group probability of being uninsured applies to the midpoint of the age range, and extrapolate linearly for individual years within categories.[3] The comparison group of interest is individuals with private health insurance coverage.

Determining the Intervention

This analysis assumes that the intervention is to provide lifetime health insurance to each uninsured person at a given age. That is, the individual will be covered from his or her current age until age 65, at which time Medicare coverage

---

[2]See Fronstin (2001a, pp. 25–28) for a discussion of the questions and their limitations.

[3]An alternative specification would be to assume that the percentage remains constant for individual years within age-group categories. Using this specification does not substantially alter the results; the extrapolation method leads to slightly more conservative estimates.

begins. Because not all insurance plans are alike, the actual impact on health is likely to vary with the design of the particular plan. Without the detailed data to construct health capital measures that vary by plan feature, the effective comparison is that uninsured individuals have the "average" private health plan.

In order to determine accurately the impact of the intervention of providing health insurance, one needs to know the counterfactual. This is problematic because of great heterogeneity in the duration and frequency of spells without insurance. Some people are uninsured for only a short period of time, and others lack coverage more often than not (IOM, 2001a; Short, 2001). Not surprisingly, the impact on health is greater for those who are uninsured for longer periods of time (Ayanian et al., 2000; Kasper et al., 2000). Although there is a fairly large literature that examines duration and frequency of periods without coverage,[4] there is not enough information to map out expected patterns of insurance over a lifetime and incorporate the differential effect of duration of uninsurance on health outcomes.[5]

Given the practical need to make some generalizing assumptions, I will measure the difference in health between the insured and uninsured under two scenarios. In the first, the counterfactual is that the individual would have otherwise remained uninsured until age 65, at which point Medicare coverage would begin. In the second, I assume that being uninsured in time t is independent of the probability of being uninsured in period $t + 1$. Thus the counterfactual for the individual receiving the intervention is that his expected health in the year occurring at age a is $\text{pr}(uninsured_a) *H_{unins} + (1 - \text{pr}(uninsured_a)) *H_{ins}$, where pr(uninsured) is the proportion uninsured at age a. This assumes that the overall rate of insurance at a particular age will remain constant over time.

Reality probably lies somewhere in between these two scenarios. Few individuals will actually remain uninsured until age 65 in the absence of the intervention. Many will eventually obtain private or public insurance coverage and realize health benefits from doing so. Therefore this approach will overestimate the impact of providing lifetime insurance, assuming that there are health gains to be made that in fact have already occurred as people transition back into the insured state. On the other hand, insurance status is not a random draw every year. The latter scenario captures the fact that the probability of being without health insurance is not constant across the lifespan. It does not, however, account for any difference in the probability of being uninsured in the future conditional on being uninsured now. It also ignores any residual effects on health of being uninsured in the previous period. If the effect of insurance status were instantaneous and nonpersistent, this method would accurately capture the average difference in health capital by insurance status. However, if being uninsured now increases the prob-

---

[4]See Institute of Medicine (2001a) and Short (2001) for summaries of this literature.

[5]Even if we did have this information, such a mapping would be a monumental undertaking.

ability of being uninsured in the future and the length of uninsured spell has an adverse impact on health outcomes, this scenario will lead to an underestimate of the benefit from providing health insurance. Furthermore, if rates of uninsurance continue on an upward trend, this scenario will provide a conservative estimate of the gains from providing insurance.[6]

I compute health capital under three sets of assumptions, which will be described. I calculate each set of estimates for the two alternative insurance scenarios. Because one approach will overestimate the health gains from insurance and the other will underestimate these gains, we can use the results from each scenario to bracket the actual effect we would expect to see under each set of assumptions.

HEALTH CAPITAL: A FRAMEWORK FOR MEASURING HEALTH

We are interested in measuring the gains in health from insuring the uninsured. But "health" has many dimensions, and is a difficult concept to define and measure. One component of health is generally straightforward: Is the person alive? Health has other physical and mental attributes as well. Is the person in pain? Does the person need help caring for herself, or is she unable to work or otherwise function normally? Is the person happy and well adjusted? We need to combine all of these elements into a single measure of health.

One approach combines these elements into a measure of quality-adjusted life. In previous work, we employed such a methodology to measure changes in the health of the U.S. population over time (Cutler and Richardson, 1997). Consider $H(a)$ to be an individual's health at age a. Because health has no natural units, we can scale H however we want. Suppose we scale H from 0 to 1, where 0 is death and 1 is perfect health. Any diseases or impairments the person has will reduce his quality of life so that it falls somewhere in the 0 to 1 range. This definition of H is frequently referred to as a health-related quality of life (HRQL) weight (Gold et al., 1996a). A year in a health state with a particular HRQL weight is referred to as a "quality-adjusted life year," or QALY (Zeckhauser and Shepard, 1976). Because a dead person has $H = 0$, expected health is simply Pr[alive at a]*$Q(a)$ where $Q(a)$ is the average quality of life among those who are alive at that age.

We then defined *health capital* as the utility[7] resulting from the stock of current and future quality-adjusted life years:

---

[6]Conversely, if rates of uninsurance go down, the gains from insurance estimated under this approach will be biased upward. Given historical patterns, however, it seems unlikely that rates of uninsurance will decline dramatically in the future.

[7]Utility is an economic term meaning the satisfaction or benefit that people receive from consuming goods and services.

$$HealthCapital(a) = V \bullet E\left[\sum_{k=0}^{\infty} \frac{H(a+k)}{(1+r)^k}\right]$$

where r is the discount rate and V is the marginal rate of substitution between health and other goods and services. Because health is measured in life years, V is the value of an additional year in perfect health. The bracketed term in the above equation is simply the discounted value of the expected number of QALYs that a person has remaining at age a.

Health capital can be thought of as analogous to human capital, a concept frequently used in labor economics. Human capital is the present value of the income one can expect to receive over the course of one's life as a function of educational attainment. Having a better education allows a person to earn more in the future. Similarly, having more health makes a person happier (and possibly more productive). Health capital is the present value of the utility resulting from a person's health.

For this paper, we are interested in finding the difference between the health capital of an insured person and an uninsured person at age a, and summing these differences over the current population of the uninsured. Note that in theory we want to isolate the difference in average health capital that is caused by lack of insurance, and not differences that arise as a result of different distributions of underlying characteristics, such as gender or income. In other words, we want to hold constant individual and environmental factors, and change only the variables that are affected by insurance coverage.

The change in health capital can be decomposed into two terms: the change in the present value of the number of quality-adjusted life years times the dollar value of those life years. We are making two different assumptions about future insurance status without the intervention. In the first case, we are assuming that an uninsured person would have remained in that state until he or she reaches age 65. For a person at age a, the difference in health capital is:

$$HealthCapital_I(a) - HealthCapital_{UI}(a) = V \bullet \left[\left[\sum_{k=0}^{\infty} \frac{H_I(a+k)}{(1+r)^k}\right] - \left[\sum_{k=0}^{\infty} \frac{H_{UI}(a+k)}{(1+r)^k}\right]\right].$$

In the second case, we are assuming that the uninsured person has a probability less than 1 of being uninsured at any given year in the future. In that case the difference in health coverage from the intervention is:[8]

---

[8]In our previous work (Cutler and Richardson, 1997), we raised an important concern that can arise when determining changes in the average health capital for a population. If the health of the marginal survivor is worse than average, it will appear that health capital is declining when in fact it is

$$HealthCapital_I(a) - HealthCapital_{UI}(a) =$$

$$V \bullet \left[\left[\sum_{k=0}^{\infty} \frac{H_I(a+k)}{(1+r)^k} \right] - \left[\sum_{k=0}^{\infty} \frac{[\Pr(UI) \star H_{UI}(a+k)] + [1 - \Pr(UI) \star H_I(a+k)]}{(1+r)^k} \right] \right]$$

The Discount Rate

Which discount rate to use is a longstanding issue in economics. The appropriate discount rate is the one that trades off utility across different years. Although market interest rates are often very high, these are discount rates for dollars rather than utility. Interest rates will be higher than the discount rate for utility for a number of reasons, including taxes and risk. I use a range of discount rates that are in line with the range considered appropriate in the health literature (Lipscomb et al., 1996): 0 percent, 3 percent, and 6 percent. The benchmark assumption is a discount rate of 3 percent.

The Value of a Life Year

In addition to measuring years of life, we need to value them in dollars. The value of a human life or a quality-adjusted life year is a subject of much debate.[9] Although there is an extensive literature on the value of life, remarkably little work has been done to date on the value of a life *year*. This is true despite the fact that QALYs are frequently used as an outcome measure in cost-effectiveness analyses of medical technologies and health care programs.

One reason QALYs have become so widespread in the literature is almost certainly the appeal of being able to compare options without putting a dollar value on health. The problem with this, of course, is that it does not fully solve the problem of how to allocate resources efficiently (Johannesson and Jonsson, 1991). What is frequently done in evaluation studies is to compare the cost per QALY to commonly used medical technologies and draw a conclusion relative to accepted practice (Mason et al., 1993). One widely used benchmark (Tolley et al., 1994) set forth by Kaplan and Bush (1982) is that a policy is cost-effective if the cost per QALY is less than $34,000, updated to 1999 dollars, which is not always done

---

going up—someone is now alive who formerly was not, so the actual health of every person in the population is the same or better. To address this, we calculated average health capital over the population that is *potentially* alive, rather than actually alive. This is not an issue here because the focus changes to the health capital of people who are already alive, and we are examining the issue cross-sectionally. For simplicity, I will use the average health capital of those who are actually alive in each group.

[9] See Viscusi (1993) for a review.

when used as a benchmark (Hirth et al., 2000), and questionable if it is greater than $238,000 (1999 dollars). The area in between was deemed controversial, but acceptable by the standards of currently employed technologies. Another commonly used benchmark of acceptability is $40,000 (Bala and Zarkin, 2000). Of course, using a benchmark value for determining what is "cost-effective" is implicitly assigning a value to a life year, albeit a range of acceptable values. However, these and other benchmarks are quite arbitrary, and there is no evidence that they represent societal willingness to pay for a life year (Hirth et al., 2000; Johannesson and Meltzer, 1998).

From a welfare economics perspective, the theoretically correct way to determine whether a policy should be adopted is to compare the total benefit that would accrue to society from the policy with the total cost to society of implementing the policy (Mishan, 1972). If an individual will receive a total benefit of X from the consumption of a good, it follows that he will be willing to pay a maximum of X to obtain that good. Therefore to value the social benefit from health outcomes such as QALYs, one would need to sum each individual's willingness to pay for the QALYs gained by them and by others (i.e., any external effects that someone else's improved health might have on a particular individual). With market-produced goods, the consumer's maximum willingness to pay is the area under the demand curve for the units consumed. It is difficult enough to construct a demand curve when a market exists, but for most health outcomes there is no direct market. Thus the challenge is to determine the maximum willingness to pay for these health outcomes. In this exercise, we need to determine willingness to pay for an individual year of life.

One way to determine societal willingness to pay for a life year is to impute it from the value of a life literature. The bulk of this literature uses one of three approaches to measuring the value of life: the human capital method, revealed preference, and contingent valuation. The human capital approach (e.g., Rice and Cooper, 1967) uses the labor market to estimate the value of life. A life is worth the sum of expected future earnings. Although it is relatively easy to measure, principal limitations of this approach are as follows: indirect costs will be zero for individuals not participating in the labor market, such as retirees, homemakers, or children; it fails to consider any disutility from illness over and above forgone earnings; and it does not allow for altruism (Mishan, 1971). Furthermore, people value leisure time as well as time spent in the labor force. Keeler (2001) shows that if the average worker places the same value on leisure time and time spent in the labor force, the value of his life is 5 to 10 times the value of future earnings.[10] Thus the human capital method does not capture an individual's full willingness to pay and is likely to underestimate social benefits.

---

[10]Keeler (2001) also points out that correcting for the value of leisure time brings human capital estimates of the value of a life close to estimates obtained from the revealed preference and contingent valuation methods.

An alternative approach is to measure willingness to pay for reduction in health risks through revealed preference. By observing individuals' behavior in existing markets, we can evaluate willingness to pay indirectly for features such as automobile safety or lower risk of mortality on the job. A great deal of work has been done in examining compensating wage differentials to estimate willingness to pay for lower risk of fatal and nonfatal injury in the labor market (see Viscusi, 1993, for a review). Consumer market studies have also examined implied willingness to pay for reduced morbidity and mortality risk through the purchase of products such as smoke detectors (Dardis, 1980).

Because the consumer market studies are limited, much of what is known about the value of a statistical life comes from the labor market literature. However, this is problematic in that it represents a subset of society—primarily workers in blue-collar jobs. How much these results can be generalized to the overall population is unknown. These studies also assume unlimited job mobility, which may not be the case for workers in low-paying jobs (Lanoie et al., 1995). Furthermore, both labor and consumer market studies suffer from possible omitted variable bias due to the inherent difficulty in identifying other job or product amenities that may be highly correlated with lower risk jobs or products (Viscusi, 1993; Gerking et al., 1988). For example, someone who buys a smoke detector is not simply purchasing a reduction in the risk of death, but also a decreased chance of injury, property damage, and psychological harm. All of these elements have value, making it difficult to isolate the actual value of a life. Finally, many health interventions that need to be valued are not traded even in an implicit market (Viscusi, 1993).

The approach that is most consistent with the theoretical foundations of cost-benefit analysis is to measure willingness to pay through contingent valuation (CV) (Diener et al., 1998; O'Brien and Gafni, 1996). CV is a survey-based methodology for eliciting consumers' willingness to pay for benefits from a particular policy, usually expressed as a small change in risk. The advantage of this approach is that it directly elicits total willingness to pay for a benefit, which is precisely the theoretically desirable measure. CV studies can be conducted from different perspectives, which determine how the results are interpreted. A societal perspective asks all individuals affected by a policy about their willingness to pay for that policy. This gives the total societal benefit of the policy. On the other hand, asking an individual how much she is willing to pay for a reduction in personal risk provides that individual's valuation of her life, but theoretically will not capture any impact of this change on others.

Developed originally in environmental economics, CV is now a widely accepted tool for assessing the benefits of environmental programs (Mitchell and Carson, 1989). In the health field, CV studies have been conducted to measure a wide range of benefits, including blood donation (Lee et al., 1998; Eastaugh, 1991), arthritis treatment (Thompson et al., 1984; Blumenschein and Johannesson, 1998; Thompson, 1986), in-vitro fertilization (Neumann and Johannesson, 1994), and hypertension therapy (Johannesson and Jonsson, 1991).

Although CV provides a direct and theoretically appealing way to measure willingness to pay for a risk reduction, it can be difficult to implement in practice. It suffers from all the standard limitations of survey questions, such as anchoring, framing, and interviewer bias. In addition there may be concern about the validity of people's responses to questions that have no real implications for their lives. There is also the issue of whose willingness to pay should be considered in an analysis. For example, do we survey only those directly affected or a representative sample of the whole population, because some people may have an altruistic interest in a policy? These issues are real, but much can be done to address them. For example, O'Brien and Gafni (1996) have set forth a valuable conceptual framework for contingent valuation studies in the health field. Among their recommendations are that (1) the entire population (or a representative sample) be surveyed; (2) an ex-ante insurance framework be utilized; and (3) the question be framed as a tax referendum or some other type of compulsory payment scheme.

One criticism of both the human capital and contingent valuation methods is that they value individuals with low income or wealth less than those with high income or wealth. Indeed, how one "should" value a life year within a lifetime or across individuals is a controversial and extremely subjective subject. A good illustration of the inherent challenges is the administration of the Victim's Compensation Fund established for victims of the September 11 attacks. The grand master of the fund, Kenneth Feinberg, was directed by Congress to consider the economic loss to a victim's family in making awards. Recent articles in the popular press have documented his controversial attempt to balance the lost economic potential of each victim with some degree of equity—for example, by capping awards (Kolbert, 2002; Belkin, 2002).

Aside from an individual's valuation of her own life, there are other reasons why the value of a year of perfect health might vary across people. Society has invested more in some people than in others, and some contribute more back to society than others. Thus, one might vary the value of a life year with the amount that one contributes to society or that society has invested in a person. This is essentially the approach taken in the literature on disability-adjusted life years. In that methodology, it is assumed that society values young adults more than children or older adults, but there is no variation by other factors such as income or the number of dependents an individual is supporting.[11]

The type of weights to use, let alone the values to employ, are questions about the social welfare function. Because there is not a standard social welfare function, the choice of weights in this context does not have clear theoretical rationale. In this paper, as in previous work, I do not vary the value of a life across people, age, or time. This assumes that society values a healthy year of life the

---

[11]Murray and Lopez (1996). This is based on the empirical observation that many people express a preference for saving the lives or life years of middle-aged people more than the very young or very old. The exclusion of other criteria in valuing people is made on *a priori* grounds.

same for everyone, at any point in their life. Another way to think of this is that it defines the social value of a life year to be the average of all individual values.[12]   If as a society we value equity, this is a perfectly reasonable assumption.

In previous work, we used $100,000 as the value of a life year (Cutler and Richardson, 1997). This value came from a brief synthesis of the literature done by Tolley et al. (1994), which concluded that a range of $70,000 to $175,000 per life year is reasonable. A subsequent study by Hirth and colleagues (2000), however, reviewed the value–of-life literature more thoroughly and with the express purpose of determining the value of a QALY. Hirth and colleagues identified 42 studies that used one of the three valuation methods described earlier and were appropriate for inclusion in their analysis. To estimate the value of a QALY from this literature, they first converted all the values to 1997 dollars and determined the average remaining life expectancy of the sample population. If age was not reported in the study, they assumed an average age of 40, with a sensitivity analysis ranging from 35 to 45. They then applied age–specific HRQL weights from the literature and assumed a 3 percent discount rate (with sensitivity analysis using 0, 5, and 7 percent).

Not surprisingly, Hirth and colleagues found that the median value of a life year varied tremendously. Not only were there large differences based on the methodology used, but within methods values also varied greatly. They found that the median value per life year was approximately:

- $25,000 in the human capital studies;
- $93,000 in the revealed preference for safety studies;
- $161,000 in the contingent valuation studies; and
- $428,000 in the revealed preference for job safety studies.

The authors presented their sensitivity analysis in terms of the percentage change to the life year value of the relevant studies; for example, changing the assumption about the average age from 40 to 35 lowered the value per life year in those studies by 7 percent. I recalculated the median value per life year for each methodology, incorporating the high and low ends of the range of estimates they tested for the discount rate and the average age of the population (when it was assumed). These numbers, along with their benchmark median values, are presented in Table B.2. Under the assumption of no discounting and an average study age of 35, the value per life year ranges from $14,000 for the human capital approach to $256,000 for the revealed-preference-for-job-risk method. Under the looser assumptions of 7 percent discounting and an average study age of 45, the

---

[12]One additional problem with the value of a life literature is that market-based values of a life are marginal rather than average. Similarly, if people value their own life years unequally, the average value of a life year will depend on the number of years of life remaining. These are issues that need to be explored further in future research.

TABLE B.2 Estimates of the Value of a Life Year

Median Estimate	Human Capital	Revealed Preference:		Contingent Valuation
		Job Risk	Safety	
3% discount rate (3% discount rate, average age 40)	$24,777	$428,286	$93,402	$161,305
Low assumptions (0% discount rate, average age 35)	$14,142	$255,718	$54,123	$85,492
High assumptions (7% discount rate, average age 45)	$40,710	$685,258	$151,909	$272,605

SOURCE: Author's calculations from Hirth et al. (2000), 1997 dollars.

human capital method yields a value per life year of $41,000, while the revealed-preference-for-job-risk studies have a median value of $685,000 per life year.

As discussed earlier, I believe that the contingent valuation is the theoretically correct methodology for valuing life and health changes and use a benchmark value of $160,000 for a year in perfect health.[13] Assuming a 3 percent discount rate and a life expectancy at birth of 76 years, this translates into a value of $4.8 million for a life. This is in line with Viscusi's (1993) conclusion that reasonable value of life estimates using any approach are clustered in the $3 to $7 million dollar range.[14] For comparison, U.S. government agencies use a range of values for a life, with most falling within Viscusi's spectrum. For example, the Environmental Protection Agency recommends a baseline estimate of $6.1 million (in 1999 dollars) for benefit calculations (USEPA, 2000); the Department of Transportation (which includes the Federal Aviation Administration) recommends a value of $3 million for all its economic evaluations (U.S. Department of Transportation, 2002)[15]; and the Food and Drug Administration and Consumer Product Safety Commission use a value of $5 million (U.S. Department of Transportation, 2002).

---

[13]In reality, deriving the value of a life year from the value of life yields the value of a year in average health rather than a year in perfect health because people are presumably not assuming they will spend the rest of their life in perfect health when they respond to survey questions or make consumption decisions. Because a year in average health is worth less than a year in perfect health, my estimates are biased downward.

[14]Note that although these numbers may seem very large relative to lifetime earnings, they are typically imputed from measurements of the value of a small reduction in mortality risk. Therefore the income effects are likely to be small and wealth constraints are unlikely to be binding.

[15]In January 2002 this was raised from $2.7 million, the value that had been used since 1996 (United States Department of Transportation, 2002).

MEASURING THE CHANGE IN HEALTH CAPITAL
EMPIRICALLY: YEARS OF LIFE APPROACH

To measure health capital empirically for the insured and the uninsured, we must measure expected quality–adjusted life years for each group over a lifetime, value those years in monetary terms, and discount them to the present. A simple way to start is to dichotomize the quality–adjusted life year variable H. In this scenario there are only two values of H: 1 for someone who is alive, and 0 for someone who is dead. When the discount rate is 0, the last term in the health capital equation is simply the standard measure of life expectancy conditional on reaching age a.

Determining the probability of survival in a given year is relatively straightforward. I start with the 1999 period life table generated by the Social Security Administration (SSA). The SSA life tables are available for men and women. However, we need separate life tables by insurance status. To construct these, I use data on mortality differences by insurance status. The Committee's earlier report, *Care Without Coverage: Too Little, Too Late* (IOM, 2002a), presented a systematic review of the literature on health outcomes as a function of insurance status, and concluded that individuals without insurance experience a 25 percent higher mortality risk in future years than individuals with insurance. This conclusion is based primarily on two long–term longitudinal studies. The first study, by Franks and colleagues (1993), followed a cohort of adults for 13 to 17 years. Those that were uninsured at baseline had cumulative mortality throughout the follow–up period that was approximately 25 percent higher than those who were privately insured at baseline (with a 95 percent confidence interval ranging from 0 to 55 percent). The second study, by Sorlie and colleagues (1994), followed a large sample of adults over a 2– to 5–year period and found mortality rates were 20 to 50 percent higher for those uninsured at baseline, depending on sex and race (with 95 percent confidence intervals ranging from about 0 to more than 200 percent).

Since the confidence intervals around the mortality estimates in these two studies are wide, it is possible that the true impact of insurance on mortality is substantially greater or less than 25 percent. Furthermore, if the uninsured differ systematically from the insured along unmeasured dimensions that are associated with higher or lower mortality, then these studies will overestimate or underestimate the impact of insurance, respectively. Theoretically, it is not clear which way this bias will go. On one hand, people may opt out of insurance because they are relatively healthy and believe they do not need coverage; on the other hand, people may lose their health insurance as a result of being sick.

Evidence from two studies that explicitly try to control for unobserved heterogeneity suggests that there is some causal effect of insurance status on mortality. A recent study by Doyle (2001) uses severe automobile accidents to examine treatment patterns by insurance status. Controlling for patient, crash, and hospital characteristics, he found that the uninsured receive 20 percent less treatment and have a 37 percent higher risk of mortality. The RAND Health Insurance Experiment, which placed individuals randomly into different categories of cost sharing for health insurance, found that high-risk individuals with very high cost sharing had a 10 percent higher risk of dying than those with free care. This effect came entirely through the adverse effect of cost sharing on high blood pressure (Newhouse et al., 1993).

Several studies have also documented higher rates of infant mortality among the uninsured (Foster et al., 1992; Moss and Carver, 1998; Currie and Gruber, 1996; Howell, 2001). However, the evidence is mixed on the effectiveness of interventions designed to provide insurance to pregnant women or improve access to prenatal care, suggesting that other factors may account for the difference. Studies of individual states have found effects of various programs ranging from zero (Piper et al, 1990; Coulam et al., 1995) to declines of more than 30 percent (Foster et al., 1992). Two national studies of Medicaid expansions have also found contradictory results. Currie and Gruber (1996) found that infant mortality dropped by 8.5 percent following coverage expansions to pregnant women. However, Howell (2001) finds no significant difference in infant mortality among unmarried mothers. She argues that the differences can be explained by better hospital resources overall, rather than better access to prenatal or postnatal care.[16]

To incorporate mortality into the life tables, I assume that the cumulative risk of mortality is 25 percent higher for the uninsured of both sexes from age 1 until age 65.[17] Because of the uncertainty in the literature about the causes of the infant mortality differential, I make the conservative assumption that there is no difference in infant mortality by insurance status. At age 65, I assume that the annual mortality rate equalizes (and thus the cumulative risk difference declines). The implication of this is that life expectancy *conditional* on reaching age 65 or any older age is the same for the two groups, although fewer of the uninsured will have lived to that age.

In fact it seems likely that differences in the annual mortality rates persist even after Medicare coverage begins. Individuals who enter Medicare from an uninsured state are more likely to have conditions that have not been treated appropriately (or at all, particularly in the case of diseases that are diagnosed late as a result). Therefore, we would expect a lag before any realization of health status improvements. Although I do not have the data necessary to model such a process in this paper, this omission will bias downward the estimate of the gap in mortality. In other words, this analysis overestimates the extent to which the life expectancy

---

[16]However, as Howell (2001) notes, the improvement in neonatal intensive care is likely to be an indirect effect of Medicaid expansions to newborns, which have allowed hospitals to finance capital and staffing improvements. Needleman and Gaskin (2003) obtain a similar result for intensive care units and other services in rural hospitals.

[17]Note that the annual relative risk will vary with age. It increases from 25 percent at age 0 to 30 percent and 33 percent at age 64 for men and women, respectively.

gap narrows at age 65 without any intervention, and thus underestimates the potential gains to be made from giving insurance to the uninsured. If in fact the uninsured continue to experience higher mortality upon entering Medicare, and if the mortality estimates are not picking up any unobserved factors correlated with higher mortality for the uninsured, then the life expectancy differences presented here are too low.

Table B.3 presents life expectancy conditional on reaching selected ages, by sex and insurance status. The first column is the comparison group, individuals who have private insurance coverage from age a until they reach 65. The next two columns represent the two sets of assumptions about coverage in the absence of the intervention. The second column is life expectancy for individuals who have no insurance coverage until they reach age 65. The third column assumes that for each year in the future, the individual faces the average probability of being uninsured. That is, the expected annual mortality rate at age a is $pr(ins_a)*$ $pr(death \mid insured_a) + (1 - pr(ins_a))*pr(death \mid uninsured_a)$. Recall that these are conditional estimates; current year mortality depends only on current insurance status and everyone is assumed to have Medicare coverage at age 65. Thus life expectancy conditional on surviving to age 65 is the same for all groups.

TABLE B.3 Conditional Life Expectancy by Insurance Status

	Insured Until 65	Uninsured Until 65	Average pr(Ins) Until 65
Men Years of life remaining at age:			
0	73.2	71.5	73.0
18	56.1	54.6	55.9
25	49.6	48.2	49.4
35	40.2	39.0	40.1
45	31.1	30.1	31.0
55	22.5	21.8	22.5
65	15.0	15.0	15.0
Women Years of life remaining at age:			
0	78.6	77.5	78.5
18	61.4	60.4	61.2
25	54.5	53.6	54.4
35	44.9	44.0	44.7
45	35.4	34.7	35.3
55	26.4	25.9	26.3
65	18.1	18.1	18.1

A newborn boy with no insurance coverage until he is age 65 can expect to live 1.7 fewer years than his counterpart with continuous private insurance coverage. A newborn boy facing the average annual probability of being uninsured only loses 0.3 life year relative to a boy with lifetime private insurance coverage. For both groups the gap narrows with age. By age 55, a male who will remain uninsured for the next 10 years and then be covered under Medicare can expect 0.7 fewer years of future life than someone who will remain privately insured until age 65, while a male with an average chance of insurance from age 55 to 65 loses 0.1 life year. For females, the amount of life expectancy lost is lower: 1.1 and 0.2 years for newborns in the continuously uninsured and average probability groups, respectively. As with males, the gap narrows with age.

Converting these life expectancy numbers into health capital under this approach simply requires multiplying by the value of a life year and discounting. Table B.4 shows the health capital estimates by insurance status and sex at certain ages using the years of life approach, and the differences in health capital between the comparison group and the two groups who lack coverage. For all groups, health capital is large, between $4.6 and $4.7 million at birth, and around $2 million for someone age 65. Women have higher health capital than men at all ages, simply reflecting the higher life expectancy for women.

In contrast, the difference in health capital between a continuously insured individual and someone who is uninsured for all or part of her life seems relatively small. Recall that we can think of the two counterfactuals as bracketing the true difference in health capital between the insured and the uninsured. For a newborn, the difference in health capital ranges from $5,000 to $50,000. The difference is greatest in the mid-forties, ranging from $8,000 to $83,000. The difference peaks at this age because the annual relative mortality risk is increasing as one gets older. At younger ages, the discounting places less weight on this higher mortality risk in the future. For the people facing the average probability of being uninsured, the peak is not as dramatic; in fact, it is barely perceptible in Table B.4. This is because the increasing annual mortality risk for the uninsured is offset by the fact that one is much less likely to be uninsured at age 45 than at ages 18 to 34.

Are these differences large or small? Relative to the level of health capital, they are small. However, the present value of lifetime earnings for a newborn who works from ages 18 to 64 and earns the 2001 mean annual income of $32,000 (CPS, 2001) is just under $500,000. Thus the value of lost health from being uninsured is equal to between 1 and 10 percent of expected lifetime earnings for an infant, which seems considerably less trivial.

Naturally the differences in health capital vary with the discount rate used. The first two columns of Table B.5A show the differences using discount rates of 0 and 6 percent under this scenario. With no discounting, an uninsured infant has between $27,000 and $270,000 less health capital than an insured infant. The magnitude of the difference declines with age because remaining life expectancy also declines with age. Using a 6 percent discount rate, an insured infant has between $1,000 and $14,000 more health capital than an uninsured infant. As with

TABLE B.4 Health Capital by Insurance Status, Sex, and Age: Years of Life Approach

	Health Capital Levels and Differences (thousands of dollars)					Benefit per Year of Insurance (dollars)	
	(1)	(2)	(3)				
	Insured Until 65	Uninsured Until 65	Average pr(Ins) Until 65	Difference (1) − (2)	Difference (1) − (3)	Uninsured Until 65	Average pr(Ins) Until 65
Men							
0	4,617	4,567	4,609	50	8	1,752	1,408
18	4,205	4,141	4,194	64	11	2,568	1,841
25	3,983	3,914	3,972	69	11	3,039	2,197
35	3,583	3,504	3,572	78	11	4,069	2,952
45	3,077	2,994	3,067	83	10	5,691	3,872
55	2,473	2,404	2,465	69	8	8,244	4,466
65	1,811	1,811	1,811				
Women							
0	4,733	4,701	4,728	32	5	1,108	893
18	4,382	4,345	4,377	37	6	1,474	1,120
25	4,178	4,136	4,172	42	6	1,818	1,427
35	3,811	3,762	3,804	50	7	2,530	2,009
45	3,345	3,291	3,337	53	8	3,576	2,661
55	2,768	2,723	2,761	45	7	5,285	3,267
65	2,110	2,110	2,110				

NOTE: Calculations assume a value of a life year of $160,000 and a real discount rate of 3 percent. Benefit per year of insurance is calculated by dividing the gain in health capital by the discounted years of insurance coverage provided (see Tables B.5A, B.5B).

TABLE B.5A Differences in Health Capital by Discount Rate, YOL Approach (thousands of dollars)

	0% discount rate		6% discount rate	
	Difference, Insured– Stay Unins.	Difference, Insured– Pr(Unins)	Difference, Insured– Stay Unins.	Difference, Insured– Pr(Unins)
Men				
0	270	41	14	2
18	238	37	21	4
25	222	32	26	5
35	199	26	35	5
45	167	21	45	7
55	113	14	45	6
Women				
0	180	27	9	1
18	152	24	11	2
25	145	22	15	2
35	133	20	21	3
45	113	17	28	4
55	77	12	29	4

NOTE: Calculations assume a value of a life year of $160,000.

the 3 percent discount rate, the differences actually increase with age as the mortality differentials become more imminent. At age 55, the difference in health capital between the insured and the uninsured ranges from $4,000 to $45,000.

A useful way to think about the gain in health capital from insurance is to compare it with the additional years of health insurance that we are providing to obtain this benefit.[18] For an individual at age a, this is the total number of years that she can expect to be uninsured for the rest of her life, discounted to make it comparable to our baseline estimates.[19] This can be written as:

$$\sum_{t=0}^{\infty} \frac{pr(uninsured_{a+t}) \star pr(alive_{a+t} \mid alive_a)}{(1+r)^t}.$$

Under the scenario assuming a counterfactual of no insurance prior to Medicare, *pr(uninsured)* is equal to one before age 65, so the estimate is simply the discounted years of expected life between now and age 65. Table B.6 shows the discounted years of insurance coverage provided at different ages under the two

---

[18]I would like to thank Emmett Keeler for suggesting this approach.

[19]Recall that we assume individuals are covered by Medicare starting at age 65, so pr(uninsured)=0 from that point on.

TABLE B.5B Differences in Health Capital by Discount Rate, QALY Approach (thousands of dollars)

	QALY Approach: Lower Bound				QALY Approach: Upper Bound			
	0% discount rate		6% discount rate		0% discount rate		6% discount rate	
	Difference, Insured-Stay Unins.	Difference, Insured-Pr(Unins)	Difference, Insured-Stay Unins.	Difference, Insured-Pr(Unins)	Difference, Insured-Stay Unins.	Difference, Insured-Pr(Unins)	Difference, Insured-Stay Unins.	Difference, Insured-Pr(Unins)
Men								
0	222	34	12	2	354	55	43	7
18	193	30	18	3	294	48	50	10
25	180	26	22	4	269	40	55	10
35	160	21	29	4	230	31	63	9
45	134	17	36	5	180	22	64	8
55	90	11	36	4	112	14	53	6
Women								
0	147	22	8	1	268	40	38	5
18	122	19	10	2	213	34	39	7
25	117	18	12	2	195	29	41	6
35	107	16	17	3	168	24	46	7
45	90	13	22	3	131	19	47	7
55	61	10	23	4	80	12	37	6

NOTE: Calculations assume a value of a life year of $160,000.

TABLE B.6 Discounted Years of Insurance Provided Under Different Scenarios

	Uninsured Until 65	Average pr(Ins) Until 65
Men Years of life remaining at age:		
0	28.4	5.5
18	24.8	5.8
25	22.8	4.8
35	19.2	3.6
45	14.5	2.7
55	8.4	1.9
Women Years of life remaining at age:		
0	28.8	5.1
18	25.3	5.2
25	23.3	4.5
35	19.6	3.6
45	14.9	2.9
55	8.6	2.2

NOTE: Assumes real discount rate of 3 percent.

scenarios, discounted at 3 percent. It would require 28.4 years of insurance in present-value terms to insure a newborn boy who otherwise would be uninsured until age 65, and 28.8 years of insurance to do the same for a newborn girl. For newborns facing the *average* probability of being uninsured in each year up to age 65, it would take 5.5 years of insurance for a boy and 5.1 for a girl.

The last two columns of Table B.4 show the gain in health capital per year of health insurance provided for various ages, using the years of life approach. For a 25-year-old male, the gain in health capital for each year of insurance is $2,200 under the average probability of insurance scenario, and $3,000 under the continually uninsured scenario. For a 25-year-old female, the corresponding estimates are $1,400 and $1,800, respectively. Because we are now normalizing the change in health capital by the amount of time one otherwise would have been uninsured, the ratios are much closer than the raw differences under the two insurance scenarios. They are still quite different, however, due to the uneven distribution of mortality and insurance status over the lifespan. Specifically, there are large health benefits from being insured later in life when overall levels of mortality are higher. Yet the probability of being uninsured at this stage is much lower than at younger, healthier ages. Therefore we would expect lower estimates from the scenario that assigns a much lower probability to receiving these health benefits later in life.

Not surprisingly, the benefit per year of insurance increases substantially with age. This is true because mortality rates are larger at older ages, and therefore gains from a reduction in mortality are larger as well. The estimates for younger uninsured individuals are lowered by the years in which insurance coverage is provided, but mortality simply is not very high. Furthermore, the gains that these individuals will receive in the future take on smaller weight due to the discounting. For older people, these gains are closer and therefore the discount factor has a smaller effect. The health gains for women remain quite a bit smaller than for men, even when controlling for the fact that women are more likely to be insured. Again, this is because women have lower overall mortality, so a proportional reduction in the mortality rate simply will not have as large an impact as it will for the men.

MEASURING THE CHANGE IN HEALTH CAPITAL EMPIRICALLY: THE QALY APPROACH

The next step is to incorporate morbidity into our estimates. To compare the difference in morbidity-adjusted health capital that arises from a lack of insurance, we need to calculate the expected differences in disease presence and quality of life by insurance status. Several factors make this very difficult. First, the uninsured have different characteristics than the insured. If we observe in the population that the uninsured are more likely to have diabetes, for example, this might simply be explained by the fact that the uninsured are more likely to be male, and men report a higher prevalence of diabetes. Even if we control for a variety of characteristics, however, it is not necessarily the case that equalizing insurance status will eliminate the remaining difference in health capital. One reason for this is that we might expect some of the adverse effects of going without coverage to persist or have long-term implications. If someone with diabetes receives inadequate treatment because she lacks insurance, she may have a higher risk of developing complications later on, even after she starts receiving appropriate care. Unfortunately this is extremely complicated to model and we lack sufficient data to do so. Another reason we would not expect to eliminate the entire difference in health capital by insuring the uninsured is that there may be factors correlated with lack of insurance and worse health outcomes that are difficult or impossible to measure, such as an aversion to doctors. Therefore, if we assume that the entire health capital differential will vanish once an individual receives insurance coverage, we will overestimate the true impact of the intervention.

The issue of selection bias makes it impossible to draw inferences about causality when comparing the health of the insured and the uninsured in the cross-section. Theoretically, the direction of any measurable difference in health by insurance status is unclear. On one hand, we might expect the uninsured to have more chronic conditions due to a lack of adequate prevention (e.g., more untreated hypertension leading to more heart disease). On the other hand, they may have a lower rate of *reported* prevalence at a given age if diagnosis occurs at a later stage of the disease (e.g., cancer). The uninsured may also have a lower prevalence of disease if they are more likely to die; we may observe less cancer in the uninsured at older ages because most of them (and perhaps the sickest) have already died from heart disease. Finally, we may see a difference in health status because of adverse selection and "cream skimming." In the first case, we would expect to see better health in the uninsured if individuals choose not to buy insurance because they are healthier and do not need it. In the latter case, patients with chronic disease who lose their insurance may subsequently be unable to find affordable coverage, and we will observe worse health. Which of these effects will dominate in practice is an empirical question. However, the conclusion of the Committee (IOM, 2002a) is that overall, the uninsured suffer worse health outcomes than the insured.

Literature on the Impact of Lacking Coverage on Health

A reasonable approach toward estimating the difference in health capital caused by a lack of insurance coverage would be to examine the literature and incorporate information from well-designed studies that control for selection bias. *Care Without Coverage* (IOM, 2002a) thoroughly evaluated and synthesized the literature on this topic. The report concludes that being uninsured leads to increased mortality, lower health status, less appropriate medical care, and lower rates of screening for many conditions.

Despite the overwhelming evidence that being uninsured is not good for overall health or access to care, however, the literature that specifically addresses the components of health capital is relatively sparse. In particular, there are few high-quality studies that examine differences in the incidence or prevalence of disease by insurance status, or differences in quality of life for a particular disease or condition. Many of the disease-specific studies focus on outcomes such as treatment patterns, utilization of services, and timely access to medical care. These types of outcomes are important for understanding the problems faced by the uninsured, but they are not the final outcome of interest here. Rather, they are the mechanisms through which health might be adversely affected. The magnitude of the effect of these particular mechanisms on quality of life, functional status, and disease prevalence are rarely measured.

One outcome that is often examined in disease-specific studies is mortality. For some diseases, such as cancer, the increased mortality the uninsured face due to later diagnosis provides clear evidence that the uninsured suffer worse health outcomes (see Roetzheim et al., 1999; Ayanian et al., 1993; Lee-Feldstein et al., 2000, among others). This is something we could easily incorporate into our measure of health capital. However, in practice the usefulness of these studies is diminished by several studies that examine overall mortality differences between the uninsured and those with coverage. Because the studies that measure total mortality should in theory incorporate all the mortality differences documented in the disease-specific measures, disease-specific mortality is not needed to conduct this analysis.

There are outcomes studies that we could incorporate into measures of health capital. For example, blood pressure levels increase when hypertensive patients lose coverage (Lurie et al., 1984; Lurie et al., 1986) and vice versa (Keeler et al., 1985). Diabetics without insurance are less likely to receive appropriate monitoring and care, putting them at higher risk for serious complications (Palta et al., 1997; Beckles et al., 1998; Ayanian et al., 2000). This information could be used to simulate an expected disease path. For example, we could determine from the literature the increased probability over one's lifetime of a cardiac event from higher blood pressure or the increased probability of future blindness from untreated diabetes. Given the limitations of the literature, however, there are relatively few diseases for which this could be done, and for many diseases the population effects would be small. This would be a very complicated exercise for an estimate that would by necessity omit many of the effects we are trying to measure.

As an alternative, I use a pair of approaches to bound the differences in the value of health capital for the uninsured. First, I assume that there is no difference in morbidity between the insured and the uninsured and calculate health capital for the insured. To generate the health capital measures for the uninsured, I simply adjust the mortality risk as in the above section. As long as the uninsured are on average less healthy than the insured, and if they do have some higher morbidity that could be alleviated with coverage, this will provide a lower bound of the potential gains from the intervention.

For the second approach, I use the National Health Interview Survey (NHIS) to determine the differences in disease prevalence and quality of life by insurance status. I control for age, sex, and a number of other demographic and socioeconomic factors when estimating prevalence and health-related quality of life. Nevertheless, there may be unobservable characteristics that confound the relationship between insurance status and health outcomes. If the uninsured differ from the insured along dimensions that are correlated with worse health, then this approach is likely to yield estimates of the difference in health capital by insurance status that are too large. Providing insurance will not completely eliminate the gap in observed health outcomes between the two groups. Therefore this approach can be considered an upper bound to the gains from extending coverage to the uninsured.

Incorporating Morbidity Empirically

Incorporating morbidity empirically is complex because it is hard to measure. It is useful to consider a schematic framework for various types of disease. Diseases arise as a result of environmental and behavioral factors, often combined with some random event. A disease can progress to death, complete recovery, or a chronic state. Chronic disease can result in reduced quality of life through lower physical and mental well-being, and it can also increase future risk of death or other diseases. It is useful to distinguish three health conditions: acute conditions, chronic conditions, and risk factors. Acute conditions are characterized by short bouts of illness followed by complete recovery. Death may follow an acute illness, but in general acute disease has become less salient to people over time. The prevalence of acute illness is difficult to measure because it fluctuates considerably from year to year or even month to month (flu season, for example). This analysis ignores short-term illnesses. Chronic diseases, on the other hand, can affect mortality, long-term quality of life, or both. Because chronic conditions persist over time, they are relatively easy to measure. The health capital framework employed here focuses on chronic conditions.

The NHIS and the Surveillance, Epidemiology and End Result (SEER) database are nationally representative sources of disease prevalence for measuring chronic conditions. The NHIS offers a cross-sectional sample of the noninstitutionalized U.S. population, approximately 100,000 people each year. It is designed in part to measure disease prevalence and asks about a large number of conditions. Mental health and HIV/AIDS are conditions that are not consistently measured in the NHIS; however, SEER is a nationally representative registry of all cancers reported at nine sites, covering a population of about 40 million.

I incorporate 14 diseases or conditions from the NHIS: heart disease (defined as coronary heart disease, angina, heart attack, other heart condition), stroke, diabetes, emphysema, asthma, bronchitis, joint pain or swelling, other pain (neck, back, jaw, or head), kidney disorder, liver condition, blindness, poor vision, deafness, and bad hearing. Prevalence data were obtained from the 1998, 1999, and 2000 NHIS. The data were pooled to increase the sample size for a final adult sample of about 95,000. Cancer prevalence is measured using SEER data. The SEER data report cancer incidence and survival by year after diagnosis. From this I construct a measure of prevalence defined as having been diagnosed with cancer in the past five years.[20] I use SEER data from 1994 to 1999 to calculate the combined 1998 and 1999 prevalence of cancer under this definition.[21, 22]

In previous work, one important category of disease that we were unable to include was mental disorders (Cutler and Richardson, 1997). The current NHIS does ask some mental health questions; however, the scope and nature of these

---

[20]As part of the redesign, the NHIS greatly improved the questions about cancer prevalence. However, the questions ask if you have *ever* been diagnosed with one of approximately 30 cancers. In 1999 and 2000, respondents were also asked the age at first diagnosis for each cancer. Here, we want to measure diagnosis with cancer in the previous 5 years, regardless of whether it is an initial diagnosis or a recurrence. These questions do not adequately capture that information.

[21]2000 SEER data are not yet available.

[22]Although the data sources are the same, there are several reasons why the health capital estimates produced in this paper are not comparable to those in previous work (Cutler and Richardson, 1997).

questions are not consistent throughout the 1998–2000 surveys. Few studies have produced reliable measures of the prevalence of mental health disorders, and the few studies that do exist generally do not provide age- and sex-specific rates (Narrow et al., 2002). In any case, there is no way to examine whether prevalence varies by insurance status, and the appropriate HRQL weights for the relevant conditions are not available. As a result, information on mental health is not included in these calculations on health capital.

One question of interest in this analysis is whether the observed burden of disease varies by insurance status. We can use the NHIS to observe net differences in reported disease prevalence by insurance status, although there is not enough information to examine the underlying mechanisms in detail. To incorporate differences in disease prevalence into this measure of health capital, I take the following approach. First, one needs to control for the fact that the uninsured population differs from the insured in many ways. For example, the uninsured are more likely to be younger and male. To address this I calculate prevalence by insurance status, sex, and age, using the following age categories: under 18, 18–24, 25–34, 35–44, 45–54, and 55–64. I also control for race (Black), Hispanic origin, income (less than $5,000, $5,000–$9,999, $10,000–$14,999, $15,000–$24,999, $25,000–$34,999, $35,000–$44,999, $45,000–$54,999, and over $55,000), residing in an urban area, region of the country (Northeast, South, Midwest, West), and insurance status. I exclude individuals with public insurance from this analysis because the proper comparison is the privately insured and the uninsured. For the elderly, I use sex and 10-year age categories, but I do not differentiate by insurance status as this population is predominantly insured by Medicare.[23]

Next I calculate the prevalence of each disease by insurance status for each age–sex category and use a t-test to determine whether the prevalence rates are significantly different. If the difference is statistically significant at the 10 percent level, I use the insurance status-specific prevalence for that disease for that age–sex group.[24] If the difference is not significant, I use the combined prevalence. I use linear interpolation to calculate prevalence by year of age, with the estimated prevalence representing the middle of the age range. The SEER data do not

---

This analysis does not require diseases that are free from time-variant reporting issues. Therefore it includes some additional conditions and produces more complete measures of health capital. In addition, the NHIS questionnaire was substantially redesigned in 1997, and many conditions are not directly comparable to those reported in previous years.

[23]Certainly we might expect to see health differences between elderly individuals with supplemental private insurance and those solely on Medicare; we might also expect health differences according to prior insurance coverage status. I ignore the former in this analysis, and have no way to measure the latter with these cross-sectional data.

[24]Using insurance status-specific prevalence only when the difference is significant at the 5 percent does not have a substantial impact on the results.

TABLE B.7 Condition Prevalence per 1,000 Population, by Age and Insurance Status

	18–24		25–34	
	Insured	Uninsured	Insured	Uninsured
Heart disease	32.9	32.5	38.0	33.2
Stroke	0.6	0.6	1.5	1.4
Emphysema	0.8	0.8	1.2	1.2
Asthma	**130.4**	**96.3**	86.0	92.6
Cancer	1.0	1.0	**3.2**	**3.7**
Diabetes	**8.4**	**4.1**	11.8	11.6
Bronchitis	35.2	34.4	31.6	29.9
Kidney disorder	5.5	5.2	6.9	6.7
Liver disease	2.3	2.3	4.4	4.6
Joint pain	153.7	154.3	187.4	169.2
Deaf	1.0	0.2	0.8	0.8
Bad hearing	**53.9**	**59.9**	**62.7**	**70.7**
Blind	0.9	0.2	1.4	1.4
Bad vision	40.2	39.3	**40.0**	**58.5**
Pain	330.0	325.9	373.8	366.1

NOTE: Pairs in bold significantly differ from each other at the 10 percent level.
SOURCE: Author's calculations from the NHIS, 1998–2000.

provide information on insurance status. Therefore, I use the NHIS prevalence of ever having cancer to test for statistical differences by insurance, and then adjust the SEER prevalence numbers to reflect the difference in relative risk observed in the NHIS.

Disease prevalence differed significantly by insurance status in approximately one-quarter of the age-sex cells. In about half the significant cases the uninsured were significantly *less* likely to have a particular disease. This may reflect later diagnosis amongst the uninsured due to reduced access to medical care. For several diseases, the uninsured were less likely than the insured to report prevalence at younger ages, but equally or more likely to report it at older ages. For example, this was true for diabetes and asthma in both genders, and stroke for women. This is the pattern we would expect to see if the uninsured are diagnosed at a later stage with diseases for which early treatment reduces severity, or if they are not receiving adequate preventive care at younger ages. All significant differences in prevalence were incorporated into the analysis, regardless of direction.

Table B.7 shows the overall prevalence of the conditions used in this analysis, by age and insurance status category. Men and women are combined for ease of presentation. Some of the statistically significant differences by insurance status are confounded when men and women are combined, but the same general conclusions can be drawn. Because I assume that everyone over age 65 is insured, overall

35–44		45–54		55–64		
Insured	Uninsured	Insured	Uninsured	Insured	Uninsured	Over 65
49.6	49.1	89.9	89.9	145.3	128.6	297.4
4.7	4.3	**7.5**	**14.7**	21.5	21.3	77.1
2.9	3.0	**7.7**	**12.3**	20.1	19.8	52.7
77.8	77.1	78.1	77.9	80.0	81.7	76.0
6.6	6.5	**17.0**	**13.0**	38.4	38.5	82.5
23.3	23.1	54.1	54.2	96.2	95.4	142.9
32.5	**47.8**	42.9	42.7	50.6	50.1	60.8
7.1	7.1	10.8	10.1	14.9	15.0	28.5
9.1	9.2	14.0	14.0	12.4	12.4	11.0
255.7	255.3	350.0	349.7	410.6	390.8	484.3
1.1	1.1	1.0	1.0	2.0	1.9	7.6
100.4	99.6	159.1	141.2	**221.7**	**174.9**	370.1
1.6	1.6	2.4	2.4	2.9	2.9	10.3
55.5	**82.4**	**89.8**	**121.2**	**81.8**	**124.0**	146.6
388.4	**404.9**	405.9	405.2	384.2	389.6	372.3

prevalence for the elderly population is shown for comparison. The most prevalent conditions are joint pain and other musculoskeletal pain. At the older ages, heart disease, bad hearing, bad vision, and diabetes are also relatively common. Asthma is one of the most prevalent diseases for the 18–24 age group, especially for the insured, but the prevalence decreases somewhat with age. I was not able to detect a statistically significant difference in prevalence by insurance status for most of the diseases, but the table generally supports the theory that the uninsured are more likely to have diseases that could be prevented or minimized with appropriate care. Stroke and emphysema are both much more common among the uninsured ages 45 to 54, and pain and bronchitis are more prevalent among the uninsured ages 35 to 44. Asthma is more common among the uninsured at ages 25 to 34. Bad vision tends to be more prevalent in the uninsured. Interestingly, there is very little difference between the two groups for heart disease, except that it is more prevalent in the insured for the 55 to 64 age group.

Measuring Quality of Life

In addition to knowing the prevalence of the conditions, we also need to know quality of life conditional on having the disease. In particular, for this measure we need a HRQL weight to assign to each condition. In theory, one would want to measure the HRQL weight using standard gamble or time tradeoff methods, which have the theoretical underpinnings of von Neumann–Morganstern utility theory (Gold et al., 1996a). In practice, conducting these surveys in the population is time consuming and methodologically difficult. As a result, there are relatively few studies that measure disease–specific HRQL weights that could be used in this analysis. Furthermore, one of the concerns that frequently surfaces with this survey methodology is the difficulty that people have in answering hypothetical questions. The QALY literature often demonstrates that people in poor health rate their health status higher than do healthy people who are asked how they would rate their health if they were in that state (for example, see Epstein et al., 1989; Najman and Levine, 1981; and Sackett and Torrance, 1978).

In previous work, both of these problems were addressed by taking a different approach toward estimating the HRQL weights (Cutler and Richardson, 1997). We compared the self–reported health of people with and without a particular condition, controlling for demographics and other conditions that the person may have. Essentially what this is doing is measuring how far a particular condition moves you along the self–reported health scale, which gives you the reduction in the HRQL weight for that particular disease. A similar methodology is employed in this paper to obtain the HRQL weights.

I use data from the NHIS to calculate the HRQL weights. The NHIS contains a question on self–reported health status that asks, "Would you say your health in general is excellent, very good, good, fair or poor?"[25] I then order these responses from 1 (poor) to 5 (excellent). I assume that people have a latent measure of health $h*$, which is related to the individual's conditions (c) and demographics (X) as follows:

$$h* = c\beta_1 + X\beta_2 + \varepsilon,$$

where ε is a random error term. This is then estimated as an ordered probit, under the assumption that the error term is normally distributed.

I control for sex, age, age squared, race, ethnicity, education, income, marital status, urbanicity, and region of the country in the model, as well as all the conditions that the individual reports having. Included in this are some conditions that are not included in Table B.7. In addition to asking chronic condition questions, the NHIS also has a section that asks about activity limitations. If someone reports a limitation, they are asked whether certain conditions caused the limitation. These questions are not designed to measure prevalence, so I cannot incorporate them in the overall measure of health capital. However, I include any

---

[25]Note that this question is different from previous versions of the NHIS, which asked, "How would you rate your health as compared with other individuals your age?"

information captured in these variables to avoid spurious correlation between the conditions in which we have an interest and the other conditions someone may have. Some of the additional conditions included in the probit model are disorders of the digestive system, injuries, and mental disorders.

In order to produce an HRQL weight that falls between 0 and 1 from our regression, we must normalize the βs. It is not clear how to do this because any endpoints one chooses are somewhat arbitrary. In a previous analysis, we used the highest and lowest cut points—the values of $h*$ at which a person will move into a different category—estimated by the model. This effectively assumes that excellent health is better than 1 and poor health is worse than death, which is obviously not the case. In this paper, I adopt a different approach.[26] Instead of using the cut points, I bound the scale with the highest and lowest predicted values ($h^{\sim}$) from the probit equation. This approach assumes that the person with the worst predicted health in the sample is in a near-death state, and the person with the best predicted health is in near-perfect health. This improves greatly on previous methodology.[27] We can then estimate the HRQL weight for disease i as $HRQL_i = \beta_1 / (h^{\sim}_{max} - h^{\sim}_{min})$.

One important factor that must be considered with this methodology is the role of interactions between the conditions. We do not want to assume linearity of the HRQL weight reductions. Having heart disease and stroke will probably not be as bad as one would predict by looking at the two conditions separately because many of the implications for quality of life are the same. To address this, I calculated the joint prevalence of pairs of conditions listed in Table B.7 and selected those with a high joint prevalence. I then fit the probit model, including these condition pairs. Pairs that were not significant at the $p = 0.05$ level were subsequently dropped from the model. The condition pairs that were included in the final model were heart disease and joint pain, heart disease and other pain, heart disease and stroke, diabetes and stroke, joint pain and other pain, poor hearing and poor vision, poor hearing and diabetes, and poor hearing and cancer.

It is also possible that the HRQL weights could vary by insurance status. To test this, I interact each of the single and joint conditions with a dummy variable for not having insurance. Interactions that were not significant at the $p = 0.05$ level were dropped from the model. Only cancer and the diabetes/stroke pair turned out to differ significantly by insurance. Notably, the main effect of not having insurance was significant and negative and is discussed below.

I also estimate the HRQL reduction associated with aging and gender. These

---

[26]I am very grateful to Will Manning for suggesting this method.

[27]This assumes that the sickest person in the sample considers his or her health state as equivalent to being dead, which is probably not the case. This has the effect of shrinking the HRQL scale, which will produce overestimates of the reduction in the HRQL weight for a given condition. However, because my estimates are rather high compared with the literature, this is probably not a major concern here.

HRQL weights are capturing any omitted disease factor, as well as any age norming that people may be doing. I include in the model age, age squared, a dummy for male, and the interaction between the male dummy and both the age variables.

The coefficients from the probit model and the estimated HRQL weight for the condition are presented in Table B.8. The direction of the coefficient estimates seems quite reasonable. All the main disease effects are negative and significant, while most of the disease interaction coefficients are positive as expected. The only disease pairs that have a negative coefficient are poor vision with poor hearing, and joint pain with other pain. It seems plausible that these could be situations in which the effect of having both conditions is actually worse than additive HRQL weights would suggest. For example, people with poor vision or poor hearing often use their other senses to compensate; having both conditions limits one's ability to do that.

The last column of Table B.9 shows the implied HRQL weights (the marginal increase or decrease in the HRQL weight is shown for the interaction terms and the uninsured dummy). Because there is no gold standard for disease-specific HRQL weights, it is difficult to compare these estimates with the existing literature. Tengs and Wallace (2000) compiled 1,000 disease- and limitation-specific HRQL weights reported in the literature. The range for most of these weights is quite large (stroke, for example, has reported weights ranging from 0.37 to 0.92). My estimates are within the reported range for nearly every condition, but they tend to fall at the high end of the range. The relative magnitudes of the HRQL weights look plausible. More serious conditions such as diabetes, stroke, and mental health disorders tend to have lower HRQL weights than less severe conditions such as poor vision or poor hearing. For the diseases included in this analysis, the HRQL weights range from 0.91 to 0.99.[28]

The uninsured interaction terms are both negative and significant, implying that quality of life for cancer patients and those with both diabetes and stroke is worse for those who are uninsured. This is consistent with the literature that suggests that cancer and diabetes are two of the chronic conditions that are most adversely affected by lack of insurance. Although none of the other interactions with the uninsured dummy variable were significant, the coefficient on the dummy variable itself is significant and negative. It is associated with a reduction in the HRQL weight of 0.01, which is similar to having asthma. Unless there is a direct impact of simply being uninsured on one's perception of health, this variable is

---

[28]One possible explanation for the high HRQL weights is poor fit of the probit model. Pregibon's link test and the modified Hosmer-Lemeshow test confirmed that model does not fit the data particularly well. Several variants were tried to correct this, including ordered logit, generalized ordered logit, and polytomous logit models, but none was successful. Further analysis of the modified Hosmer-Lemeshow test suggested that the misspecification would lead to an overestimate of the impact of health insurance, but that the magnitude of this estimate is likely to be quite small.

TABLE B.8 Relationship Between Chronic Conditions and Self-Reported Health

	Coefficient	Standard Error	QALY
Disease (*Conditions included in health capital*)			
Heart disease	−0.459	(0.024)	0.93
Stroke	−0.577	(0.043)	0.91
Asthma	−0.070	(0.034)	0.99
Bronchitis	−0.129	(0.031)	0.98
Emphysema	−0.439	(0.042)	0.93
Cancer	−0.279	(0.022)	0.96
Diabetes	−0.630	(0.022)	0.91
Kidney disorder	−0.500	(0.041)	0.92
Liver disease	−0.536	(0.047)	0.92
Deaf	−0.205	(0.067)	0.97
Bad hearing	−0.113	(0.015)	0.98
Blind	−0.412	(0.066)	0.94
Bad vision	−0.172	(0.019)	0.97
Joint pain	−0.242	(0.014)	0.96
Head/back/neck pain	−0.255	(0.012)	0.96
Interactions (*Change in QALY weight*)			
Heart disease*joint pain	0.084	(0.029)	0.01
Joint pain*other pain	−0.051	(0.019)	−0.01
Heart disease*other pain	0.105	(0.029)	0.02
Poor hearing*poor vision	−0.097	(0.032)	−0.01
Poor hearing*diabetes	0.092	(0.038)	0.01
Heart disease*stroke	0.186	(0.060)	0.03
Lung disease*diabetes	0.146	(0.044)	0.02
Poor hearing*cancer	0.143	(0.040)	0.02
Diabetes*stroke	0.203	(0.070)	0.03
Cancer*uninsured	−0.293	(0.086)	−0.04
Diabetes*stroke* uninsured	−1.254	(0.495)	−0.19
Control conditions			
Hypertension	−0.321	(0.011)	0.95
Other circulatory	−0.612	(0.076)	0.91
Other lung disease	−0.185	(0.036)	0.97
Other endocrine	−0.678	(0.094)	0.90
Nervous system	−0.748	(0.047)	0.89
Ulcer	−0.190	(0.016)	0.97
Digestive disorders	−0.863	(0.081)	0.87
Skin conditions	−0.492	(0.221)	0.93
Blood conditions	−0.771	(0.194)	0.88

continued on next page

TABLE B.8 Continued

	Coefficient	Standard Error	QALY
Amputee	−0.259	(0.138)	0.96
Injuries	−0.496	(0.061)	0.93
Other musculoskeletal	−0.565	(0.048)	0.92
Genitourinary disorders	−0.709	(0.092)	0.89
Mental health disorders	−0.821	(0.038)	0.88
Uninsured (*change in QALY weight*)	−0.075	(0.027)	−0.01
Age	−0.019	(0.002)	
Age^2	0.00011	(0.00002)	
Male	0.309	(0.077)	
Male*Age	−0.011	(0.003)	
Male*Age^2	0.00009	(0.00003)	
White	0.179	(0.020)	
Black	−0.072	(0.023)	
Hispanic	−0.133	(0.015)	
High school graduate	0.301	(0.013)	
Some college	0.545	(0.015)	
College graduate	0.739	(0.020)	
Income $5–10,000	−0.060	(0.034)	
Income $10–15,000	−0.007	(0.034)	
Income $15–20,000	0.059	(0.034)	
Income $20–25,000	0.078	(0.034)	
Income $25–35,000	0.144	(0.032)	
Income $35–45,000	0.194	(0.033)	
Income $45–55,000	0.259	(0.033)	
Income >$55,000	0.281	(0.031)	
Married	0.032	(0.010)	
Lives in urban area	0.088	(0.012)	
Lives in urban area*uninsured	−0.053	(0.031)	
Northeast region	−0.038	(0.014)	
Midwest region	−0.053	(0.013)	
South region	−0.064	(0.013)	
N	84,738		
Max predicted *h*	0.985		
Min predicted *h*	−5.67		

NOTE: Model is an ordered probit of self-reported health, with categories of excellent (5), very good, good, fair, and poor (1).

TABLE B.9 Health Capital by Insurance Status, Sex, and Age: Lower-Bound QALY Approach

	Health Capital Levels and Differences (thousands of dollars)					Benefit per Year of Insurance (dollars)	
	(1)	(2)	(3)				
	Insured Until 65	Uninsured Until 65	Average pr(Ins) Until 65	Difference (1) – (2)	Difference (1) – (3)	Uninsured Until 65	Average pr(Ins) Until 65
Men							
0	4,308	4,265	4,301	42	7	1,490	1,198
18	3,707	3,654	3,698	53	9	2,121	1,536
25	3,446	3,389	3,437	57	9	2,491	1,812
35	3,023	2,959	3,014	64	9	3,304	2,403
45	2,535	2,469	2,527	67	8	4,584	3,119
55	1,996	1,941	1,989	55	7	6,582	3,565
65	1,434	1,434	1,434				
Women							
0	4,356	4,329	4,352	27	4	941	754
18	3,842	3,811	3,837	31	5	1,208	920
25	3,605	3,570	3,600	34	5	1,481	1,164
35	3,215	3,175	3,209	40	6	2,047	1,624
45	2,757	2,715	2,751	43	6	2,868	2,131
55	2,229	2,193	2,223	36	6	4,198	2,594
65	1,660	1,660	1,660				

NOTE: Calculations assume a value of a life year of $160,000 and a real discount rate of 3 percent. Benefit per year of insurance is calculated by dividing the gain in health capital by the discounted years of insurance coverage provided (see Tables B.5A, B.5B).

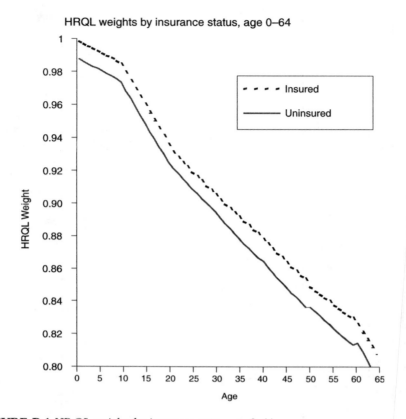

HRQL weights by insurance status, age 0–64

FIGURE B.1 HRQL weights by insurance status, age 0–64.

picking up the impact of omitted factors that are correlated with insurance status and health. This could be omitted chronic conditions, acute conditions, or personal characteristics. This negative impact of being uninsured is included in the overall HRQL weight for the uninsured state. As in previous work, I also include age factors for men and women.

Figure B.1 shows the overall expected HRQL weight for the insured state and the uninsured state from ages 1 to 64. The insured have a slightly higher HRQL weight in any given year, with a difference of about 0.01 to 0.02. The gap between them narrows throughout childhood and then gradually starts to widen a bit in the early twenties.

The QALY Approach: Lower-Bound Estimates

Table B.9 shows health capital at certain ages by sex and insurance category. In these estimates, the HRQL weights and disease prevalence are assumed to be the same for the uninsured and the insured. These estimates differ from those in Table B.4 only in that they are adjusted for morbidity. If morbidity were evenly distributed by age, this would only affect the level of health capital and not the relative difference in health capital between the uninsured and the insured. Because the disease burden is not constant over the lifespan, however, the difference is likely to change as well.

Because we are incorporating morbidity, the levels of health capital should be lower at every age for every group. Table B.9 shows that they are lower, but still very high. Health capital for an insured infant is about $4.3 million, slightly lower than it was using the years of life method. There are much larger decreases in health capital as one ages, however, compared with the Table B.4 estimates. At age 65, health capital is $1.4 million for men, and $1.7 million for women, quite a bit lower than the YOL method. Again, this is because the burden of disease increases with age. At birth the decrease in health capital once morbidity has been incorporated gets relatively little weight once we discount, whereas the decline in QALYs is more imminent at older ages.

Incorporating morbidity under this conservative approach actually decreases the differences in health capital between the insured and the uninsured. For a newborn, the forgone health capital from lacking insurance ranges from $4,000 to $42,000. As before, the difference is greatest in late middle age, reaching $6,000 to $67,000 at age 45. The left-hand columns of Table B.5B show the impact on the health capital differences by insurance of using a range of interest rates. The pattern is exactly like that observed under the YOL approach. With no discounting, the magnitude of the difference declines with age, while the difference increases slightly with age when a higher discount rate is used. The health capital difference between insured and uninsured 45-year-olds is between $3,000 and $36,000, using a 6 percent discount rate, and between $13,000 and $134,000 with a discount rate of zero.

The last two columns of Table B.9 show the gain in health capital per year of insurance coverage provided. Because the increases in health capital from insurance are lower with this approach than with the years of life method, the gain per year of insurance will be correspondingly lower as well. A 25-year-old male realizes an improvement in health capital of between $1,800 and $2,500 per incremental year of coverage. A 25-year-old female experiences gains of between $1,200 and $1,500 for each additional year of health insurance provided. A large difference in the health gains for men and women remains. The improvements in health capital are still driven by mortality because morbidity does not vary by insurance status.

Health Capital Estimates: Upper-Bound QALY Approach

Table B.10 shows the analogous results to Table B.9 when we allow the HRQL weight to differ by insurance status. As expected, the differences in health

TABLE B.10 Health Capital by Insurance Status, Sex, and Age: Upper-Bound QALY Approach

	Health Capital Levels and Differences (thousands of dollars)					Benefit per Year of Insurance (dollars)	
	(1) Insured Until 65	(2) Uninsured Until 65	(3) Average pr(Ins) Until 65	Difference (1) − (2)	Difference (1) − (3)	Uninsured Until 65	Average pr(Ins) Until 65
Men							
0	4,308	4,210	4,292	98	16	3,435	2,842
18	3,707	3,602	3,688	105	19	4,239	3,288
25	3,446	3,337	3,428	109	18	4,753	3,646
35	3,023	2,912	3,007	111	15	5,758	4,286
45	2,535	2,433	2,523	102	13	7,012	4,766
55	1,996	1,921	1,987	75	9	8,879	4,806
65	1,434	1,434	1,434				
Women							
0	4,356	4,276	4,344	79	12	2,759	2,273
18	3,842	3,763	3,828	78	13	3,090	2,482
25	3,605	3,526	3,593	79	12	3,400	2,705
35	3,215	3,135	3,204	81	12	4,099	3,191
45	2,757	2,684	2,747	74	11	4,958	3,610
55	2,229	2,176	2,220	52	8	6,134	3,780
65	1,660	1,660	1,660				

NOTE: Calculations assume a value of a life year of $160,000 and a real discount rate of 3 percent. Benefit per year of insurance is calculated by dividing the gain in health capital by the discounted years of insurance coverage provided (see Tables B.5A, B.5B).

capital between the insured and the uninsured increase dramatically; they are generally 2 to 3 times larger once morbidity is allowed to vary. For an uninsured newborn, the reduction in health capital relative to an insured newborn ranges from $12,000 to $98,000. At age 35, the difference is between $12,000 and $111,000. The distribution of the difference over the lifespan changes as well. The difference in health capital is now greater at the younger ages and generally declines with age. This reflects the differences in the relative risk of disease by age as well as the fact that the decreased quality of life from being uninsured is felt more heavily at the younger ages. The last four columns of Table B.5B show that, without discounting, the value of health capital is between $40,000 and $354,000 greater for an insured newborn; the difference shrinks to $5,000 to $43,000 with a 6 percent discount rate.

Looking at the last two columns of Table B.10, we see some big differences in the health capital benefits per year of insurance under this approach compared with the previous two approaches. First, the gains are much larger, reflecting the improvements in morbidity from obtaining insurance coverage. Now a 25-year-old male has a gain in health capital of between $3,600 and $4,800 per year of coverage, while a 25-year-old female has an increase in health of between $2,700 and $3,400 per year of insurance. Now that morbidity gains are incorporated, the change in women's health capital is much closer to the change in the health capital of men.

To summarize, our benchmark estimates of the reduction in health capital from being uninsured range from $27,000 to $98,000 for a newborn who will remain uninsured until age 65 and from $4,000 to $16,000 for an uninsured newborn who faces the average probability of being uninsured each year. These results are quite sensitive to the discount rate. The overall range of estimates we get by varying the discount rate from 0 to 6 percent widens to $8,000 to $354,000 for a newborn who will remain uninsured until age 65, and to a range of $1,000 to $55,000 for an uninsured newborn who faces the average probability of being uninsured each year. This is obviously an extremely wide range of estimates. Figure B.2 shows the pattern of health capital across the lifespan using the different approaches and scenarios. This simply presents more clearly the patterns that were visible in the tables.

If we normalize the gains in health capital from insurance by the number of years of insurance coverage provided, a newborn who will remain uninsured until age 65 sees an increase in health of between $940 and $3,400 per year. An uninsured newborn facing the average probability of being uninsured realizes a gain in health capital of $750 to $2,800 per year of coverage. For a 25-year-old, the corresponding increases per year of insurance range from $1,500 to $4,800 and from $1,200 to $3,600, respectively.

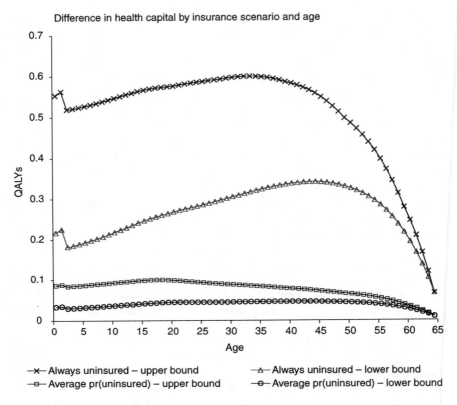

FIGURE B.2 Difference in health capital by insurance scenario and age.

CONCLUSION: TOTAL COST OF HEALTH FORGONE BY THE UNINSURED

The previous section presented a range of estimates for the difference in health capital between the insured and the uninsured at various ages. If we suddenly gave a lifetime of health insurance to the 40 million people who are currently uninsured, how much health would we gain? One key question is how much of the difference in health capital or other measures of health status would disappear and how much would persist. In constructing the health capital measures described earlier, I have tried to focus only on the difference that arises purely from a lack of insurance. The two measures of health capital using the QALY approach should provide an upper and lower bound to this impact.

If that is the case, then to estimate the total value of the health that society would gain from insuring the uninsured, we simply multiply the average gain in health capital at age *a* by the number of uninsured at that age and sum over all ages. Table B.11 presents the results of that exercise. The total value of forgone health

TABLE B.11 Total Cost of Health Forgone by Lack of Insurance

	Assume Otherwise Remain Uninsured	Assume Faces Average pr(Unins)
3% discount rate		
Total cost ($ millions)		
Health capital, YOL approach	2,087,157	306,097
Health capital, lower-bound QALY approach	1,698,366	250,049
Health capital, upper-bound QALY approach	3,266,083	498,595
Cost per year of insurance ($)		
Health capital, YOL approach	2,783	2,014
Health capital, lower-bound QALY approach	2,265	1,645
Health capital, upper-bound QALY approach	4,356	3,280
0% discount rate		
Total cost ($ millions)		
Health capital, YOL approach	6,269,248	913,831
Health capital, lower-bound QALY approach	5,053,450	738,543
Health capital, upper-bound QALY approach	7,771,782	1,157,662
6% discount rate		
Total cost ($ millions)		
Health capital, YOL approach	895,041	141,256
Health capital, lower-bound QALY approach	735,379	109,174
Health capital, upper-bound QALY approach	1,777,432	277,677

NOTE: Calculated by summing the average difference in health capital by age over all uninsured people under age 65 in the United States in 2000. Assumes value of a life year of $160,000.

is extremely large. Using the benchmark discount rate of 3 percent, the conservative estimate of the value of this health is between $250 billion and $499 billion. This assumes that each uninsured individual faces the average probability of being uninsured each year in the future. If they otherwise would have remained uninsured until age 65, the value of this health would be between $1.7 and $3.3 trillion. In reality, the value probably falls somewhere in between. This corresponds to an average increase in health capital per year of insurance coverage provided of between $1,600 and $4,400. Using a range of discount rates from 0 to 6 percent, the conservative estimate of the total value of health is between $109 billion and $1.2 trillion. The highest upper-bound estimate is nearly $7.8 trillion.

Even using the most conservative measures, the estimates of lost health capital are substantial. There is no doubt that this forgone health imposes tremendous disutility on our society. Furthermore, it is important to remember that measure of health capital only captures the value of an individual's health *to that individual*. It does not include any possible spillover effects to others in society from that one person being in better health.

There are numerous limitations to a study such as this one. Obviously, great uncertainty is inherent in all the numbers presented. Many implicit and explicit assumptions could shift the numbers in either direction. For example, the results are sensitive to the choice of discount rate, the value of a life year, the magnitude of any mortality reduction, and estimates of the HRQL weight. Also, we cannot be certain how much of the difference in observed health capital can truly be attributed to lack of insurance coverage. There may be omitted variable bias from unobservable differences between the insured and uninsured that are correlated with health outcomes. Even if there were a causal relationship, there is no guarantee that providing coverage will restore health outcomes to a preuninsured state. A related point is that this analysis also assumes that expanding coverage to a large number of people will not have any macroeconomic effects that would influence health outcomes. In reality, a large-scale expansion might have a measurable impact on access to care by insured individuals, incomes of health-sector workers, the productivity of society in general, and any number of other things, all of which might in turn affect population health.

Another limitation is the assumption that differences in mortality and morbidity by insurance status are eliminated once someone turns 65 and becomes eligible for Medicare. In fact, individuals who lack insurance suffer morbidity consequences that cannot be rectified immediately. Therefore, providing insurance coverage prior to Medicare is likely to lead to additional gains after age 65 that are not measured in this analysis.

This assumption is true for the under-65 population as well. Permanent decreases to health capital as a result of previous spells of uninsurance are not taken into account. Conditional on reaching a certain age, any adverse events prior to that age have no bearing on future health. This is an unrealistic but necessary assumption, given the data limitations. Consequently, the levels of health capital for individuals with a history of being uninsured are overestimated, although it is unclear *a priori* what effect this will have on changes in health capital.

I also make several assumptions about the uninsured population. I extrapolate rates of uninsurance within age categories to obtain uninsurance rates by year of age. The specification in which each individual faces the average probability of being uninsured assumes that rates of uninsurance will not change, when in fact they appear to be on an upward trend. Wherever possible, all these assumptions were made conservatively, that is, to understate the loss in health capital to the uninsured.

The estimates of health capital depend heavily on the value assigned to a life year. In this analysis, $160,000 per life year is the value used, which is derived from the literature on stated willingness to pay for a statistical life. This value falls in the middle of the range of estimates considered appropriate in the literature and used by government agencies. However, one feature of this measure of health capital is that it is quite straightforward to revise the value of a life year. One need only divide the health capital estimate of interest by \$160,000 and multiply it by a different value for a single life year.

Even by conservative estimates, the lost health capital due to lack of health insurance is substantial. Further research is necessary to increase the precision of each component of this analysis. This will better enable us to examine changes in population health from public policies, improvements in medical technology, or any number of health-related interventions.

C

Biographical Sketches

Mary Sue Coleman, Ph.D., *Co-chair,* is president of the University of Michigan. She is professor of biological chemistry in the University of Michigan Medical School and professor of chemistry in the College of Literature, Science and the Arts. She previously was president of the University of Iowa and president of the University of Iowa Health Systems (1995–2002). Dr. Coleman served as provost and vice president for academic affairs at the University of New Mexico (1993–1995) and dean of research and vice chancellor at the University of North Carolina at Chapel Hill (1990–1992). For 19 years, she was both faculty member and Cancer Center administrator at the University of Kentucky in Lexington, where her research focused on the immune system and malignancies. Dr. Coleman is a member of the Institute of Medicine (IOM) and a fellow of the American Association for the Advancement of Science and of the American Academy of Arts and Sciences. She serves on the Life Sciences Corridor Steering Committee for the State of Michigan, the Executive Committee of the American Association of Universities, and other voluntary advisory bodies and corporate boards.

Arthur L. Kellermann, M.D., M.P.H., *Co-chair,* is professor and director, Center for Injury Control, Rollins School of Public Health, Emory University, and professor and chairman, Department of Emergency Medicine, School of Medicine, Emory University. Dr. Kellermann has served as principal investigator or co-investigator on several research grants, including federally funded studies of handgun-related violence and injury, emergency cardiac care, and the use of emergency room services. Among many awards and distinctions, he is a fellow of the American College of Emergency Physicians (1992), is the recipient of a meritorious service award from the Tennessee State Legislature (1993) and the Hal Jayne Academic Excellence Award from the Society for Academic Emergency Medicine (1997), and was elected to membership in the Institute of Medicine (1999). In addition, Dr. Kellermann is a member of the Editorial Board of the journal *Annals of Emergency Medicine,* and has served as a reviewer for the *New England Journal of Medicine,* the *Journal of the American Medical Association,* and the *American Journal of Public Health.*

Ronald M. Andersen, Ph.D. is the Fred W. and Pamela K. Wasserman Professor of Health Services and professor of sociology at the University of California at Los Angeles School of Public Health. He teaches courses in health services organization, research methods, evaluation, and leadership. Dr. Andersen received his Ph.D. in sociology at Purdue University. He has studied access to medical care for his entire professional career of 30 years. Dr. Andersen developed the Behavioral Model of Health Services Use that has been used extensively nationally and internationally as a framework for utilization and cost studies of general populations as well as special studies of minorities, low-income populations, children, women, the elderly, the homeless, the HIV-positive population, and oral health. He has directed three national surveys of access to care and has led numerous evaluations of local and regional populations and programs designed to promote access to medical care. Dr. Andersen's other research interests include international comparisons of health services systems, graduate medical education curricula, physician health services organization integration, and evaluations of geriatric and primary care delivery. He is a member of the Institute of Medicine and was on the founding board of the Association for Health Services Research. He has been chair of the Medical Sociology Section of the American Sociological Association. In 1994 he received the association's Leo G. Reeder Award for Distinguished Service to Medical Sociology; in 1996 he received the Distinguished Investigator Award from the Association for Health Services Research; and in 1999 he received the Baxter Allegiance Health Services Research Prize.

John Z. Ayanian, M.D., M.P.P. is associate professor of medicine and health care policy at Harvard Medical School and Brigham and Women's Hospital, where he practices general internal medicine. His research focuses on quality of care and access to care for major medical conditions, including colorectal cancer and myocardial infarction. He has extensive experience in the use of cancer registries to assess outcomes and evaluate the quality of cancer care. In addition, he has studied the effects of race and gender on access to kidney transplants and on quality of care for other medical conditions. Dr. Ayanian is deputy editor of the journal *Medical Care*, director of the general internal medicine fellowship at Brigham and Women's Hospital, and a fellow of the American College of Physicians.

Norman Daniels, Ph.D.★ is professor of ethics and population health at Harvard School of Public Health, formerly having served as Goldthwaite professor and former chair of the Tufts Philosophy Department and professor of medical ethics at Tufts Medical School. He has written widely in the philosophy of science, ethics, political and social philosophy, and medical ethics. His most recent books include *Seeking Fair Treatment: From the AIDS Epidemic to National Health Care Reform* (Oxford, 1995); (with Donald Light and Ronald Caplan) *Benchmarks of Fairness for Health Care Reform* (Oxford, 1996); (with Allen Buchanan, Dan Brock, and Dan Wikler) *From Chance to Choice: Genetics and Justice* (Cambridge, 2000); (with Bruce Kennedy and Ichiro Kawachi) *Is Inequality Bad for Our Health?* (Beacon Press, 2000); and (with James Sabin) *Setting Limits Fairly: Can We Learn to Share Medical Resources?* (Oxford, 2002). He is also working on *Just Health*, a substantial revision and expansion of *Just Health Care*. Professor Daniels is a fellow of the Hastings Center, a member of the Institute of Medicine, and a founding member of the National Academy of Social Insurance and of the International Society for Equity in Health.

Sheila P. Davis, B.S.N., M.S.N., Ph.D. is associate professor in the School of Nursing at the University of Mississippi Medical Center. She is also vice president of Davis, Davis & Associates, a health maintenance consultant company. Her research focuses on minority health issues, especially cardiovascular risk among ethnic populations. Dr. Davis is the founder and chair of the Cardiovascular Risk Reduction in Children Committee at the University of Mississippi. This is a multidisciplinary committee committed to reducing cardiovascular risks in children. Dr. Davis is a member of the American Nurses Association and has written numerous publications on the profession and the experiences of ethnic minorities in the health professions. She is author of a faith-based program, Healthy Kid's Seminar, which is used to promote adoption of healthy lifestyle choices by children. Dr. Davis serves on the editorial review board of the *Journal of Cultural Diversity* and the *Association of Black Nursing Faculty Journal*. She is also founder and editor in chief of the *Online Journal of Health Ethics*.

George C. Eads, Ph.D. is vice president of Charles River Associates (CRA) Washington, D.C., office and is an internationally known expert in the economics of the automotive and airlines industries. Prior to joining CRA, Dr. Eads was vice

---

★Member, Subcommittee on the Societal Costs of Uninsured Populations.

president and chief economist at General Motors Corporation. He frequently represented the corporation before congressional committees and federal regulatory agencies. He has served as a member of the President's Council of Economic Advisers and as a special assistant to the assistant attorney general in the Antitrust Division of the U.S. Department of Justice. Dr. Eads has published numerous books and articles on the impact of government on business and has taught at several major universities, including Harvard and Princeton.

Sherry Glied, Ph.D.* is associate professor and chair of the Department of Health Policy and Management of Columbia University's Joseph L. Mailman School of Public Health. In 1992–1993, she served as a senior economist for health care and labor market policy to the President's Council of Economic Advisers. Dr. Glied's principal areas of research are health policy reform and mental health care policy. Her research on health policy has focused on the financing of health care services in the United States. She is an author of recently published articles and reports on managed care, women's health, child health, and health insurance expansions. Her book on health care reform, *Chronic Condition*, was published by Harvard University Press in 1998. She is a recipient of a Robert Wood Johnson Foundation Investigator Award through which she is currently studying the U.S. employer-based health insurance system. Dr. Glied is also conducting research sponsored by the Commonwealth Fund on the characteristics of uninsured Americans and on strategies to expand health insurance coverage.

Jack Hadley, Ph.D.* is a senior fellow at the Center for Studying Health System Change (HSC) and a principal research associate at The Urban Institute. He is a past president of the Association for Health Services Research and a former editor of the journal *Inquiry*. His work with HSC focuses on studies of the market for health insurance and of physicians' behavior. His research emphasizes the application of econometric analysis to health care problems in physician and hospital payment, medical education financing, hospital efficiency, access to care, assessment of the outcomes of medical treatment, and effects of managed care on health delivery systems. Much of his work has analyzed large databases such as Medicare claims and national hospital data in order to understand patient, provider, or system responses to policy changes.

Ruby Hearn, Ph.D.* recently retired from her position as senior vice president of The Robert Wood Johnson Foundation after 25 years. For most of her career, her efforts have focused on children's health. She was the leading developer of the Infant Health and Development Program, the first randomized trial to look for

---

*Member, Subcommittee on the Societal Costs of Uninsured Populations.

interventions to improve outcomes for low-birthweight infants. Dr. Hearn also played a key role in formulating Foundation programs on AIDS, substance abuse, and minority medical education. Her interests and influence have helped inform the Foundation's approach to health. Dr. Hearn is a member of the Institute of Medicine (IOM) and the National Academy of Sciences Committee on Science, Engineering, and Public Policy. She currently serves on the IOM Board on Health Care Services, the Board of Directors of the Council on Foundations, and the Science Board for the Food and Drug Administration.

Sandra R. Hernández, M.D. is chief executive officer of the San Francisco Foundation, a community foundation serving California's five Bay Area counties. It is one of the largest community foundations in the country. Dr. Hernández is a primary care internist who previously held a number of positions within the San Francisco Department of Public Health, including director of the AIDS Office, director of community public health, county health officer, and director of health for the City and County of San Francisco. She was appointed to and served on President Clinton's Advisory Commission on Consumer Protection and Quality in the Healthcare Industry. She currently serves on the boards of the National Alliance for Hispanic Health and the California Managed Risk Medical Insurance Board, which is the governing body for the California Children's Health Insurance Program. Among the many honors and awards bestowed on her, Dr. Hernández was named by *Modern Healthcare* magazine as one of the top ten health care leaders for the next century. Dr. Hernández is a graduate of Yale University, Tufts School of Medicine, and the John F. Kennedy School of Government at Harvard University. She is on the faculty of the University of California at San Francisco School of Medicine and maintains an active clinical practice at San Francisco General Hospital in the AIDS Clinic.

Emmett B. Keeler, Ph.D.* is a senior mathematician who joined RAND in 1968. He is currently leading a large study of 40 organizations to evaluate interventions to improve care for chronic illness. He also leads a project that supplies cost-effectiveness analyses to a variety of University of California at Los Angeles (UCLA) geriatric interventions. Dr. Keeler teaches health economics for physicians at UCLA and analytic methods at The RAND Graduate School and has taught at Harvard and the University of Chicago. Together with his RAND co-authors, he has received article-of-the-year awards three times from the Association for Health Services Research for papers on outlier payments, on the costs to others of bad health habits, and on whether poor medical patients receive worse care in hospitals than other patients. Dr. Keeler presently serves on the National Research Council's Panel to Review the Scientific Evidence on the Polygraph.

---

*Member, Subcommittee on the Societal Costs of Uninsured Populations.

Willard G. Manning, Ph.D. is professor in the Department of Health Studies, Pritzker School of Medicine, and in the Harris School of Public Policy at The University of Chicago. His primary research focus has been the effects of health insurance and alternative delivery systems on the use of health services and health status. He is an expert in statistical issues in cost-effectiveness analysis and small area variations. His recent work has included examination of mental health services use and outcomes in a Medicaid population, and cost-effectiveness analysis of screening and treating depression in primary care. Dr. Manning is a member of the Institute of Medicine.

James J. Mongan, M.D.† is president and chief executive officer of Partners HealthCare, Inc., and was previously president of Massachusetts General Hospital. Dr. Mongan served as assistant surgeon general in the Department of Health and Human Services; as former associate director for health and human resources, domestic policy staff, the White House; and as former deputy assistant secretary for health policy, Department of Health, Education and Welfare. Dr. Mongan is chair of the Task Force on the Future of Health Insurance for Working Americans, a nonpartisan effort of the Commonwealth Fund to address the implications of the changing U.S. workforce and economy for the availability and affordability of health insurance. He is also a member of the Kaiser Commission on Medicaid and the Uninsured and a past board member of the Kaiser Family Foundation.

Jack Needleman, Ph.D. is assistant professor of economics and health policy in the Department of Health Policy and Management at Harvard University. Dr. Needleman's research examines the impact of changes in the health care market and regulation on health care providers and consumers. Recent work has focused on whether nonprofit and for-profit hospitals have responded in similar ways to tighter reimbursement; examined the extent and impact of changes in hospital ownership from nonprofit or public to for-profit corporations; and examined the influence of diagnosis and expected payment source on patient flows among hospitals of differing ownership. Dr. Needleman is currently conducting two studies examining nurse staffing and hospital quality issues. He also teaches and conducts program evaluation. Other work under way includes studies of increased competition for Medicaid patients between safety-net and community hospitals in Florida, the impact of market change on hospitalization patterns for patients with psychiatric conditions, and the relationship between nurse staffing and hospital quality.

Christopher Queram, M.A. has been chief executive officer of the Employer Health Care Alliance Cooperative (The Alliance) of Madison, Wisconsin, since

---

*Member, Subcommittee on the Societal Costs of Uninsured Populations.
†Chair, Subcommittee on the Societal Costs of Uninsured Populations.

1993. The Alliance is a purchasing cooperative owned by more than 160 member companies that contracts with providers; manages and reports cost and utilization data; performs consumer education and advocacy; and designs employer and provider quality initiatives and reports. Prior to his current position, Mr. Queram served as vice president for programs at Meriter Hospital, a 475-bed hospital in Madison. Mr. Queram is a member of the board of The Leapfrog Group and serves as treasurer. He is also a member and past chair of the board of the National Business Coalition on Health. Mr. Queram was a member of the President's Advisory Commission on Consumer Protection and Quality in the Health Care Industry, served as a member of the Planning Committee for the National Quality Forum, and continues as chair of the Purchaser Council and board member of the Forum. He is a member of the Wisconsin Board on Health Information and the Board of the Wisconsin Private Employer Health Care Coverage program. He holds a master's degree in health services administration from the University of Wisconsin at Madison and is a fellow in the American College of Healthcare Executives.

Shoshanna Sofaer, Dr.P.H. is the Robert P. Luciano Professor of Health Care Policy at the School of Public Affairs, Baruch College, in New York City. She completed her master's and doctoral degrees in public health at the University of California, Berkeley; taught for six years at the University of California, Los Angeles, School of Public Health; served on the faculty of George Washington University Medical Center, where she was professor, associate dean for research of the School of Public Health and Health Services, and director of the Center for Health Outcomes Improvement Research. Dr. Sofaer's research interests include providing information to individual consumers on the performance of the health care system; assessing the impact of information on both consumers and the system; developing consumer-relevant performance measures; and improving the responsiveness of the Medicare program to the needs of current and future cohorts of older persons and persons with disabilities. In addition, Dr. Sofaer studies the role of community coalitions in pursuing public health and health care system reform objectives and has extensive experience in the evaluation of community health improvement interventions. She has studied the determinants of health insurance status among the near-elderly, including early retirees. Dr. Sofaer served as co-chair of the Working Group on Coverage for Low Income and Non-Working Families for the White House Task Force on Health Care Reform in 1993 and co-chair of the Task Force on Medicare of the Century Foundation in New York City. She is a member of the Health Systems Study Section of the Agency for Healthcare Research and Quality.

Gordon R. Trapnell, B.A. ★ is president of the Actuarial Research Corporation. He is a nationally recognized expert in analyzing the feasibility and estimating the

---

★Member, Subcommittee on the Societal Costs of Uninsured Populations.

cost of private and public insurance programs. Mr. Trapnell also has extensive experience in analyzing the actuarial problems of existing public-sector insurance and employee benefit programs, including Medicaid and Medicare. Mr. Trapnell maintains a consulting practice for private health insurance programs, rate setting by health maintenance organizations and other managed care organizations, prescription drug insurance programs, and long-term care insurance. Prior to forming Actuarial Research, Mr. Trapnell was the senior actuary for Medicare in the Social Security Administration.

Stephen J. Trejo, Ph.D.* is associate professor in the Department of Economics at the University of Texas at Austin. His primary research focus has been in the field of labor economics. He has examined the response of labor market participants to the incentives created by market opportunities, government policies, and the institutional environment. Specific research topics include the economic effects of overtime pay regulation; immigrant labor market outcomes and welfare recipiency; the impact of labor unions on compensation, employment, and work schedules; the importance of sector-specific skills; and the relative economic status of Mexican Americans.

Reed V. Tuckson, M.D. is senior vice president of consumer health and medical care advancement at UnitedHealth Group. Formerly, he was senior vice president, professional standards, at the American Medical Association. Dr. Tuckson was president of Charles R. Drew University School of Medicine and Science from 1991 to 1997. From 1986 to 1990, he was commissioner of public health for the District of Columbia. Dr. Tuckson serves on a number of health care, academic, and federal boards and committees and is a nationally known lecturer on topics concerning community-based medicine, the moral responsibilities of health professionals, and physician leadership. He currently serves on the IOM Roundtable on Research and Development of Drugs, Biologics, and Medical Devices and is a member of the Institute of Medicine.

Edward H. Wagner, M.D., M.P.H., F.A.C.P. is a general internist–epidemiologist and director of the W.A. (Sandy) MacColl Institute for Healthcare Innovation at the Center for Health Studies, Group Health Cooperative. He is also professor of health services at the University of Washington School of Public Health and Community Medicine. Current research interests include the development and testing of population-based care models for diabetes, frail elderly, and other chronic illnesses; the evaluation of the health and cost impacts of chronic disease and cancer interventions; and interventions to prevent disability and reduce depressive symptoms in older adults. Dr. Wagner has written two books and more than 200 journal articles. He serves on the editorial boards of *Health Services*

---

*Member, Subcommittee on the Societal Costs of Uninsured Populations.

Research and the *Journal of Clinical Epidemiology* and acts as a consultant to multiple federal agencies and private foundations. He recently completed a stint as senior advisor on managed care initiatives in the Director's Office of the National Institutes of Health. Dr. Wagner directs Improving Chronic Illness Care (ICIC), a national program of The Robert Wood Johnson Foundation. The overall goal of ICIC is to assist health systems in improving their care of chronic illness through quality improvement and evaluation, research, and dissemination. Dr. Wagner is also principal investigator of the Cancer Research Network, a National Cancer Institute-funded consortium of 10 health maintenance organizations conducting collaborative cancer effectiveness research.

Lawrence Wallack, Dr.P.H. is professor of public health and director, School of Community Health, at Portland State University. He is also professor emeritus of public health, University of California, Berkeley. Dr. Wallack's primary interest is in the role of mass communications, particularly the news media, in shaping public health issues. His current research is on how public health issues are framed in print and broadcast news. He is principal author of *Media Advocacy and Public Health: Power for Prevention and News for a Change: An Advocate's Guide to Working with the Media.* He is also co-editor of *Mass Communications and Public Health: Complexities and Conflicts.* Dr. Wallack has published extensively on topics related to prevention, health promotion, and community interventions. Specific content areas of his research and intervention work have included alcohol, tobacco, violence, handguns, sexually transmitted diseases, cervical and breast cancer, affirmative action, suicide, and childhood lead poisoning. Dr. Wallack was also a member of the IOM Committee on Communication for Behavior Change in the 21st Century: Improving the Health of Diverse Populations.

Institute of Medicine Staff

Wilhelmine Miller, M.S., Ph.D. is a senior program officer in the Division of Health Care Services. She served as staff to the Committee on Immunization Finance Policy and Practices, conducting and directing case studies of health care financing and public health services. Prior to joining the Institute of Medicine, Dr. Miller was an adjunct faculty member in the Departments of Philosophy at Georgetown University and Trinity College, teaching political philosophy, ethics, and public policy. She received her doctorate from Georgetown, with studies and research in bioethics and issues of social justice. In 1994–1995, Dr. Miller was a consultant to the President's Advisory Committee on Human Radiation Experiments. Dr. Miller was a program analyst in the Department of Health and Human Services for 14 years, responsible for policy development and regulatory review in areas including hospital and health maintenance organization payment, prescription drug benefits, and child health. Her M.S. from Harvard University is in health policy and management.

Dianne Miller Wolman, M.G.A. joined the Health Care Services Division of the Institute of Medicine in 1999 as a senior program officer. She directed the study that resulted in the IOM report *Medicare Laboratory Payment Policy: Now and in the Future,* released in 2000. Her previous work experience in the health field has been varied and extensive, focused on finance and reimbursement in insurance programs. She came to IOM from the U.S. General Accounting Office, where she was a senior evaluator on studies of the Health Care Financing Administration, its management capacity, and its oversight of Medicare contractors. Prior to that, she was a reimbursement policy specialist at a national association representing non-profit providers of long-term care services. Her earlier positions included policy analysis and management in the Office of the Secretary in the Department of Health and Human Services and work with a peer review organization, a governor's task force on access to health care, and a third-party administrator for very large health plans. In addition, she was policy director for a state Medicaid rate-setting commission. She has a bachelor's degree in sociology from Brandeis University and a master's degree in government administration from Wharton Graduate School, University of Pennsylvania.

Lynne Page Snyder, Ph.D., M.P.H. is a program officer in the IOM Division of Health Care Services. She came to IOM from the Department of Health and Human Services, where she worked as a public historian, documenting and writing about past federal activities in medicine, health care, and public health. In addition, she has worked for the Social Science Research Council's Committee on the Urban Underclass and served as a graduate fellow at the Smithsonian Institution's National Museum of American History. She has published on 20th-century health policy, occupational and environmental health, and minority health. Current research interests include health literacy and access to care by low-income seniors. She earned her doctorate in the history and sociology of science from the University of Pennsylvania (1994), working under Rosemary Stevens, and received her M.P.H. from the Johns Hopkins School of Hygiene and Public Health (2000).

Tracy McKay, B.A. is a research associate in the IOM Division of Health Care Services. She has worked on several projects, including the National Roundtable on Health Care Quality; Children, Health Insurance, and Access to Care; Quality of Health Care in America; and a study on non-heart-beating organ donors. She has assisted in the research for the National Quality Report on Health Care Delivery, Immunization Finance Policies and Practices, and Extending Medicare Coverage for Preventive and Other Services and helped develop this project on the consequences of uninsurance from its inception. Ms. McKay received her B.A. in sociology from Vassar College in 1996.

Ryan Palugod, B.S. is a senior program assistant in the IOM Division of Health Care Services. Prior to joining the project staff in 2001, he worked as an administrative assistant with the American Association of Homes, Services for the Aging. He graduated with honors from Towson University in 1999 with a degree in health care management.

Consultants to the Committee on the Consequences of Uninsurance

Hanns Kuttner, M.A. is a senior research associate with the Economic Research Initiative on the Uninsured, a research program on the causes and consequences of uninsurance funded by the Robert Wood Johnson Foundation and located at the University of Michigan. Mr. Kuttner is a Ph.D. candidate in the Irving B. Harris Graduate School of Public Policy Studies at the University of Chicago, from which he already holds an M.A. Prior to his graduate studies, Mr. Kuttner was a research affiliate of the Governor's Task Force on Human Services Reform in Illinois, a member of the domestic policy staff in the Office of Policy Development at the White House during the presidency of George H. W. Bush, and special assistant to the administrator of the Health Care Financing Administration.

M. Eugene Moyer, Ph.D. received his doctorate in economics from the University of Wisconsin. After teaching at the University of Illinois for four years, he joined the Department of Health, Education and Welfare in 1970. He was an economist with the Social Security Administration Office of Research and the Office of the Secretary in the Department of Health and Human Services (DHHS) until his retirement from federal service in 1999. His work there included the modeling of national health insurance and other programmatic coverage expansions, and analyses of the status of uninsured persons from survey data. He served as a DHHS project officer and managed numerous actuarial and economic research projects for the Office of the Secretary. For several years, he calculated the Federal Medical Assistance Percentage, used to determine the amount of the federal government's contribution toward state Medicaid expenditures. Recently he has been an economic consultant to DHHS, the University of Southern California, and the Institute of Medicine.

Elizabeth Richardson Vigdor, Ph.D. is assistant professor of public policy studies in the Terry Sanford Institute of Public Policy at Duke University. Her research focuses on health economics, public economics, and applied microeconomics. She has co-authored several papers on the measurement and valuation of health in publications such as *American Economic Review, Frontiers of Health Policy Research*, and *Brookings Papers on Economic Activity*. Dr. Vigdor has a Ph.D. in Health Policy from Harvard University and a Master of Science in Health Policy and Management from Harvard School of Public Health.

References

Academy for Health Services Research and Health Policy. 2000. *Glossary of Terms Commonly Used in Health Care.* Accessed February 4, 2002. Available at: http://www.academyhealth.org/publications.glossary.pdf.

AcademyHealth. 2002. *State Coverage Matrix.* Accessed November 5, 2002. Available at: http://www.statecoverage.net/matrix.htm.

Aday, Lu Ann, G.V. Fleming, and Ronald Andersen. 1984. *Access to Medical Care in the U.S.: Who Has It, Who Doesn't.* Chicago: Pluribus Press.

Agency for Healthcare Research and Quality (AHRQ). 2001. *Health Care Expenses in the U.S. Civilian Non-institutional Population, 1997.* Accessed April 16, 2002. Available at: http://www.meps.ahrq.gov/Papers/RF_01-R035/Tables/Tables1_8.pdf.

Andersen, Ronald, and Pamela Davidson. 2001. Improving Access to Care in America: Individual and Contextual Indicators. Pp. 3-30 in: *Changing the U.S. Health Care System: Key Issues in Health Services, Policy and Management,* Ronald Andersen, Thomas Rice, and Gerald Kominski, eds. San Francisco: Jossey-Bass.

Anderson, Elizabeth S. 1999. What Is the Point of Equality? Pp. 287-337 in: *Ethics,* vol. 109, John Deigh (ed.). Chicago: University of Chicago.

Andrulis, Dennis, Lisa Duchon, Carol Pryor, and Nanette Goodman. 2003. *Paying for Health Care When You're Uninsured: How Much Support Does the Safety Net Offer?* Boston: The Access Project.

Arons, Bernard S. 2000. Mental Health and Criminal Justice: Testimony by Bernard S. Arons, M.D. Accessed December 5, 2002. Available at: http://www.hhs.gov/asl/testify/t000921a.html.

Asplin, Brent R., and Robert K. Knopp. 2001. A Room With a View: On-Call Specialist Panels and Other Health Policy Challenges in the Emergency Department. *Annals of Emergency Medicine* 37(5):500-503.

Ayanian, John Z., Betsy A. Kohler, Toshi Abe, and Arnold M. Epstein. 1993. The Relation Between Health Insurance Coverage and Clinical Outcomes Among Women With Breast Cancer. *New England Journal of Medicine* 329(5):326-331.

Ayanian, John Z., Joel S. Weissman, Eric C. Schneider, Jack A. Ginsburg, and Alan M. Zaslavsky. 2000. Unmet Health Needs of Uninsured Adults in the United States. *Journal of the American Medical Association* 284(16):2061-2069.

Baker, David W., Carl D. Stevens, and Robert H. Brook. 1994. Regular Source of Ambulatory Care and Medical Care Utilization by Patients Presenting to a Public Hospital Emergency Department. *Journal of the American Medical Association* 271(24):1909-1912.

Baker, David W., Joseph J. Sudano, Jeffrey M. Albert, Elaine A. Borawski, et al. 2001. Lack of Health Insurance and Decline in Overall Health in Late Middle Age. *New England Journal of Medicine* 345(15):1106-1112.

Bala, Mohan V., and Gary A. Zarkin. 2000. Are QALYs an Appropriate Measure for Morbidity in Acute Diseases? *Health Economic Letters* 9(2):177-180.

Bamezai, Anil, Jack Zwanziger, Glenn A. Melnick, and Joyce M. Mann. 1999. Price Competition and Hospital Cost Growth in the United States (1989-1994). *Health Economics* 8(3):233-243.

Bartel, Ann, and Paul Taubman. 1986. Some Economic and Demographic Consequences of Mental Illness. *Journal of Labor Economics* 4(2):243-256.

Bazelon Center for Mental Health Law. 2003. *Criminalization of People With Mental Illnesses: The Role of Mental Health Courts in System Reform.* Washington, DC: Judge David L. Bazelon Center for Mental Health Law.

Becker, Gary S. 1964. *Human Capital.* New York: Columbia University Press.

Beckles, Gloria L. A., Michael M. Engelgau, K. M. V. Narayan, William H. Herman, et al. 1998. Population-Based Assessment of the Level of Care Among Adults With Diabetes in the U.S. *Diabetes Care* 21(9):1432-1438.

Belkin, Lisa. 2002, December 8. Just Money. *The New York Times.* Section 6, p. 92.

Bellah, Robert, Richard Madsen, William Sullivan, Ann Swidler, et al. 1985. *Habits of the Heart: Individualism and Commitment in American Life.* Berkeley: University of California Press.

Berndt, Ernst R., Howard L. Bailit, Martin B. Keller, Jason C. Verner, et al. 2000. Health Care Use and At-Work Productivity Among Employees With Mental Disorders. *Health Affairs* 19(4):244-256.

Berndt, Ernst R., Stan N. Finkelstein, Paul E. Greenberg, Alison Keith, et al. 1997. *Illness and Productivity: Objective Workplace Evidence.* Cambridge, MA: MIT Sloan School.

Billings, John, Nina Parikh, and Tod Mijanovich. 2000. *Emergency Room Use: The New York Story.* New York: The Commonwealth Fund.

Birnbaum, Howard G., William E. Berger, Paul E. Greenberg, Michael Holland, et al. 2002. Direct and Indirect Costs of Asthma to an Employer. *Journal of Allergy and Clinical Immunology* 109(2):264-270.

Bitterman, Robert. 2002. Explaining the EMTALA Paradox. *Annals of Emergency Medicine* 40(5):470-475.

Blau, David M., and Donna B. Gilleskie. 2001. Retiree Health Insurance and the Labor Force Behavior of Older Men in the 1990's. *Review of Economics and Statistics* 83(1):64-80.

Bloom, David E., David Canning, and Jaypee Sevilla. 2001. *The Effect of Health on Economic Growth: Theory and Evidence.* NBER Working Paper 8587. Cambridge, MA: National Bureau of Economic Research.

Blough, D. K., C. W. Madden, and Mark C. Hornbrook. 1999. Modeling Risk Using Generalized Linear Models. *Journal of Health Economics* 18:153-171.

Blumenschein, Karen, and Magnus Johannesson. 1998. Relationship Between Quality of Life Instruments, Health State Utilities, and Willingness to Pay in Patients With Asthma. *Annals of Allergy, Asthma, and Immunology* 80:189-194.

Bound, John, Michael Schoenbaum, Todd R. Stinebricker, and Timothy Waidmann. 1999. The Dynamic Effects of Health on the Labor Force Transitions of Older Workers. *Labour Economics* 6(2):179-202.

Briscoe, Daren, and Charles Ornstein. 2003, February 8. Health Systems Gets an Extra $100 Million. Davis Surprises County by Tacking Federal Funds Onto a New Aid Package. Officials Hope Money Buys Hospitals Time to Escape. *Los Angeles Times.*

Brown, E. Richard, Ninez Ponce, Thomas Rice, and Shana Alex Lavarreda. 2002. *The State of Health Insurance in California: Findings from the 2001 California Health Interview Survey.* Los Angeles: UCLA Center for Health Policy Research.

Buchanan, Joan L., Emmett B. Keeler, John E. Rolph, and Martin R. Holmer. 1991. Simulating Health Expenditures Under Alternative Insurance Plans. *Management Science* 37(9):1067–1090.

Buchmueller, Thomas C. 2000. *The Business Case for Employer-Provided Health Benefits: A Review of the Relevant Literature.* Irvine, CA: California HealthCare Foundation.

Bulger, Ruth E., Elizabeth M. Bobby, and Harvey V. Fineberg (eds.). 1995. *Society's Choices: Social and Ethical Decision Making in Biomedicine.* Washington, DC: National Academy Press.

Bureau of Labor Statistics (BLS). 2002. *Producer Price Indexes: November 2002.* Accessed January 6, 2003. Available at: http://www.bls.gov/news.release/archives/ppi_12132002.pdf.

Burman, Leonard. 2003. *Tax Incentives for Health Insurance.* Tax Policy Discussion Paper. Washington, DC: The Urban Institute.

Campbell, Ellen S., and Michael W. Ahern. 1993. Have Procompetitive Changes Altered Hospital Provision of Indigent Care? *Health Economics* 2(3):281–289.

Card, David, and Brian P. McCall. 1996. Is Workers' Compensation Covering Uninsured Medical Costs: Evidence From the Monday Effect. *Industrial and Labor Relations Review* 49(4):690–706.

Cardenas, Jose, and Darren Briscoe. 2002, September 25. County OKs 25% Cut in Subsidies for Health Clinics. Budget: Dozens Will Be Eliminated From 'Public-Private Partnership' Program. Some Fear Strain on Emergency Rooms. *Los Angeles Times.*

Centers for Disease Control and Prevention (CDC). 1996. Asthma Mortality and Hospitalization Among Children and Young Adults—United States, 1980–1993. *Morbidity and Mortality Weekly Report* 45(17):350–353.

_____. 1999. *Chronic Diseases and Their Risk Factors: The Nation's Leading Causes of Death.* Atlanta, GA: Centers for Disease Control and Prevention.

_____. 2000. *Measuring Healthy Days.* Atlanta, GA: Centers for Disease Control and Prevention.

_____. 2001. Preventing and Controlling Tuberculosis Along the U.S.-Mexico Border. *Morbidity and Mortality Weekly Report* 50(RR-1):1–6.

Chaikind, Stuart, and H. Corman. 1991. The Impact of Low Birthweight on Special Education Cost. *Journal of Health Economics* 10(3):291–311.

Chirikos, Thomas N., and Gilbert Nestel. 1985. Further Evidence on the Economic Effects of Poor Health. *Review of Economics and Statistics* 67(1):61–69.

Chollet, Deborah, and Adele Kirk. 1998. *Understanding Individual Health Insurance Markets: Structure, Practices, and Products in Ten States.* Menlo Park, CA: The Kaiser Family Foundation.

Chollet, Deborah J. 2000. Consumers, Insurers, and Market Behavior. *Journal of Health Politics, Policy and Law* 25(1):27–44.

Christensen, Rachel, Paul Fronstin, Karl Polzer, and Ray Werntz. 2002. *Employee Attitudes and Practices Affecting Health Benefits and the Uninsured.* Washington, DC: Employee Benefit Research Institute.

Christianson, Jon B., Stephen T. Parente, and Ruth Taylor. 2002. Defined-Contribution Health Insurance Products: Development and Prospects. *Health Affairs* 21(1):49–64.

Coate, Stephen. 1995. Altruism, the Samaritan's Dilemma, and Government Transfer Policy. *American Economic Review* 85(1):46–57.

Coburn, Andrew F. 2002. Insurance Coverage in Rural Populations and Places. *Presentation to the Subcommittee on Community Effects of Uninsured Populations.* Washington, DC.

Cohn, Jonathan. 2002, December 12. The White House Abandons L.A. Ill Treatment. *The New Republic.*

Colgan, Charles S. 2002. *The Economic Effects of Rural Hospital Closures.* Portland, ME: University of Southern Maine, Edmund S. Muskie School of Public Service. Unpublished paper.

Commonwealth Fund Task Force on Academic Health Centers. 2001. *A Shared Responsibility: Academic Health Centers and the Provision of Care to the Poor and Uninsured.* New York: The Commonwealth Fund.

Congressional Budget Office (CBO). 2002. *CBO March 2002 Baseline: Medicaid and State Children's Health Insurance Program Fact Sheet.* Washington, DC: Congressional Budget Office.

_____. 2002. *Glossary of Budgetary and Economic Terms.* Accessed November 25, 2002. Available at: http://www.cbo.gov/showdoc.cfm?index=3280&sequence=0.

Conover, Christopher J. 1998. *Health Care for the Medically Indigent of South Carolina: Final Report.* Raleigh, NC: Duke University, North Carolina Center for Health Policy, Law, and Management.

Cooper, Barbara S., and Dorothy P. Rice. 1976. The Economic Cost of Illness Revisited. *Social Security Bulletin* 39:21-36.

Cooper, Philip F., and Barbara S. Schone. 1997. More Offers, Fewer Takers for Employer-Based Health Insurance: 1987 and 1996. *Health Affairs* 16(6):142-149.

Cooper-Patrick, Lisa, Rosa M. Crum, Laura A. Pratt, William W. Eaton, et al. 1999. The Psychiatric Profile of Patients With Chronic Disease Who Do Not Receive Regular Medical Care. *International Journal of Psychiatry* 29(2):165-180.

Cordes, Sam M. 1998. Health Care and the Rural Economy. *Forum for Applied Research and Public Policy* 13(2):90-93.

Cordes, Sam M., Evert Van der Sluis, Charles Lamphear, and Jerry Hoffman. 1999. Rural Hospitals and the Local Economy: A Needed Extension and Refinement of Existing Empirical Research. *Journal of Rural Health* 15(2):189-201.

Coulam, Robert, Thomas R. Cole, et al. 1995. *Final Report of the Medicare Catastrophic Coverage Act: Impacts on Maternal and Child Health Programs and Beneficiaries.* Cambridge, MA: Abt Associates.

Culyer, Anthony J. 1991. The Normative Economics of Health Care Finance and Provision. Pp. 65-98 in: *Providing Health Care: The Economics of Alternative Systems of Finance and Delivery,* Alistair McGuire, Paul Penn, and Ken Mayhew (eds.). New York: Oxford University Press.

Cunningham, Peter J. 2002. *Mounting Pressures: Physician Serving Medicaid Patients and the Uninsured, 1997-2001.* Tracking Report No. 6. Results from the Community Tracking Study. Washington, DC: Center for Studying Health System Change.

Cunningham, Peter J., and Paul B. Ginsburg. 2001. What Accounts for Differences in Uninsurance Rates Across Communities? *Inquiry* 38(10):6-21.

Cunningham, Peter J., Jerome M. Grossman, Robert F. St. Peter, and Cara S. Lesser. 1999. Managed Care and Physicians' Provision of Charity Care. *Journal of the American Medical Association* 281(12):1087-1092.

Current Population Survey (CPS). 2001. *Annual Demographic Survey: March Supplement.* Accessed March 27, 2003. Available at: http://ferret.bls.census.gov/macro/032001/health/toc.htm.

Currie, Janet, and Jonathan Gruber. 1996. Saving Babies: The Efficacy and Cost of Recent Changes in the Medicaid Eligibility of Pregnant Women. *Journal of Political Economy* 104(6):1263-1296.

Currie, Janet, and Brigitte C. Madrian. 1999. Health, Health Insurance, and the Labor Market. Pp. 3309-3416 in: *Handbook of Labor Economics, Vol. 3,* Orley Ashenfleder and David Card (eds.). Amsterdam: Elsevier.

Cutler, David M. 2002. *Employee Costs and the Decline in Health Insurance Coverage.* Boston, MA: Harvard University and National Bureau of Economic Research.

Cutler, David M., and Mark McClellan. 2001. Is Technological Change in Medicine Worth It? *Health Affairs* 20(5):11-29.

Cutler, David M., and Richard J. Zeckhauser. 2000. The Anatomy of Health Insurance. Pp. 563-644 in: *Handbook in of Health Economics, Vol. 1A,* Anthony J. Culyer and Joseph P. Newhouse (eds.). Amsterdam: Elsevier.

Cutler, David M., and Elizabeth Richardson. 1997. Measuring the Health of the United States Population. *Brookings Papers on Economic Activity. Microeconomics:* 217-271.

_____. 1999. Your Money and Your Life: The Value of Health and What Affects It. Pp. 99-132 in: *Frontiers in Health Policy Research 2,* Alan M. Garber (ed.). Cambridge, MA: MIT Press.

Daniels, Norman. 1985. *Just Health Care.* Cambridge, England: Cambridge University Press.

Dardis, Rachel. 1980. The Value of a Life: New Evidence From the Marketplace. *American Economic Review* 70:1077–1082.

Davidoff, Amy J., A. B. Garrett, Diane M. Makuc, and Matthew Schirmer. 2000. Medicaid-Eligible Children Who Don't Enroll: Health Status, Access to Care, and Implications for Medicaid Enrollment. *Inquiry* 37:203–218.

Davison, David. 2001. *Is Philanthropy Dying at the Hospital?* Accessed October 28, 2002. Available at: http://philanthropyroundtable.org/magazines/2001/august/davison.html.

DeBuono, Barbara A. 2000. Vaccine Coverage: Access and Administration. *American Journal of Preventive Medicine* 19(3 Suppl.):21–23.

de Meza, David. 1983. Health Insurance and the Demand for Medical Care. *Journal of Health Economics* 2:47–54.

Derlet, Robert W. 1992. ED Overcrowding in New York City. *Journal of Emergency Medicine* 10(1):93–94.

Derlet, Robert W., John R. Richards, and Richard L. Kravitz. 2001. Frequent Overcrowding in U.S. Emergency Departments. *Academic Emergency Medicine* 8(2):151–155.

Desonia, Randy. 2002. *Running on Empty: The State Budget Crisis Worsens.* Washington, DC: The George Washington University.

Diamond, P., and John Hausman. 1984. The Retirement and Unemployment Behavior of Older Men. Pp. 97–134 in: *Retirement and Economic Behavior*, Henry J. Aaron and Gary Burtless (eds.). Washington, DC: Brookings Institution.

Diener, Alan, Bernie O'Brien, and Amiram Gafni. 1998. Health Care Contingent Valuation Studies: A Review and Classification of the Literature. *Health Economics* 7:313–326.

Dionne, E. J., Jr. 1998. Social Insurance Commentary. In: *Medicare: Preparing for the Challenges of the 21st Century.* Robert D. Reischauer, Stuart Butler, and Judith R. Lave (eds.). Washington, DC: Brookings Institution Press.

Ditton, Paula M. 1999. *Mental Health and Treatment of Inmates and Probationers.* NCJ 174463. Washington, DC: U.S. Department of Justice.

Dixon, Lee, and James Cox. 2002. *State Management and Allocation of Tobacco Settlement Revenues.* Washington, DC: National Conference of State Legislatures.

Doeksen, Gerald A., Tom Johnson, and Chuck Willoughby. 1997. *Measuring the Economic Importance of the Health Sector on a Local Economy: A Brief Literature Review and Procedures to Measure Local Impacts.* Mississippi State, MS: The Southern Rural Development Center.

Doyle, Joseph J. 2001. *Does Health Insurance Affect Treatment Decisions and Patient Outcomes? Using Automobile Accidents as Unexpected Health Shocks.* Chicago: University of Chicago.

Dranove, David. 1988. Pricing by Non-Profit Institutions: The Case of Hospital Cost Shifting. *Journal of Health Economics* 7(1):47–57.

———. 1995. Measuring Costs. Pp. 61–75 in: *Valuing Health Care: Costs, Benefits, and Effectiveness of Pharmaceuticals and Other Medical Technologies*, Frank A. Sloan (ed.). New York: Cambridge University Press.

Dranove, David, and William D. White. 1998. Medicaid-Dependent Hospitals and Their Patients: How Have They Fared? *Health Services Research* 33(2 Pt 1):163–185.

Drummond, Michael F., Bernie J. O'Brien, Greg L. Stoddart, and George W. Torrance. 1997. Methods for the Economic Evaluation of Health Care Programmes. Pp. 53–81 in: *Cost Analysis.* 2nd ed. Oxford: Oxford University Press.

Druss, Benjamin G., Steven C. Marcus, Mark Olfson, Terri Tanielian, et al. 2001. Comparing the National Economic Burden of Five Chronic Conditions. *Health Affairs* 20(6):233–242.

Duan, Naihua, Willard G. Manning, C. N. Morris, and Joseph P. Newhouse. 1983. A Comparison of Alternative Models for the Demand for Health Care. *Journal of Business and Economic Statistics* 1(2):115–126.

Eastaugh, Steven R. 1991. Valuation of the Benefits of Risk-Free Blood: Willingness to Pay for Hemoglobin Solutions. *International Journal of Technology Assessment in Health Care* 7(1):51–57.

Ehrenreich, Barbara. 1989. *Fear of Falling.* New York: Pantheon Books.

Emmons, David W. 1995. Uncompensated Physician Care. Pp. 11–14 in: *Socioeconomic Characteristics of Medical Practice, 1995*, Martin L. Gonzalez (ed.). Chicago: American Medical Association, Center for Health Policy Research.

Epstein, Arnold M., J. A. Hall, J. Tognetti, L. H. Son, Jr., and L. Conant. 1989. Using Proxies to Evaluate Quality of Life. Can They Provide Valid Information and Patients' Health Status and Satisfaction With Medical Care? *Medical Care* 27:S91-98.

Epstein, Richard A. 1997. *Mortal Peril: Our Inalienable Right to Health Care?* Reading, MA: Addison-Wesley.

Ettner, Susan L., Richard G. Frank, and Ronald C. Kessler. 1997. The Impact of Psychiatric Disorders on Labor Market Outcomes. *Industrial and Labor Relations Review* 51(1):64–81.

Fairbrother, Gerry, Hanns Kuttner, Wilhelmine Miller, R. Hogan, et al. 2000. Findings From Case Studies of State and Local Immunization Programs. *American Journal of Preventive Medicine* 19(3 Suppl.):54–77.

Farber, Henry, and Helen Levy. 2000. Recent Trends in Employer-Sponsored Health Insurance Coverage: Are Bad Jobs Getting Worse? *Journal of Health Economics* 19:93-119.

Federal Trade Commission. 1999. *FTC Facts for Consumers: Fair Credit Reporting.* Accessed July 18, 2002. Available at: http://www.ftc.gov/bcp/conline/pubs/credit/fcra.pdf.

Feenberg, Daniel R., and Elizabeth Coutts. 1993. An Introduction to TAXSIM Model. *Journal of Policy Analysis and Management* 12(1):189-194.

Foster, David C., David S. Guzick, and Robert P. Pulliam. 1992. The Impact of Prenatal Care on Fetal and Neonatal Death Rates for Uninsured Patients: A "Natural Experiment" in West Virginia. *Obstetrics and Gynecology* 79(1):40–45.

Frank, Richard G., and David S. Salkever. 1991. The Supply of Charity Services by Nonprofit Hospitals: Motives and Market Structure. *RAND Journal of Economics* 13(2):430-445.

Franks, Peter, Carolyn M. Clancy, and Marthe R. Gold. 1993. Health Insurance and Mortality: Evidence From a National Cohort. *Journal of the American Medical Association* 270(6):737-741.

Freedman, Vicki A., and Linda Martin. 1998. Understanding Trends in Functional Limitations Among Older Americans. *American Journal of Public Health* 88(10):1457-1462.

Fronstin, Paul. 2001a. *Employment-Based Health Benefits: Trends and Outlook.* Washington, DC: Employee Benefit Research Institute.

———. 2001b. *Sources of Health Insurance and Characteristics of the Uninsured: Analysis of the March 2001 Current Population Survey.* Washington, DC: Employee Benefit Research Institute.

———. 2002. *Sources of Health Insurance: Analysis of the March 2002 Current Population Survey.* Washington, DC: Employee Benefit Research Institute.

Fronstin, Paul, and Ruth Helman. 2000. *Small Employers and Health Benefits: Findings From the 2000 Small Employer Health Benefits Survey.* EBRI Issue Brief No. 226. Washington, DC: Employee Benefit Research Institute.

Fronstin, Paul, and Alphonse G. Holtmann. 2000. Productivity Gains From Employment-Based Health Insurance. *The Economic Costs of the Uninsured: Implications for Business and Government.* Washington, DC: Employee Benefit Research Institute.

Fuchs, Victor R. 1996. Economics, Values, and Health Care Reform. *American Economic Review* 86(1):1-24.

Garber, Alan M. 2000. Advances in Cost-Effectiveness Analysis of Health Interventions. *Handbook of Health Economics*, Anthony J. Culyer and Joseph P. Newhouse (eds.). New York: Elsevier.

Garber, Alan M., M. C. Weinstein, G. W. Torrance, and M. S. Kamlet. 1996. Theoretical Foundations of Cost-Effectiveness Analysis. Pp. 25–53 in: *Cost-Effectiveness in Health and Medicine.* Marthe R. Gold, et al. (eds.). New York: Oxford University Press.

Gaskin, Darrell J. 1999. *Safety Net Hospitals: Essential Providers of Public Health and Specialty Services.* New York: The Commonwealth Fund.

Gaskin, Darrell J., and Jack Hadley. 1999a. Are Subsidies Allocated to Urban Hospitals in Accordance with Their Safety Net Roles? Washington, DC: Institute for Health Care Research and Policy, Georgetown University.

Gaskin, Darrell, and Jack Hadley. 1999b. Population Characteristics of Markets of Safety Net and Non-Safety Net Hospitals. *Journal of Urban Health* 76(3): 351-370.

Gaskin, Darrell J., and Jack Needleman. 2003. The Impact of Uninsured Populations on the Availability of Hospital Services and Financial Status in Hospitals in Urban Areas. Pp. 205-220 in: *A Shared Destiny: Community Effects of Uninsurance*, Institute of Medicine. Washington, DC: National Academies Press.

Geiter, Lawrence (ed.). 2000. *Ending Neglect: The Elimination of Tuberculosis in the United States.* Washington, DC: National Academy Press.

Gerking, Shelby, Menno De Haan, and William Schulze. 1988. The Marginal Value of Job Safety: A Contingent Valuation Study. *Journal of Risk and Uncertainty* 1(2):185-199.

Gilleskie, Donna B. 1998. A Dynamic Stochastic Model of Medical Care Use and Work Absence. *Econometrica* 66(1):1-45.

Glied, Sherry, and Dahlia Remler. 2002. What Every Public Finance Economist Needs to Know About Health Economics: Recent Advances and Unresolved Questions. *National Tax Journal* 55(4):771-788.

Glied, Sherry, Dahlia K. Remler, and Joshua Graff Zivin. 2002. Inside the Sausage Factory: Improving Estimates of the Effects of Health Insurance Expansion Proposals. *The Milbank Quarterly* 80(4):603-635.

Gold, Marthe R., David L. Patrick, G. W. Torrance, D. G. Fryback, et al. 1996a. Identifying and Valuing Outcomes. Pp. 82-134 in: *Cost-Effectiveness in Health and Medicine*, Marthe R. Gold, Joanna E. Siegel, Louise B. Russell, and Milton C. Weinstein (eds.). New York: Oxford University Press.

Gold, Marthe R., Joanna E. Siegel, Louise B. Russell, and Milton C. Weinstein (eds.). 1996b. *Cost-Effectiveness in Health and Medicine.* New York, NY: Oxford University Press.

Goldberg, Bruce W. 1998. Managed Care and Public Health Departments: Who Is Responsible for the Health of the Population? *Annual Reviews in Public Health* 19:527-537.

Goldman, Dana P., Jayanta Bhattcharya, Daniel F. McCaffery, Naihua Duan, et al. 2001. Effect of Insurance on Mortality in an HIV-Positive Population in Care. *Journal of the American Statistical Association* 96(455):883-894.

Graham, John D. 1999. *An Investor's Look at Life-Saving Opportunities.* Accessed March 21, 2003. Available at: http://www.hcra.harvard.edu/pdf/February1999.pdf.

Greenberg, Paul, Stan N. Finkelstein, and Ernst R. Berndt. 1995. Economic Consequences of Illness in the Workplace. *Sloan Management Review* 36(4):26-38

Greenberg, Paul E., Tamar Sisitsky, Ronald C. Kessler, Stan N. Finkelstein, et al. 1999. The Economic Burden of Anxiety Disorders in the 1990s. *Journal of Clinical Psychiatry* 60(7):427-435.

Grossman, Michael. 1972. *The Demand for Health: A Theoretical and Empirical Investigation.* New York: National Bureau of Economic Research.

Gruber, Jonathan. 1994. The Incidence of Mandated Maternity Benefits. *American Economic Review* 84(3):622-641.

Gruber, Jonathan, and Brigitte C. Madrian. 2001. *Health Insurance, Labor Supply, and Job Mobility: A Critical Review of the Literature.* Ann Arbor: University of Michigan.

Grumbach, Kevin, Dennis Keane, and Andrew Bindman. 1993. Primary Care and Public Emergency Department Overcrowding. *American Journal of Public Health* 83(3):372-378.

Hadley, Jack. 2002. *Sicker and Poorer: The Consequences of Being Uninsured.* Washington, DC: Kaiser Family Foundation.

Hadley, Jack, and Judith Feder. 1985. Hospital Cost Shifting and Care for the Uninsured. *Health Affairs* 4(3):67-80.

Hadley, Jack, and John Holahan. 2003a. How Much Medical Care Do the Uninsured Use and Who Pays for It? *Health Affairs* Web Exclusive (1):W66-W81.

———. 2003b. Covering the Uninsured: How Much Would It Cost? Forthcoming in *Health Affairs*.

Hadley, Jack, and James D. Reschovsky. 2002. Small Firms' Demand for Health Insurance: The Decision to Offer Insurance. *Inquiry* 39(2):118-137.

Hadley, Jack, Stephen Zuckerman, and Lisa I. Iezzoni. 1996. Financial Pressure and Competition: Changes in Hospital Efficiency and Cost-Shifting Behavior. *Medical Care* 34(3):205-219.

Hanson, Karla L. 1998. Is Insurance for Children Enough? The Link Between Parents' and Children's Health Care Use Revisited. *Inquiry* 35(3):294-302.

Hartley, David, and Mark B. Lapping. 2000. *Case Report: Old West County Montana*. Portland, ME: Maine Rural Health Research Center.

Haveman, Robert, Barbara Wolfe, Lawrence Buron, and Steven C. Hill. 1995. The Loss of Earnings Capability From Disability/Health Limitations: Toward a New Social Indicator. *Review of Income and Wealth* 41(3):289-308.

Health Care Financing Administration (HCFA). 2000. *A Profile of Medicaid*. Baltimore: Health Care Financing Administration.

Heidenreich, Paul, and Mark McClellan. 2003. Biomedical Research and Then Some: The Causes of Technological Change in Heart Attack Treatment. In: *Measuring the Gains from Medical Research: An Economic Approach*, Kevin Murphy and Robert H. Topel (eds.). Chicago: University of Chicago Press.

Herkimer, Alan G. 1993. *Patient Financial Services: Organizing and Managing a Cost-Effective Patient Financial Services Operation*. Chicago: Probus.

Hirth, Richard A., Michael E. Chernew, Edward Miller, A. M. Fendrick, and William G. Weissert. 2000. Willingness to Pay for a Quality-Adjusted Life Year: In Search of a Standard. *Medical Decision Making* 20:332-342.

Holahan, John. 2002. *Variations Among States in Health Insurance Coverage and Medical Expenditures: How Much Is Too Much?* Washington, DC: The Urban Institute.

Hovey, Harold A. 1991. Who Pays When State Health Care Costs Rise? Pp. 71-129 in: *State Governments: The Effects of Health Care Program Expansion in a Period of Fiscal Stress*, Advisory Council on Social Security. Washington, DC: Advisory Council on Social Security.

Howell, Embry M. 2001. The Impact of the Medicaid Expansions for Pregnant Women: A Synthesis of the Evidence. *Medical Care Research and Review* 58(1):3-30.

Hubbell, Bryan J. 2002. Implementing QALYs in the Analysis of Air Pollution Regulations. U.S. Environmental Protection Agency, Innovative Strategies and Economics Group, draft MS. Accessed March 23, 2003. Available at: http://www.rff.org.

Hurley, Jeremiah. 2000. An Overview of the Normative Economics of the Health Sector. Pp. 56-110 in: *Handbook of Health Economics*, A.J. Culyer and Joseph P. Newhouse (eds.). New York: Elsevier Science.

Institute of Medicine (IOM). 1988. *The Future of Public Health*. Washington, DC: National Academy Press.

———. 2000. *Calling the Shots: Immunization Finance Policies and Practices*. Washington, DC: National Academy Press.

———. 2001a. *Coverage Matters: Insurance and Health Care*. Washington, DC: National Academy Press.

———. 2001b. *Crossing the Quality Chasm: A Health System for the 21st Century*. Washington, DC: National Academy Press.

———. 2002a. *Care Without Coverage: Too Little, Too Late*. Washington, DC: National Academy Press.

———. 2002b. *Health Insurance Is a Family Matter*. Washington, DC: The National Academies Press.

———. 2003a. *A Shared Destiny: Community Effects of Uninsurance*. Washington, DC: The National Academies Press.

———. 2003b. *The Future of the Public's Health in the 21st Century*. Washington, DC: The National Academies Press.

———. 2003c. *Unequal Treatment: Confronting Racial and Ethnic Disparities in Health Care*. Washington, DC: The National Academies Press.

Johannesson, Magnus, and Bengt Jonsson. 1991. Economic Evaluation in Health Care: Is There a Role for Cost-Benefit Analysis? *Health Policy* 17:1-23.

Johannesson, Magnus, and David Meltzer. 1998. Some Reflections on Cost-Effectiveness Analysis. *Health Economics* 7:1-7.

Johnson, Kay A., Alice Sardell, and Barbara Richards. 2000. Federal Immunization Policy and Funding: A History of Responding to Crises. *American Journal of Preventive Medicine* 19(3S):99-113.

Kahneman, Daniel, and Carol Varey. 1991. Notes on the Psychology of Utility. Pp. 127-163 in: *Interpersonal Comparisons of Well-Being*, Jon Elster and John E. Roemer (eds.). Cambridge, England: Cambridge University Press.

Kaiser Family Foundation. 2003. *Kaiser HealthPoll Report.* Accessed March 17, 2003. Available at: http://www.kff.org/healthpollreport.

Kaiser Family Foundation and Health Research & Educational Trust (HRET). 2002. *Employer Health Benefits, 2002: Summary of Findings.* Washington, DC: The Henry J. Kaiser Family Foundation.

Kane, Carol. 2002. *Physician Marketplace Report. Physician Provision of Charity Care, 1988-1999.* Chicago: American Medical Association, Center for Health Policy Research.

Kaplan, Robert M., and J. W. Bush. 1982. Health-Related Quality of Life Measurement for Evaluation Research and Policy Analysis. *Health Psychology* 1:61-80.

Kasper, Judith D., Terence A. Giovannini, and Catherine Hoffman. 2000. Gaining and Losing Health Insurance: Strengthening the Evidence for Effects on Access to Care and Health Outcomes. *Medical Care Research Review* 57(3):298-318.

Kausz, Annamaria T., Gregorio T. Obrador, Pradeep Arora, Robin Ruthazer, et al. 2000. Late Initiation of Dialysis Among Women and Ethnic Minorities in the United States. *Journal of the American Society of Nephrology* 11(12):2351-2357.

Kawachi, Ichiro, and Bruce P. Kennedy. 1997. The Relationship of Income Inequality to Mortality: Does the Choice of Indicator Matter? *Social Science & Medicine* 45(7):1121-1127.

Keeler, Emmett B. 2001. The Value of Remaining Lifetime Is Close to Estimated Values of Life. *Journal of Health Economics* 20:141-143.

Keeler, Emmett B., Robert H. Brook, George A. Goldberg, Caren J. Kamberg, et al. 1985. How Free Care Reduced Hypertension in the Health Insurance Experiment. *Journal of the American Medical Association* 254(14):1926-1931.

Keeler, Emmett B., Glenn A. Melnick, and Jack Zwanziger. 1999. The Changing Effects of Competition on Non-Profit and For-Profit Hospital Pricing Behavior. *Journal of Health Economics* 18(1):69-86.

Kershaw, Sarah. 2002, May 20. The New Front in the Battle Against TB. *The New York Times*.

Kessler, Ronald C., Paul E. Greenberg, Kristin D. Mickelson, Laurie Meneades, et al. 2001a. The Effects of Chronic Medical Conditions on Work Loss and Work Cutback. *Journal of Occupational and Environmental Medicine* 43(3):218-225.

Kessler, Ronald C., Kristin D. Mickelson, Catherine Barber, Philip Wang. 2001b. The Association Between Chronic Medical Conditions and Work Impairment. Pp. 403-426 in: *Caring and Doing for Others: Social Responsibility in the Domains of Family, Work, and Community*, Alice S. Rossi (ed.). Chicago: University of Chicago Press.

Kessler, Ronald C., Catherine Barber, Howard G. Birnbaum, Richard G. Frank, et al. 1999. Depression in the Workplace: Effects on Short-Term Disability. *Health Affairs* 18(5):163-171.

Kolbert, Elizabeth. 2002, November 25. The Calculator. *The New York Times*. p. 42.

Kozak, Lola J., Margaret J. Hall, and Maria F. Owings. 2001. Trends in Avoidable Hospitalizations, 1980-1998. *Health Affairs* 20(2):225-232.

Kraus, Lewis E., Susan Stoddard, and David Gilmartin. 1996. *Chartbook on Disability in the United States, 1996.* Washington, DC: National Institute on Disability and Rehabilitation Research.

Kuehl, Karen S., Jeanne M. Baffa, and Gary A. Chase. 2000. Insurance and Education Determine Survival in Infantile Coarctation of the Aorta. *Journal of Health Care for the Poor and Underserved* 11(4):400-411.

Lagnado, Lucette. 2003a, March 13. Twenty Years and Still Paying. *Wall Street Journal*. pp. B1-B2.

————.2003b, March 17. One Critical Appendectomy Later, Young Woman Has a $19,000 Debt. *The Wall Street Journal Online*.

Lakdawalla, Darius, Jay Bhattacharya, and Dana Goldman. 2001. *Are the Young Becoming More Disabled?* NBER Working Paper No. 8247. Cambridge, MA: National Bureau of Economic Research.

Lanoie, Paul, Carmen Pedro, Robert Latour. 1995. The Value of a Statistical Life: A Comparison of Two Approaches. *Journal of Risk and Uncertainty* 10 (3): 235-257.

Lave, Judith R., Christopher R. Keane, J. L. Chyongchiou, et al. 1998. The Impact of Lack of Health Insurance on Children. *Journal of Health and Social Policy* 10(2):57-73.

Lee, Stephanie J., Bengt Lilias, Peter J. Neumann, Milton C. Weinstein, and Magnus Johannesson. 1998. The Impact of Risk Information on Patients' Willingness to Pay for Autologous Blood Donation. *Medical Care* 36(8):1162-1173.

Lee-Feldstein, Anna, Paul J. Feldstein, Thomas Buchmueller, and Gale Katterhagen. 2000. The Relationship of HMOs, Health Insurance, and Delivery Systems to Breast Cancer Outcomes. *Medical Care* 38(7):705-718.

Levit, Katherine, Cynthia Smith, Cathy Cowan, Helen Lazenby, et al. 2003. Trends in U.S. Health Care Spending, 2001. *Health Affairs* 22(1):154-164.

Levy, Helen. 2002. *The Economic Consequences of Being Uninsured.* ERIU Working Paper 12. Ann Arbor, MI: Economic Research Initiative on the Uninsured.

Lewin Group. 2002. *Emergency Department Overload: A Growing Crisis.* Washington, DC: American Hospital Association, American College of Emergency Physicians.

Lewin, Marion E., and Stuart Altman (eds.). 2000. *America's Health Care Safety Net: Intact but Endangered.* Washington, DC: National Academy Press.

Lipscomb, Joseph, Milton C. Weinstein, and George W. Torrance. 1996. Time Preference. Pp. 214-246 in: *Cost-Effectiveness in Health and Medicine,* Marthe R. Gold, Joanna E. Siegel, Louise B. Russell, and Milton C. Weinstein (eds.). New York: Oxford University Press.

Lochner, Kimberly, Ichiro Kawachi, and Bruce P. Kennedy. 1999. Social Capital: A Guide to Its Measurement. *Health and Place* 5(4):259-270.

Long, Stephen H., and M. Susan Marquis. 1994. The Uninsured "Access Gap" and the Cost of Universal Coverage. *Health Affairs* 13(2):211-220.

Luce, B. R., Willard G. Manning, J. E. Siegel, and J. Lipscomb. 1996. Estimating Cost in Cost-Effectiveness Analysis. Pp. 176-213 in: *Cost-Effectiveness in Health and Medicine,* Marthe R. Gold, Joanna E. Siegel, Louise B. Russell, and Milton C. Weinstein (eds.). New York: Oxford University Press.

Lurie, Nicole, N. B. Ward, Martin F. Shapiro, and Robert Brook. 1986. Termination of Medi-Cal Benefits: A Followup Study One Year Later. *New England Journal of Medicine* 314(19):1266-1268.

Lurie, Nicole, N. B. Ward, Martin F. Shapiro, and Robert H. Brook. 1984. Termination From Medi-Cal: Does It Affect Health? *New England Journal of Medicine* 311(7):480-484.

Lutzky, Amy W., John Holahan, and Joshua M. Wiener. 2002. *Health Policy for Low-Income People: Profiles of 13 States.* Washington, DC: The Urban Institute.

Lynch, Wendy, and John E. Riedel. 2001. *Measuring Employee Productivity: A Guide to Self-Assessment Tools.* Scottsdale, AZ: William M. Mercer and Institute for Health and Productivity Management.

Macinko, James, and Barbara Starfield. 2001. The Utility of Social Capital in Research on Health Determinants. *Milbank Quarterly* 79(3):387-427.

Madrian, Brigitte C. 1994. Employment-Based Health Insurance and Job Mobility: Is There Evidence of Job-Lock? *The Quarterly Journal of Economics* 109:27-54.

Mann, Joyce M., Glenn Melnick, Anil Bamezai, and Jack Zwanziger. 1995. Uncompensated Care: Hospitals' Responses to Fiscal Pressures. *Health Affairs* 14(1):263-270.

Manning, Willard G., Emmett B. Keeler, Joseph P. Newhouse, Elizabeth M. Sloss, et al. 1991. *The Cost of Poor Health Habits.* Cambridge, MA: Harvard University Press.

Manning, Willard G., Emmett B. Keeler, Joseph P. Newhouse, Elizabeth M. Sloss, and Jeffrey Wasserman. 1989. The Taxes of Sin: Do Smokers and Drinkers Pay Their Way? *Journal of the American Medical Association* 261(11):1604-1609.

Manning, Willard G., and M. Susan Marquis. 1996. Health Insurance: The Tradeoff Between Risk Pooling and Moral Hazard. *Journal of Health Economics* 15(5):609-639.

Manton, Kenneth G., Larry Corder, and Eric Stallard. 1997. Chronic Disability Trends in Elderly United States Populations: 1982–1994. *Proceedings of the National Academies of Sciences* 94(6):2593-2598.

Martin, Joyce A., Brady E. Hamilton, Stephanie J. Ventura, Fay Menacker, et al. 2002. *Births: Final Data for 2000*. National Vital Statistics Reports 50(5). Atlanta, GA: Centers for Disease Control and Prevention.

Mason, J., M. F. Drummond, and G. W. Torrance. 1993. Some Guidelines on the Use of Cost-Effectiveness League Tables. *British Journal of Medicine* 306:570.

McAlpine, Donna D., and David Mechanic. 2000. Utilization of Specialty Mental Health Care Among Persons With Severe Mental Illness: The Roles of Demographics, Need, Insurance, and Risk. *Health Services Research* 35(1):277-282.

McCormick, Marie C., Robin M. Weinick, Anne Elixhauser, Marie N. Stagnitti, et al. 2001. Annual Report on Access to and Utilization of Health Care for Children and Youth in the United States—2000. *Ambulatory Pediatrics* 1(1):3-15.

Medicare Payment Advisory Commission (MedPAC). 2001. *Report to the Congress: Medicare Payment Policy*. Washington, DC: Medicare Payment Advisory Commission.

Medoff, James L., Howard B. Shapiro, Michael Calabrese, and Andrew D. Harless. 2001. *How the New Labor Market Is Squeezing Workforce Health Benefits*. New York: The Commonwealth Fund.

Merlis, Mark. 2001. Public Subsidies for Employees: Contributions to Employer-Sponsored Insurance. *Inquiry* 38(2):121-132.

Messonnier, Mark L., Phaedra S. Corso, Steven M. Teutsch, Anne C. Haddix et al. 1999. An Ounce of Prevention. . . What Are the Returns? *American Journal of Preventive Medicine* 16(3):248-263.

Miller, G. Edward, Jessica S. Banthin, and John F. Moeller. 2003. *Covering the Uninsured: Estimates of the Impact on Total Health Expenditures for 2002*. Rockville, MD: Agency for Healthcare Research and Quality.

Miller, Victor. 2002a. *Most States Adopt New Breast and Cervical Cancer Treatment Option*. Issue Brief 02-53. Washington, DC: Federal Funds Information for States.

———. 2002b. *The States, Medicaid, and Health Care Spending*. Washington, DC: Unpublished presentation to the IOM Committee on the Consequences of Uninsurance.

Mills, Robert J. 2002. Health Insurance Coverage: 2001. *Current Population Reports*. Washington, DC: U.S. Census Bureau.

Minkovitz, Cynthia S., Patricia J. O'Campo, Yi-Hua Chen, and Holly A. Grason. 2002. Associations Between Maternal and Child Health Status and Patterns of Medical Care Use. *Ambulatory Pediatrics* 2(2):85-92.

Mishan, E. J. 1972. *Elements of Cost-Benefit Analysis*. London: George Allen and Unwin.

———. 1971. Evaluation of Life and Limb: A Theoretical Approach. *Journal of Political Economy* 79:687-705.

Mitchell, Jean M., and J.S. Butler. 1986. Arthritis and the Earnings of Men: An Analysis Incorporating Selection Bias. *Journal of Health Economics* 5(1):81-98.

Mitchell, Jean M., and Richard V. Burkhauser. 1990. Disentangling the Effect of Arthritis on Earnings: A Simultaneous Estimate of Wage Rates and Hours Worked. *Applied Economics* 22(10):1291-1309.

Mitchell, R. C., and R. T. Carson. 1989. *Using Surveys to Value Public Goods: The Contingent Valuation Method*. Washington, DC: Resources for the Future.

Moffitt, Robert. 1983. An Economic Model of Welfare Stigma. *American Economic Review* 73(5):1023-1035.

Moore, Michael, and W. Kip Viscusi. 1988. The Quantity-Adjusted Value of Life. *Economic Inquiry* 26:369-388.

Morrisey, Michael A. 1993. Hospital Pricing: Cost-Shifting and Competition. *EBRI Issue Brief* 137:1-17.

————. 1994. *Cost Shifting in Health Care: Separating Evidence From Rhetoric.* Washington, DC: AEI Press.

————. 1996. Hospital Cost Shifting: A Continuing Debate. *EBRI Issue Brief* 180:1-13.

Moss, Nancy E., and Karen Carver. 1998. The Effect of WIC and Medicaid on Infant Mortality in the United States. *American Journal of Public Health* 88(9):1354-1361.

Mulkey, M. R., and Jill M. Yegian. 2001. Small Businesses, Information, and the Decision to Offer Health Insurance. *Health Affairs* 20(5):278-282.

Murphy, Kevin M., and Robert H. Topel. 1999. *The Economic Value of Medical Research.* Chicago: University of Chicago Press.

Murphy, Kevin M., and Robert H. Topel (eds.). 2003. *Measuring the Gains from Medical Research: An Economic Approach.* Chicago: University of Chicago Press.

Murray, Christopher J. L., and Alan D. Lopez (eds.). 1996. *The Global Burden of Disease: A Comprehensive Assessment of Mortality and Disability From Diseases, Injuries, and Risk Factors in 1990 and Projected to 2020.* Cambridge, MA: Harvard University Press.

Musgrave, Richard A. 1959. *The Theory of Public Finance.* New York: McGraw-Hill.

Najman, J. M., and S. Levine. 1981. Evaluating the Impact of Medical Care and Technologies on the Quality of Life: A Review and Critique. *Social Science and Medicine* 15:107-115.

Narrow, William E., Donald S. Rae, Lee N. Robins, and Darrel A. Regier. 2002. Revised Prevalence Estimates of Mental Disorders in the United States. *Archives of General Psychiatry* 59(2):115-123.

National Academy of Social Insurance (NASI). 1999. *Medicare and the American Social Contract.* Washington, DC: National Academy of Social Insurance.

National Academy on an Aging Society (NAAS). 2000. Who Are Young Retirees and Older Workers? Washington, DC: National Academy on an Aging Society.

National Association of State Budget Officers (NASBO). 2001. *1998–1999 State Health Care Expenditure Report.* New York: Milbank Memorial Fund.

————. 2002. *Medicaid and Other State Health Care Issues: The Current Situation: A Supplement to the Fiscal Survey of the States.* Washington, DC: NASBO.

Needleman, Jack. 1994. *Cost Shifting or Cost Cutting: Hospital Responses to High Uncompensated Care.* Cambridge, MD: Malcolm Weiner Center for Social Policy.

Needleman, Jack, and Darrell J. Gaskin. 2003. The Impact of Uninsured Discharges on the Availability of Hospital Services and Hospital Margins in Rural Areas. Pp. 221-235 in: *A Shared Destiny: Community Effects of Uninsurance,* Institute of Medicine. Washington, DC: National Academies Press.

Neumann, Peter J., and Magnus Johannesson. 1994. The Willingness to Pay for In-Vitro Fertilization: A Pilot Study Using Contingent Valuation. *Medical Care* 32:686-699.

Newacheck, Paul W., and Neal Halfon. 1986. The Association Between Mother's and Children's Use of Physician Services. *Medical Care* 24(1):30-38.

Newhouse, Joseph P., and The Insurance Experiment Group. 1993. *Free For All? Lessons From the RAND Health Insurance Experiment.* Cambridge, MA: Harvard University Press.

Nichols, Len M. 2000. State Regulation: What Have We Learned So Far? *Journal of Health Policy, Politics and Law* 25(1):175-196.

Nozick, Robert. 1974. *Anarchy, State and Utopia.* New York: Basic Books.

Nussbaum, Martha, and Amartya Sen (eds.). 1993. *The Quality of Life.* Oxford: Clarendon Press.

Nyman, John A. 1999a. The Economics of Moral Hazard Revisited. *Journal of Health Economics* 18:811-824.

————. 1999b. The Value of Health Insurance: The Access Motive. *Journal of Health Economics* 18:141-152.

Obrador, Gregorio T., Robin Ruthazer, Arora Pradeep, Annamaria T. Kausz, et al. 1999. Prevalence of and Factors Associated With Suboptimal Care Before Initiation of Dialysis in the United States. *Journal of the American Society of Nephrology* 10(8):1793-1800.

O'Brien, Bernie, and Amiram Gafni. 1996. When Do the "Dollars" Make Sense? Towards a Conceptual Framework for Contingent Valuation Studies in Health Care. *Medical Decision Making* 16:288-299.

O'Brien, Ellen. 2003. Employers' Benefits From Workers' Health Insurance. *Milbank Quarterly* 81(1):5-43.

Office of Management and Budget (OMB). 2003. *Draft 2003 Report to Congress on the Costs and Benefits of Federal Regulations; Notice.* Washington, DC: Office of Management and Budget.

Ormond, Barbara A., Susan Wallin, and Susan M. Goldenson. 2000. *Supporting the Rural Health Care Safety Net.* Occasional Paper No. 36. Washington, DC: The Urban Institute.

Ornstein, Charles. 2003, February 5. Hospitals to Get $150 Million Infusion. U.S. Officials Approve Extra Funds for Ailing County Health System, Saving Two Medical Centers From Closure. *Los Angeles Times.*

Palta, Mari, Tamara LeCaire, Kathleen Daniels, Guanghong Shen, et al. 1997. Risk Factors for Hospitalization in a Cohort With Type I Diabetes. *American Journal of Epidemiology* 146(8):627-636.

Pappas, Gregory, Wilbur C. Hadden, Lola Jean Kozak, and Gail F. Fisher. 1997. Potentially Avoidable Hospitalizations: Inequities in Rates Between US Socioeconomic Groups. *American Journal of Public Health* 87(5):811-816.

Patrick, D.L., and P. Erickson. 1993. *Health Status and Health Policy: Allocating Resources to Health Care.* New York: Oxford University Press.

Pauly, Mark V. 1997. *Health Benefits at Work: An Economic and Political Analysis of Employment-Based Health Insurance.* Ann Arbor: University of Michigan Press.

Pauly, Mark V., and Allison M. Percy. 2000. Cost and Performance: A Comparison of the Individual and Group Health Insurance Markets. *Journal of Health Politics, Policy and Law* 25(1):9-26.

Piper, Jeanna M., Wayen A. Ray, and Marie R. Griffin. 1990. Effects of Medicaid Eligibility Expansion on Prenatal Care and Pregnancy Outcome in Tennessee. *Journal of the American Medical Association* 264(17):2219-2223.

President's New Freedom Commission on Mental Health. 2002. *Interim Report of the President's New Freedom Commission on Mental Health.* Washington, DC: Executive Office of the President.

Rabinowitz, Jonathan, Evelyn Bromet, Janet Lavelle, G. Carlson, et al. 1998. Relationship Between Type of Insurance and Care During Early Course of Psychosis. *American Journal of Psychiatry* 155(10):1392-1397.

Rabinowitz, Jonathan, Evelyn J. Bromet, Janet Lavelle, Kimberly J. Hornak, et al. 2001. Changes in Insurance Coverage and Extent of Care During the Two Years After First Hospitalization for a Psychotic Disorder. *Psychiatric Services* 52(1):87-91.

Ramsey, Scott, Kent H. Summers, Stephanie A. Leong, Howard A. Birnbaum, et al. 2002. Productivity and Medical Costs of Diabetes in a Large Employer Population. *Diabetes Care* 25(1):23-29.

Rawls, John. 1971. *Theory of Justice.* Cambridge, MA: Harvard University Press.

Reed, Marie C., Peter J. Cunningham, and Jeffrey J. Stoddard. 2001. Physicians Pulling Back From Charity Care. *Issue Brief, Center for Studying Health System Change* 42:1-4.

Riccardi, Nicholas. 2002, October 28. Health Care Out of Hope? Two Federal Bailouts Delayed a Reckoning for the County's Troubled System. But Lack of Reform May Doom Aid This Year. *Los Angeles Times.*

Riccardi, Nicholas, and Charles Ornstein. 2002, October 2. Official Calls Bailout for County Dead. Health: U.S. Won't Give $350 Million to Keep Hospitals Open, Bush Aide Says. Expected Next Is a Battle Over Funds in Sacramento. *Los Angeles Times.*

Rice, Dorothy P. 1966. *Estimating the Cost of Illness.* Health Economic Series, No. 6. DHEW Pub. No. (PHS) 947-6. Rockville, MD: U.S. Department of Health, Education and Welfare.

Rice, Dorothy P., and Barbara S. Cooper. 1967. The Economic Value of Human Life. *American Journal of Public Health* 57:1954-1966.

Rice, Dorothy P., Thomas A. Hodgson, and Andrea N. Kopstein. 1985. The Economic Costs of Illness: A Replication and Update. *Health Care Financing Review* 6(1):61-80.

Rice, Dorothy P., Sander Kelman, and Leonard S. Miller. 1991. Estimates of Economic Costs of Alcohol and Drug Abuse and Mental Illness, 1985 and 1998. *Public Health Reports* 106(3):280-292.

Richards, John R., Misty L. Navarro, and Robert W. Derlet. 2000. Survey of Directors of Emergency Departments in California on Overcrowding. *Western Journal of Medicine* 172(6):385-388.

Roetzheim, Richard G., Naazneen Pal, Colleen Tennant, Lydia Voti, et al. 1999. Effects of Health Insurance and Race on Early Detection of Cancer. *Journal of the National Cancer Institute* 91(16):1409-1415.

Roetzheim, Richard G., Eduardo C. Gonzalez, Jeanne M. Ferrante, Naazneen Pal, et al., 2000a. Effects of Health Insurance and Race on Breast Carcinoma Treatments and Outcomes. *Cancer* 89(11):2202-2213

Roetzheim, Richard G., Naazneen Pal, Eduardo C. Gonzalez, Jeanne M. Ferrante, et al., 2000b. Effects of Health Insurance and Race on Colorectal Cancer Treatments and Outcomes. *American Journal of Public Health* 90(11)1746-1754.

Rosenbaum, Sara. 2000. The Public-Private Dynamics of National Immunization Policy. *American Journal of Preventive Medicine* 19(3S):19-27.

Rubin, Lillian B. 1994. *Families on the Fault Line.* New York: HarperCollins.

Rundle, Rhonda L. 2002, July 15. Garthwaite Aims To Revamp Los Angeles Health System. *Wall Street Journal.*

Russell, Louise B., Marthe R. Gold, Joanna E. Siegel, Norman Daniels, et al. 1996. The Role of Cost-Effectiveness Analysis in Health and Medicine. *Journal of the American Medical Association* 276(14):1172-1177.

Sackett, D. L., and G. W. Torrance. 1978. The Utility of Different Health States As Perceived by the General Public. *Journal of Chronic Diseases* 31:697-704.

Sanchez, Rene. 2002, December 31. Los Angeles Tax Hike Shows Growing Voter Concerns on Health Care. *The Washington Post.* p. A5.

Schneider, Andy. 2002. *The Medicaid Resource Book.* Washington, DC: The Kaiser Commission on Medicaid and the Uninsured.

Schneider, Mike. 2003, January 28. Nonprofit Group Puts Hospitals on Notice About Price-Gouging. *Naples Daily News.*

Schoen, Cathy, and Catherine DesRoches. 2000. Uninsured and Unstably Insured: The Importance of Continuous Insurance Coverage. *Health Services Research* 35(1):187-206.

Scitovsky, Anne A., and Dorothy P. Rice. 1987. Estimates of the Direct and Indirect Costs of Acquired Immunodeficiency Syndrome in the United States, 1985, 1986, 1991. *Public Health Reports* 102(1):5-17.

Selden, Thomas M., Katherine R. Levit, Joel W. Cohen, Samuel H. Zuvekas, et al. 2001. Reconciling Medical Expenditure Estimates From the MEPS and the NHA, 1996. *Health Care Financing Review* 23(1):161-178.

Sen, Amartya. 1993. Capability and Well-Being. In: *The Quality of Life.* Martha Nussbaum and Amartya Sen (eds.). Oxford: Clarendon Press.

Sheils, John, Paul Hogan, and Randall Haught. 1999. *Health Insurance and Taxes: The Impact of Proposed Changes in Current Federal Policy.* Washington, DC: The National Coalition on Health Care.

Short, Pamela F. 2001. *Counting and Characterizing the Uninsured.* Ann Arbor, MI: Economic Research Initiative on the Uninsured.

Singer, Burton H., and Kenneth G. Manton. 1998. The Effects of Health Changes on Projections of Health Service Needs for the Elderly Population of the United States. *Proceedings of the National Academy of Sciences* 95:15618-15622.

Sisk, Jane E. 2000. The Best and Worst of Times: Use of Adult Immunizations. *American Journal of Preventive Medicine* 19(3 Suppl.):26-28.

Sloan, Frank A. 1995a. Introduction. Pp. 1-14 in: *Valuing Health Care: Costs, Benefits, and Effectiveness of Pharmaceuticals and Other Medical Technologies*, Frank A. Sloan (ed.). New York: Cambridge University Press.

Sloan, Frank A. (ed.). 1995b. *Valuing Health Care: Costs, Benefits, and Effectiveness of Pharmaceuticals and Other Medical Technologies*. New York: Cambridge University Press.

Smith, David H., Daniel C. Malone, Kenneth A. Lawson, Lynn J. Okamoto, Carmelina Battista, and William B. Saunders. 1997. A National Estimate of the Economic Costs of Asthma. *American Journal of Respiratory and Critical Care Medicine* 156(3):787-793.

Smith, Vernon, Eileen Ellis, Kathy Gifford, Rekha Ramesh, et al. 2002. *Medicaid Spending Growth: Results From a 2002 Survey*. Pub. No. 4064. Washington, DC: The Henry J. Kaiser Family Foundation.

Social Security Administration (SSA). 2002. *Annual Statistical Report on the Social Security Disability Insurance Program, 2001*. Accessed January 20, 2003. Available at: http://www.ssa.gov/statistics.

———. 2003. *2003 Social Security Changes Fact Sheet*. Accessed March 13, 2003. Available at: http://www.ssa.gov/cola/colafacts2003.htm.

Sorlie, Paul D., Norman J. Johnson, Eric Backlund, and Douglas D. Bradham. 1994. Mortality in the Uninsured Compared With That in Persons With Public and Private Health Insurance. *Archives of Internal Medicine* 154(21):2409-2416.

Starr, Paul. 1982. *The Social Transformation of American Medicine*. New York: Basic Books.

Strunk, Bradley C., Paul B. Ginsburg, and Jon R. Gabel. 2002. Tracking Health Care Costs: Growth Accelerates Again in 2001. *Health Affairs*. Accessed November 1 2002. Available at: http://www.healthaffairs.org/Library.

Sturm, Roland, and Kenneth B. Wells. 2000. Health Insurance May Be Improving—But Not for Individuals With Mental Illness. *Health Services Research* 35(1, Pt. II):253-262.

Sullivan, Teresa A., Elizabeth Warren, and Jay L. Westbrook. 2000. *The Fragile Middle Class*. New Haven, CT: Yale University Press.

Szilagyi, Peter G., Jack Zwanziger, Lance E. Rodewald, Jane L. Holl, et al. 2000. Evaluation of a State Health Insurance Program for Low-Income Children: Implications for State Child Health Insurance Programs. *Pediatrics* 105(2):363-371.

Szpiro, G. 1986. Measuring Risk Aversion: An Alternative Approach. *Research Statistics* 68:156-159.

Taylor, Amy K., Joel W. Cohen, and Steven R. Machlin. 2001. Being Uninsured in 1996 Compared to 1987: How Has the Experience of the Uninsured Changed Over Time? *Health Services Research* 36(6, Pt. II):16-31.

Tengs, Tammy O., and Amy Wallace. 2000. One Thousand Health-Related Quality-of-Life Estimates. *Medical Care* 38(6):583-637.

The Kaiser Commission on Medicaid and the Uninsured (Kaiser). 2000. *In Their Own Words: The Uninsured Talk About Living Without Health Insurance*. Washington, DC: The Kaiser Commission on Medicaid and the Uninsured.

Thompson, Mark J. 1986. Willingness to Pay and Accept Risks to Cure Chronic Disease. *American Journal of Public Health* 74(4):392-396.

Thompson, Mark J., Leighton Read, and Matthew Liang. 1984. Feasibility of Willingness-to-Pay Measurement in Chronic Arthritis. *Medical Decision Making* 4(2):195-215.

Tolley, George, Donald Kenkel, and Robert Fabian (eds.). 1994. *Valuing Health for Policy: An Economic Approach*. Chicago: University of Chicago Press.

U.S. Department of Transportation. 2002. *Revised Departmental Guidelines: Treatment of Value of Life and Injuries in Preparing Economic Evaluations*. Accessed January 31, 2003. Available at: http://ostpxweb.dot.gov/VSL_2002_guidance.pdf.

U.S. Environmental Protection Agency (USEPA). 2000. *Guidelines for Preparing Economic Analyses*. EPA-240-R-00-003. Washington, DC: U.S. Environmental Protection Agency.

———. 2001. *Control of Air Pollution from New Motor Vehicles: Heavy-Duty Engine and Vehicle Standards and Highway Diesel Fuel Sulfur Control Requirements: Final Rule*. AMS-FRL6923-7. Washington, DC: United States Environmental Protection Agency.

U.S. Preventive Services Task Force (USPSTF). 1996. Appendix A: Task Force Ratings. *Guide to Clinical Preventive Services*. 2nd ed. Baltimore: Williams & Wilkins.

Valdez, Robert B., Anne Leibowitz, J. E. Ware, et al. 1986. Health Insurance, Medical Care, and Children's Health. *Pediatrics* 77(1):124-128.

Vigdor, Elizabeth R. 2003. *Coverage Does Matter: The Value of Health Forgone by the Uninsured*. Raleigh, NC: Duke University. Sanford Institute of Public Policy.

Viscusi, W. Kip. 1993. The Value of Risks to Life and Health. *Journal of Economic Literature*:1912-1946.

Viscusi, W. Kip, and Joseph E. Aldy. 2002. *The Value of Statistical Life: A Critical Review of Market Estimates Throughout the World*.

Vladeck, Bruce. 2003. Universal Health Insurance in the United States: Reflections on the Past, the Present, and the Future. *American Journal of Public Health* 93(1):16-19.

Walzer, Michael. 1983. *Spheres of Justice: A Defense of Pluralism and Equality*. New York: Basic Books.

Wang, Philip S., Patricia Berglund, and Ronald C. Kessler. 2000. Recent Care of Common Mental Disorders in the United States. *Journal of General Internal Medicine* 15:284-92.

Weinstein, Milton C., and Willard G. Manning. 1997. Theoretical Issues in Cost-Effectiveness Analysis. *Journal of Health Economics* 16(1):121-128.

Weiss, Kevin B., Sean D. Sullivan, and Christopher S. Lyttle. 2000. Trends in the Cost of Illness for Asthma in the United States, 1985-1194. *Journal of Allergy and Clinical Immunology* 106(3):493-499.

Wielawski, Irene. 2000. Gouging the Medically Uninsured: A Tale of Two Bills. *Health Affairs* 19(5):180-185.

Wolfe, Barbara L. 1985. The Influence of Health on School Outcomes: A Multivariate Approach. *Medical Care* 23(10):1127-1138.

Wunderlich, Gooloo S., Dorothy P. Rice, and Nicole L. Amado (eds.). 2002. *The Dynamics of Disability: Measuring and Monitoring for Social Security Programs*. Washington, DC: National Academy Press.

Wyatt, Richard J., Ioline de Saint Ghislaine, Megan C. Leary, and Edward Taylor. 1995. An Economic Evaluation of Schizophrenia. *Social Psychiatry and Psychiatric Epidemiology* 30(5):196-205.

Yaari, M. E., and M. Bar-Hillel. 1984. On Dividing Justly. *Social Choice and Welfare* 1(1):1-24.

Zeckhauser, Richard J., and Donald S. Shepard. 1976. Where Now For Saving Lives? *Law and Contemporary Problems* 40(4):5-45.

Zwanziger, Jack, Glenn A. Melnick, and Anil Bamezai. 2000. Can Cost Shifting Continue in a Price Competitive Environment? *Health Economics* 9(3):211-226.

———. 1994. Costs and Price Competition in California Hospitals, 1980–1990. *Health Affairs* 13(4):118-126.

Zweifel, P. J., and Willard G. Manning. 2000. Handbook of Health Economics: Consumer Incentives in Health Care. In: *Handbook of Health Economics*, Anthony J. Culyer and Joseph P. Newhouse (eds.). Amsterdam: Elsevier.